Woman's Day Book of BEST-LOVED Toys & Dolls

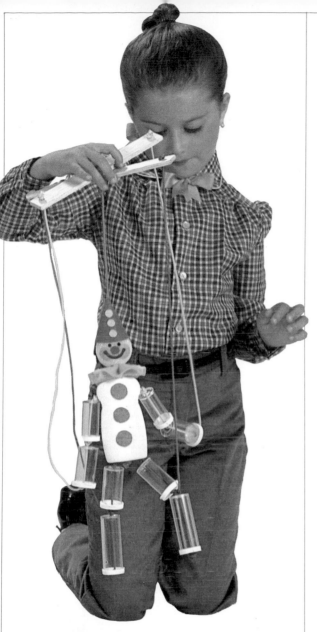

Woman's Day

Book of BEST-LOVED Toys & Dolls

COMPILED AND EDITED

by Julie Houston

SEDGEWOOD PRESS

NEW YORK

For CBS Inc.

Editorial Director: *Dina von Zweck*

Editor: *Julie Houston*

Project Coordinator: *Lisa Le Fever*

For Sedgewood Press

Editorial Director, Sedgewood Press: *Jane Ross*

Project Director: *Virginia Colton*

Supervising Editor: *Gale Kremer*

Designer: *Bentwood Studio/Jos. Trautwein*

Production Manager: *Bill Rose*

Distributed in the Trade by Van Nostrand Reinhold.
ISBN 0-442-29238-4
Library of Congress Catalog Number 81-85170.
Manufactured in the United States of America.

Contents

Editor's Introduction   6

Reminders about Safety   9

CHAPTER 1

    Precious Stuffed Animals   12-33

CHAPTER 2

    Adorable Dolls   34-55

CHAPTER 3

    Just-for-fun
    Activity Toys   56-79

CHAPTER 4

    Wooden Playthings   80-111

CHAPTER 5

    Settings for
    Fantasy Play   112-175

CHAPTER 6

    General Instructions   176-185

Index   187

Editor's Introduction

Many of us have felt the tug at the heart and twinge of nostalgia that comes with discovering a once-beloved but long-forgotten toy or doll tucked away in an attic or storage closet. For a moment, precious childhood memories come flooding back, even though we couldn't say just what the toy or doll meant to us all those years ago.

To a child, cherished playthings are an essential of life, the tools that open up a vast world of knowledge. For play is discovering what the world is all about, and toys are incomparable companions on that exploratory journey.

It has been said that play is a child's work. To see how true this is, notice how seriously children take their toys, and how differently they "profit" from them. The infant concentrates all its senses on the colorful objects that bounce and flicker and roll and chime; the toddler-scientist rejoices in the newfound ability to organize, to sort things out and classify; the pre-school child imagines and peoples a makebelieve world with the toys of that time. At each fast-moving stage of childhood, toys and dolls enrich the process of development. Activity toys stimulate curiosity, challenge skills and give children a feeling of accomplishment; soft animals and dolls, made to cuddle and squeeze, give them a warm sense of security.

Woman's Day Book of Best-Loved Toys & Dolls is packed with over one hundred playthings selected for immediate appeal and potential to delight. The collection is divided into five chapters, beginning with the softest of stuffed animals and the most endearing dolls. It goes on to ingenious activity toys for all interest levels, both classic and innovative wooden toys and dramatic backdrops for fantasy play. From the tiniest teddy bear to the complex and provocative Outer-space Station, they are the kind of toys that could *only* be made by hand. And all they ask of you, by way of investment, is a generous helping of love.

If you are experienced at sewing, yarn craft or woodworking, chances are you have scraps of material just right for any number of projects. Even if you are a newcomer to making things on your own, whatever you need to create the toys is readily, and inexpensively, available. Do, however, scout around before you buy. You might be surprised at what proves usable—a still bright but worn sheet, an outmoded sweater, a too-short nubby skirt. Looked at this new way, these might well be material for toys.

In choosing toys for children, you need not focus too narrowly on age levels, provided the end result suits a particular child. Any attractive doll, toy or animal will intrigue an infant; if it's a bit advanced at the moment, it will be welcomed later, like an old friend, for active play. Visual stimulation alone, however, won't suffice long for toddlers or pre-schoolers. Their interest is better sustained by toys that demonstrate some aspect of cause and effect. That's the charm of Squiggly Dragon, Socko the Hobbyhorse and the Foam ball Finger Puppets. (Nobody's ever too grown-up, though, to hug a dear little stuffed animal or doll. After all, a person sometimes has to relax!)

So begin now to make toys for the child, or children, closest to your heart. All the instructions are here for a wide range of the best designs ever collected in one place. The time and effort you invest will be infinitely small compared to the joy these gifts will bring, now, and perhaps again in some not-so-distant future, when childhood is just a memory.

—*Julie Houston*

Reminders about Safety

- Toymaking is one of the most satisfying ways to use scrap materials — and an incentive for keeping them on hand. Be sure, however, that all materials are fresh and clean before you begin any project. Fabrics can become soiled just lying around. Pay special attention, of course, to anything that has ever been worn or used.

- Wooden toys, by definition, are sturdy, but take care that they are smooth and splinter-free as well. Devote the necessary time to careful sanding — you will be rewarded in peace of mind.

- When paint is suggested, use only non-toxic, lead-free types. Research has shown that lead is perilous to children, especially to little ones still putting things in their mouths.

- In general, when making toys for infants and toddlers, it is better to eliminate anything that can be swallowed (buttons, beans, beads, buckles, etc.) rather than simply securing them in place. On animal or doll faces, sew felt features in place if necessary. Or embroider them instead, if that's practical.

- Watch out for sharp things, too. And not just in finished toys, but while you are making them. If you will be doing work of any kind with children nearby, remember that the implements you use can be dangerous to them, and take appropriate precautions. Even sewing, surely a harmless activity in every other way, has its pins, needles and scissors — all potential hazards to the young.

- As an extra safeguard, you may want to double-stitch seams of toys that are stuffed with synthetic batting. In any case, make certain that seams are strong.

- Nothing so fascinates a young baby as the toys of older brothers and sisters. If toys are intended for a family's older children, they should be made with one eye on the safety of younger ones.

- Large, soft toys are lots of fun for any age but should never be put into or near a crib, where an infant might inadvertently use them as a leg-up-and-over onto the floor.

—J.H.

Woman's Day Book of BEST-LOVED Toys & Dolls

CHAPTER 1

Precious Stuffed Animals

Stuffed animals have a very special place in a child's heart. In the crib or on a bed, lined up on a shelf or tucked in the toybox, these are the soft toys that children want always in sight and close at hand for a loving pat or a squeeze of security.

This chapter presents a marvelous menagerie of cuddly friends for children of all ages, from infants to adolescents. There are wonderful variations of old-time favorite play-mates — teddy bears of every shape and size, bright-eyed bunnies and frisky pups — even Rudolph the Red-Nosed Reindeer comes along for the ride. And there's lots more — a dazzling crocheted zebra and tiger, fuzzy hand puppets and the Uggie Wuggies, a pair of totally original fantasy creatures with amusing, interchangeable faces.

Every project here is quick and easy to create, requiring only a little of this and a little of that. So pick your favorite little critter and begin cutting out a pattern — you'll see right away why a stuffed animal is a scrap-saver's dream and a child's priceless treasure.

Note *In making your choice of stuffed animal projects, consider also the darling frog and bunny "pets" — and the puffy little spider and ladybug — that appear with the Family of Elves at the beginning of Chapter 2.*

Contents

A bevy of bears **14**

Pinky the Pig **17**

Tumbly Tiger **18**

Zippy Zebra **19**

Floppy Pup, Hopalong Bunny
& Brown Bear **20**

Switch-a-roo Uggie Wuggies **22**

Dachshund pals **24**

Rudolph **25**

Honey bunnies **26**

Lonely Leo **28**

Satin-smooth teddy **29**

Velour teddy friends **30**

Shaggy Sheep **31**

Fake-fur hand puppets **32**

A Bevy of Bears

*A bevy of bears — the more
the merrier! Simple shapes to cut for clothes
patterns and bear bodies make this
lively troupe quick and simple to
create, at a cost of just pennies whether you
reach for the scrap bag or
buy new fabric and stuffing.
Best of all, with so many dress-up combinations,
kids never run out of games to play.*

Note *If the bears are intended for a small child, substitute small pieces of felt for the buttons; tack all trims securely.*

SIZE About 7″ tall.

MATERIALS You will need a 9″ x 18″ piece of cotton-blend fabric for each bear. Use small amounts of assorted fabrics, laces, ribbons, etc., for clothes (see individual directions). Use black embroidery floss for features and polyester fiberfill for stuffing.

GENERAL DIRECTIONS

PATTERNS Enlarge according to instructions, page 16. Cut out paper patterns, adding ⅜″ to all edges for seam allowance.

BASIC BEAR

Cut out 2 bear pieces from fabric. Using 2 strands floss, on one piece embroider mouth and nose in backstitch and each eye in one tiny straight stitch (see stitch diagrams, page 184). With right sides facing, stitch bear pieces together, leaving opening along one side between dots. Clip curves and turn. Stuff; close opening.

Dresses and Shirts Cut out 2 fabric pieces. **Note** *Broken lines indicate various lengths of garments and sleeves; be sure to add seam allowance when following these lines. Stitch shoulder and side seams. Topstitch ¼″ finished hems on all raw edges.*

Pants Cut out 2 fabric pieces (see note immediately above). Stitch center front and back seams; stitch inner leg seams. Topstitch finished waist and leg hems.

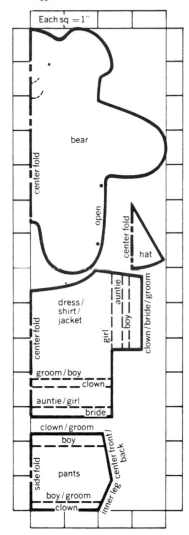

Each sq = 1"

bear

center fold

open

center fold

hat

dress/shirt/jacket

auntie

girl

boy

clown / bride / groom

center fold

groom / boy

clown

auntie / girl

bride

clown / groom

boy

side fold

pants

boy / groom

clown

inner leg center front / back

HOW TO ENLARGE PATTERNS

You will need brown wrapping paper (pieced if necessary to make a sheet large enough for a pattern), a felt-tipped marker, pencil and ruler. (When pattern you are enlarging has a grid around it, you must first connect lines across pattern with a colored pencil to form a grid over the picture.) Mark paper with grid as follows: First cut paper into a true square or rectangle. Then mark dots around edges, 1" or 2" apart or whatever is indicated on pattern, making same number of spaces as there are squares around the edges of pattern diagram. Form a grid by joining the dots across opposite sides of paper. Check to make sure you have the same number of squares as diagram. With marker, draw in each square the same pattern lines you see in corresponding squares on diagram.

BOY

7" x 8" piece knit fabric for shirt; 5" x 5" piece felt for pants. See General Directions for shirt and pants, above.

GIRL

6" x 9" piece print fabric for dress; 10" length baby rickrack; scrap yarn. See General Directions to make dress. Trim lower edge with rickrack. Make 2 small yarn bows and sew 1 over each ear.

AUNTIE

6" x 9" plaid or print fabric for dress; scrap velveteen; 3½" x 8" piece veiling; tiny flowers and ball-headed straight pin for hat (optional); about 10½"-long string of tiny beads.

See General Directions to make dress. Cut out 2 fabric pieces for hat, stitch sides together, hem raw edge and push in top point. Curve one long edge of veiling and gather other long edge to point so piece resembles fan. Sew gathers securely, tuck into top of hat and add flowers. Sew hat to head and insert pin. (For small child omit pin and simply tack fold in hat with hand stitches.) Slip beads around neck and sew ends together. (For small child substitute ribbon for beads; tack on securely.)

CLOWN

12" x 22" piece print fabric for suit and hat; 3" x 26" length white organdy for ruff (pieced if necessary); 12" length narrow white cord; red button or felt; pinking shears; large-eyed tapestry needle (blunt point).

See General Directions to make shirt and pants. Cut 2 hat pieces from fabric, stitch sides together and hem raw edge.

Using pinking shears, trim organdy to 2½" wide. Fold and press ¼"-wide pleat lengthwise along center of strip. Topstitch both edges of pleat so that it forms casing. Thread cord in needle and insert through casing. Pull up to form ruff around clown's neck; tie in back. Sew hat to head and button or felt nose to face.

BRIDE

8" x 10" piece eyelet fabric for dress; 7" square organdy for veil; 1 yd. narrow lace; bunch of about 11 tiny flowers; 6"-length narrow ribbon.

See General Directions to make dress. Trim all edges with lace, then add 2 lengths, spaced 1" apart, down front. Topstitch ⅛" hem all around organdy square. Twist stems of about 5 flowers together to make 2" length. Roll one corner of veil for about 1½" and whipstitch, gathering veil slightly. Lay flower strip along roll, pinch rolled fabric over stems and sew. Tack across top of head. Tie remaining flowers together in bunch with ribbon; tack to paw.

GROOM

9" x 14" piece velveteen and 4" x 7" piece satin for suit; tiny flower; 5" length ¼"-wide ribbon; 2 small buttons or felt circles; 2 snaps (optional).

From velveteen, cut jacket back on fold, then cut 2 fronts, reversing one, adding seam allowance to front edges. Cut 2 fronts from satin in same manner. With right sides facing, stitch a satin front to each velveteen front along front and neck edges. Turn. Stitch fronts and back together at shoulders and sides, catching satin lining in side and shoulder seams. Topstitch finished hems at lower and sleeve edges. Turn back revers and tack; pin flower to one rever. Sew buttons or felt to left front. (Optional: Sew snaps inside left front and outside right front edges to close jacket.) Fold 2½" length ribbon with ends overlapping at center; tack. Fold ¾" length ribbon in half lengthwise, wrap around other piece to simulate bow; tack. Sew bow to bear's neck.

See General Directions to make pants from velveteen.

BABY

Form 10" length ⅝"-wide plaid taffeta ribbon into a bow; notch ends. Tack to the baby bear's neck.

Pinky the Pig

Here's the best-dressed, best-behaved piggy of them all, about 12" long, with crocheted posies appliquéd on a soft, huggable crocheted body.

SIZE About 12" long.

MATERIALS Synthetic knitting worsted, 4 oz. pink for the pig, small amounts of purple, rose and lavender for flowers and green for leaves; aluminum crochet hook size H (or Canadian hook No. 8) **or the size that will give you the correct gauge;** 2 sew-on movable eyes or buttons ½" in diameter (or cut eyes from felt, if toy is for an infant); polyester fiberfill for stuffing. For crochet refresher course, see Chapter 6.

GAUGE 4 sc = 1".

Body Starting at tail end, ch 4. Join with sl st to form ring. **1st rnd** Work 6 sc ring. Do not join, but work around spiral fashion and mark beg of rnds. **2nd rnd** 2 sc in each sc around. **3rd rnd** * Sc in each sc around, increasing 6 sc evenly spaced, being careful not to work increases directly over those on the previous rnd. Repeat last rnd 7 times more (60 sc). Work 18 rnds even. **29th rnd** * Sc in next 8 sc; pull up lp in each of next 2 sc, yo hook and draw through 3 lps on hook (1 sc decreased). Repeat from * around. **30th rnd** * Sc in next 7 sc, dec 1 sc. Repeat from *

around. Work 7 more rnds in this manner, decreasing 6 sts evenly spaced and being careful not to work decreases directly over those on previous rnd (6 sc). Break off, leaving 6" end. Stuff; sew opening closed.

Head (make 2 pieces) Work as for body through 8th rnd (48 sc). Work 2 rnds even. Break off.

Snout Work as for body through 3rd rnd (18 sc). **4th rnd** Working through back lps only, sc in each sc around. Working through both lps, work 2 rnds even. Break off.

Ear back (make 2) Starting at tip, ch 2. **1st row** Work 3 sc in 2nd ch from hook; ch 1, turn. **2nd row** Sc in each sc across; ch 1, turn. **3rd row** 2 sc in first sc, sc in each sc to last sc, 2 sc in last sc; ch 1, turn. (Work 2 rows even, repeat 3rd row) three times (11 sc). Break off.

Ear front (make 2) Work same as for back. Sl st sides of ears together, leaving edges along last row open.

Front legs (make 2) Starting at center of bottom, work as for body through 4th rnd (24 sc). Work 8 rnds even. Break off. With bottom of foot facing you, form lp on hook.

Work 1 sc over each sc of 4th rnd to form ridge; join. Break off.

Back legs (make 2) Work as for body through 4th rnd. Work 5 rnds even. Break off. Make ridge as for front legs.

FINISHING Sew head pieces together, leaving opening for stuffing. Stuff and sew opening closed. Sew snout to face and feet to body, following photograph for position and stuffing lightly. Pad ears and sew to head. Sew eyes to face. Sew head in place.

Tail Ch 13, work 2 sc in 2nd ch from hook and each ch across. Break off. Sew in place.

Flowers (make 1 purple, 2 lavender and 2 rose) Starting at center, ch 12. Join with sl st to form ring. **1st rnd** * 2 dc in each of next 2 ch, sl st in next ch. Repeat from * 3 times more. Break off.

Leaves (make 7) Ch 10. **1st rnd** Sl st in 2nd ch from hook; * sc in next ch, hdc in next ch, dc in each of next 3 ch, hdc in next ch, sc in next ch, * 3 sc in last ch. Working along opposite side of starting ch, repeat from * to * once; join. Break off. Sew flowers and leaves to back of pig.

SIZE About 12″ high.

MATERIALS Rug yarn, 1 (70-yd.) skein each orange (color A) and black (B); aluminum crochet hook size J (or international size 6:00 mm) **or the size that will give you the correct gauge;** tapestry needle; felt scraps for features; white yarn scraps for whiskers; polyester fiberfill for stuffing.

GAUGE 4 sts = 1″, before stuffing.

Note *Crochet in back lp only of each st throughout. Side of work facing you is outside of tiger. Alternate A and B rnds throughout. For crochet refresher course, see Ch. 6.*

Head and Body Starting at top of head with color A, ch 4. Work as for zebra through 2nd rnd. **3rd rnd** * Sc in each of next 2 sc, work 2 sc in next sc. Repeat from * around, ending sc in last sc (21 sc). **4th rnd** * Sc in each of next 2 sc, work 2 sc in next sc. Repeat from * around (28 sc). **5th through 8th rnd** Sc in each sc around. **9th rnd** * Skip next sc, sc in each of next 3 sc. Repeat from * around (21 sc). **10th rnd** * Skip next sc, sc in each of next 2 sc (14 sc). Stuff head; continue to stuff as you work.

11th rnd * Sc in next sc, work 2 sc in next sc. Repeat from * around (21 sc). **12 rnd** Repeat 4th rnd (28 sc). **13 through 20th rnd** Sc in each sc around for body. **21st rnd** Sc in next sc, * skip next sc, sc in each of next 2 sc (19 sc). **22nd rnd** Skip next sc, * sc in next sc, skip next sc. Repeat from * around (9 sc). **23rd rnd** Sl st in next sc, * skip next sc, sl st in next sc. Repeat from * around. Break off, leaving 8″ end. Draw opening closed.

Hind legs (make 2) Starting with ch 10, work as for zebra legs for 6 rnds. **7th rnd** Mark center of rnd. Work 5 sc (back of paw); work 2 sc in each of next 5 sc for front of paw (15 sc). **8th rnd** Sc in each sc around. **9th and 10th rnds** Work same as 22nd and 23rd rnds of head and body. Break off; stuff; draw opening closed. Sew legs to body.

Front legs (make 2) Work same as for hind legs through 5th rnd. **6th through 9th rnd:** Work same as 7th through 10th rnd of hind legs. Break off; stuff; sew opening closed. Sew legs to body.

Finishing Tail With A, ch 6. Make ring. Alternating colors as before, sc in each sc around (5 sc) for 14 rnds. **Next rnd** Sl st in next sc, (skip next sc, sc in next sc) twice. Break off; draw opening closed. Sew tail to body.

Ears With A, sl st into top of head, ch 2, work 7 dc and 1 sc into sl st. Break off. Work other ear in same manner.

Ruff With A, sl st in front neck, * ch 4, working around face edge, skip ¼″ on face, sc into head. Repeat from * around face, working behind ears. Break off.

Features Cut felt scraps for features (see photograph); glue securely in place. Knot on small yarn whiskers.

This is one roly-poly cat who's as tame as can be — crocheted in orange and black rug yarn and brought to life with felt scrap features and yarn scrap whiskers. He's about 12″ high.

Tumbly Tiger

Zippy Zebra

Here's a bold, black-and-white zebra you crochet with rug yarn, adding felt scraps for features. He's about 13" long, and bound to be a big attraction among any child's pet playthings.

SIZE About 13" long.

MATERIALS Rug yarn, 1 (70-yd.) skein each white (color A) and black (B); aluminum crochet hook size J (or international size 6:00 mm) **or size that gives correct gauge;** tapestry needle; felt scraps; polyester fiberfill.

GAUGE 4 sts = 1", before stuffing.

Note *Crochet in back lp only of each st throughout. Facing side is inside of zebra.*

Head and Body Starting at nose with color A, ch 4. Sl st in 1st ch to form ring. **1st rnd** Work 2 sc in same place as sl st and in each remaining ch around (8 sc). Do not join but work around and around. Mark beg of rnds. Drop A; attach B. **2nd rnd** With B, work 2 sc in each sc around (16 sc). Continue to alternate A and B rnds throughout. **3rd through 5th rnd** Sc in each sc around. **6th rnd** Sc in each of next 6 sc, work 2 sc in each of next 4 sc (forehead), sc in each remaining sc (20 sc). **7th rnd** Sc in each of next 9 sc, work 2 sc in each of next 2 sc, sc in each remaining sc (22 sc). Work even for 2 rnds. **10th rnd** Skip next sc, sc in each sc to last 2 sc, skip next sc, sc in next sc (20 sc). Stuff head; continue to stuff as you work. Work even for 13 rnds for neck.

24th rnd Sc in next sc, * work 2 sc in next sc, sc in next sc. Repeat from * around (30 sc). Work even for 13 rnds for body. **38th rnd** Sc in 1st sc, * skip next sc, sc in each of next 2 sc. Repeat from * to last 2 sc, skip next sc, sc in last sc (20 sc). **39th rnd** Repeat 38th rnd to last sc, sc in last sc (14 sc). **40th rnd** Sl st in next st, * skip next sc, sl st in next sc. Repeat from * to last sc. Break off, leaving 8" end. Draw opening closed.

Legs (make 4) With pins mark position for 4 legs on body (see photograph). Starting at top of leg with A, ch 13 and form ring. Working as for body, sc in each st around (12 sts) for 9 rnds. Break off A. With B only, work even for 3 more rnds for hooves. **Next rnd** With B, * skip next sc, sl st in next sc. Repeat from * around. Break off; draw opening closed. Work remaining legs in same manner. Stuff legs, pinch tops closed and sew to body.

FINISHING To shape head, tack 10th rnd under chin to 15th rnd of neck (see photo). To arch neck, tack 17th rnd at back neck to 24th rnd on back of body. **Mane** With B, sl st in back of neck at tack. Ch 4, sc in same place as sl st; working in neck sts along back of neck to forehead, * ch 4, skip ¼" along neck, sc into neck, ch 4, sc in same place. Repeat from * to forehead. Break off.

Ears With B, sl st into head at one side of mane, work sc, hdc, dc, hdc and sc all in same place as sl st. Break off. Work other ear.

Tail With both A and B, sl st in end of body, ch 6. Break off A. * With B only, ch 6, sc in last A and B ch. Repeat from * 3 times more. Break off. Sew tail to body.

Features Cut felt eyes and nose; glue on.

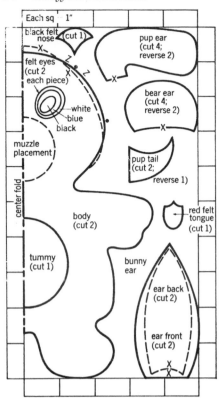

Floppy Pup

With extra-furry tummies for **Hopalong Bunny & Brown Bear** *extra-nice patting, this cheerful, starry-eyed trio in knit velour is cut from the same simple pattern, then given individual felt features and embroidered smiles.*

Each baby animal is about 10″ tall.

SIZE About 10″ from head to toe.

MATERIALS For each toy: ⅜ yd. 45″-wide knit velour fabric; scraps pink velour for bunny's tummy and ear fronts; scraps white fur fabric for pup and bear tummies; scraps felt for eyes, nose, teeth (bunny) and tongues; 6-strand black embroidery floss for mouth; ½ yd. satin ribbon; polyester fiberfill stuffing; optional small bell (not advisable if toy is for a small child); fabric glue.

PATTERNS Enlarge patterns according to adjacent instructions, adding ½″ to all edges for seam allowance. (Do not add to felt pieces.) For head, follow solid line for pup and bear and broken line for bunny. Cut out fabric pieces. Also cut 3″-diam. velour circle for muzzle and for bear's and bunny's tails.

STITCHING

Note *For help with embroidery stitches, see stitch diagrams, page 184.* Turn under seam allowance and appliqué tummy to front. Sew running stitches around bunny's and bear's tail pieces ¼″ from edge, draw up to form pouch, stuff and sew to body back. For pup's tail, stitch pieces together, right sides facing, leaving straight end open. Turn, stuff and sew straight end to body back.

Turn under ¼″ around muzzle and slipstitch to face, stuffing as you go. Stack and glue eye pieces together. Embroider white French knot to center. Glue eyes to face. Following photograph for placement, slipstitch nose to muzzle and embroider mouth in outline stitch. Glue tongue to bear and pup; cut two ½″-square white felt teeth and glue to bunny.

For bear's and pup's ears, stitch matching ear pieces together, leaving edge X open. For bunny's ears, stitch fronts to backs, leaving edge X open, then pleat edge X slightly on ear front. Turn all ears and pad lightly. Place ears on body front, matching raw edges to raw edges of head between dots for bear, X's for bunny and Z's for pup; pin. Stitch body pieces together, ears sandwiched between, leaving opening on one side. Turn and stuff. Close opening. Tie bow around neck and sew on bell if desired.

SIZES Orange is 15″ tall, blue is 20″ tall.

MATERIALS 45″-wide looped (unsheared) terry cloth, ⅝ yd. orange or ½ yd. blue; scraps of felt in assorted colors; pieces of snag-loop fastening tape (hooked part only; tape will stick to terry cloth); cardboard; gift-wrap yarn; fabric glue; polyester fiberfill.

PATTERNS Enlarge patterns following adjacent instructions and cut, adding ½″ seam allowance to all edges. Cut orange arms shorter; add seam allowance to cut edge.

Body With right sides facing, stitch pairs of matching pieces together (bodies, arms, legs), leaving opening (bottom on blue) for turning. Turn and stuff. Baste closed tops of arms and legs. Insert arms in body between dots and blue legs in bottom of body. Topstitch (on blue, stitch right across bottom of body and across X lines on arms and legs; omit X lines for orange). Bend each foot forward at broken line, making pleat. Hand-sew pleat to form foot.

Features: Hair Cut yarn into 4″ lengths. Tie 20 to 25 lengths together tightly around center to form shaggy pompon. Cut 1¼″ square of matching felt and, pushing all cut ends of pompon upward, glue square to center bottom of pompon and fastening tape to other side of felt.

Eyes, Mouths, Cheeks Following photograph, cut pieces of each feature from felt and glue together. Place each finished feature on cardboard, trace around it and cut out. Glue feature to cardboard; glue fastening tape to other side of cardboard.

Round nose Cut 4″-diam. felt circle. Sew running stitches around circle close to edge, pulling up to form pouch. Stuff firmly; sew closed. Glue fastening tape over gathers.

Carrot nose Following pattern, cut nose from orange terry. Stitch pieces together, leaving base open. Turn; stuff. Cut 2″-diam. cardboard circle, insert in nose; pull terry over and glue to form flat base. Glue fastening tape to base. Glue ¼″-wide strips of darker orange felt in rings around cone.

Horns Following pattern, cut horns from felt. Stitch pairs together, leaving base open. Trim and clip seams; turn and stuff firmly. Cut two 1″-diam. cardboard circles; insert 1 in each horn and finish as for carrot nose.

Hat Use empty 2″-long sewing thread spool for crown. Glue strip of red felt around spool and circle of felt to 1 end. For brim, cut 3″-diam. cardboard circle and cover both sides with felt. Glue crown to center of brim. Glue ⅜″-wide yellow felt strip around crown; glue fastening tape to bottom of brim.

Bow tie Cut 3½″ x 16″ strip yellow felt. Fold in half crosswise, overlapping ends at center. Wrap and glue (or sew) ¾″ x 5″ felt strip around middle. Glue fastening tape to back of tie.

Switch-a-roo Uggie Wuggies

There's nothing more fun than making a face, and nothing easier with this wonderfully gruesome twosome! They're easy, funny terry cloth dolls you sew, stuff and then fit out with interchangeable eyes, noses, mouths, hats and clumps of yarn hair.

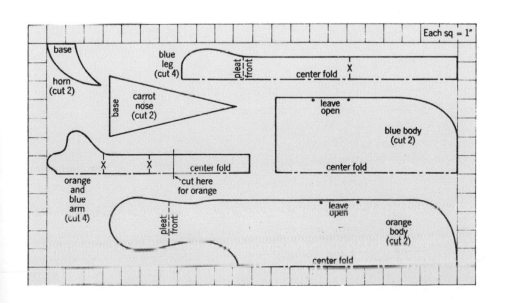

Each sq = 1"

base

horn
(cut 2)

blue
leg
(cut 4)

pleat
front

center fold

X

base

carrot
nose
(cut 2)

leave
open

blue body
(cut 2)

orange
and
blue
arm
(cut 4)

X   X

center fold

cut here
for orange

center fold

pleat
front

leave
open

orange
body
(cut 2)

center fold

center fold

HOW TO ENLARGE PATTERNS

You will need brown wrapping paper (pieced if necessary to make a sheet large enough for a pattern), a felt-tipped marker, pencil and ruler. (When pattern you are enlarging has a grid around it, you must first connect lines across pattern with a colored pencil to form a grid over the picture.) Mark paper with grid as follows: First cut paper into a true square or rectangle. Then mark dots around edges, 1″ or 2″ apart or whatever is indicated on pattern, making same number of spaces as there are squares around the edges of pattern diagram. Form a grid by joining the dots across opposite sides of paper. Check to make sure you have the same number of squares as diagram. With marker, draw in each square the same pattern lines you see in corresponding squares on diagram.

DACHSHUND PALS

To double a toddler's fun, simple overalls are appliquéd with a dachshund pattern that matches the floppy-eared stuffed doggy.

SIZES Dachshund measures 18″ long. Appliqué measures 11″ long.

MATERIALS Plain blue or other solid-color denim overalls, new or hand-me-down; ½ yd. 45″-wide red cotton fabric with large polka dots (A); 6″ x 24″ piece red cotton fabric with small polka dots (B); scraps of blue felt and blue denim, small yellow pompon; matching sewing threads; polyester fiberfill for stuffing; fabric cement.

OVERALLS Appliqué: Enlarge appliqué pattern according to adjacent instructions, and cut out the dog and two small ear pieces, adding ¼″ seam allowance all around. For tail cut a 2″ x 2½″ strip of B.

Fold tail in half lengthwise, wrong side out. Stitch 1 end and raw long edges together with ¼″ seam. Turn. With right sides facing, sew ear pieces together, leaving top edge open. Turn.

Press seam allowance to wrong side of dog body. Following photograph for placement, pin dog body to side section of overalls. Insert raw end of tail between body and overalls at dot and raw edge of ear between dots. Fold ear down over body and press. Using red thread and an overhand stitch, appliqué dog's body in place. Cut denim eye and with blue thread appliqué eye in place; stitch mouth.

TOY DACHSHUND Enlarge patterns and cut out the toy dog and four of the large ear pieces, adding ½″ seam allowance all around. For tail cut 2″ x 6″ strip of B. From felt, cut eyes and mouth.

Fold tail in half lengthwise, wrong side out. Stitch 1 end and raw long edges together with ½″ seam. Turn and stuff lightly. With right sides facing, sew ear pieces together, leaving top edge open. Turn.

With right sides facing, pin body pieces together, sandwiching tail at dot. Pleat ears to fit and sandwich between dots. Stitch around dog, leaving 5″ opening. Clip curves and turn. Stuff; slipstitch opening closed. Glue on features.

HOW TO ENLARGE PATTERNS

You will need brown wrapping paper (pieced if necessary to make a sheet large enough for a pattern), a felt-tipped marker, pencil and ruler. (When pattern you are enlarging has a grid around it, you must first connect lines across pattern with a colored pencil to form a grid over the picture.) Mark paper with grid as follows: First cut paper into a true square or rectangle. Then mark dots around edges, 1″ or 2″ apart or whatever is indicated on pattern, making same number of spaces as there are squares around the edges of pattern diagram. Form a grid by joining the dots across opposite sides of paper. Check to make sure you have the same number of squares as diagram. With marker, draw in each square the same pattern lines you see in corresponding squares on diagram.

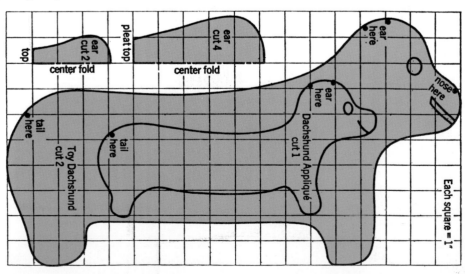

rudolph

A holiday visitor sure of a welcome, especially when he lands under the Christmas tree.

SIZE About 25″ tall including antlers.

MATERIALS ⅝ yd. 45″-wide green corduroy for body; 36″-wide cotton-blend printed fabrics as follows: ⅝ yd. red-dotted white fabric for underbody (includes inner legs), scraps white-dotted red fabric for nose, ¼ yd. yellow calico for antlers; scraps felt as follows: black and white for eyes, yellow and white for collar; 1 oz. white knitting-worsted-weight yarn or bulky yarn for tail; 6 jingle bells (not advisable for very small child's toy); polyester fiberfill stuffing; white glue.

PATTERNS Enlarge patterns according to instructions opposite, adding ½″ to all edges for seam allowance (do not add to felt eyes). Cut out fabric pieces.

ASSEMBLING Underbody Stitch darts in underbody pieces. With right sides facing, matching points on chest, stitch shaped edges (A) of front underbodies together. Matching points on rear, stitch shaped edges (B) of back underbodies together. Join front and back underbodies at C (seam crosses center of tummy).

Body Slipstitch dotted nose pieces to corduroy body pieces. Stitch body pieces together from dot on chest, around head, along back, to circle on rear. Stitch underbody to 1 body piece, matching chest point on front underbody to dot and rear point on back underbody to circle, stitching around front leg, along tummy and around hind leg. Stitch free edge of underbody to other body piece, leaving tummy from D to E open for turning. Clip seam allowance at curves. Turn and stuff firmly so Rudolph stands.

Ears Stitch ear pieces together, leaving 3″ open on 1 side. Turn and pad pointed ends lightly. Tie ear unit tight at center to pleat; sew tied center to head at F.

Antlers and Eyes Stitch matching halves of antlers together, leaving straight ends open. Turn and stuff firmly; sew openings closed. Following photograph, hold antlers together near base so they fan out slightly; sew where they touch. Sew to head in front of ears. Glue eyes to head.

Tail For pompon, wrap yarn around 4″-wide piece of cardboard about 60 to 80 times, depending on thickness of yarn. Cut yarn along 1 edge of cardboard and tie strands together tight at center. Trim pompon and sew to rear.

Collar From felt, cut 2″-wide yellow band and ¾″-wide white band to fit around Rudolph's neck. Topstitch white band along center of yellow band. Cut 2 strips rickrack to fit along edges of collar and stitch in place. Sew bells around white band (omit if toy is for very small child; you might substitute felt or embroidered decorations). Turn in ends of collar and sew around neck, shaping to fit slant of back neck.

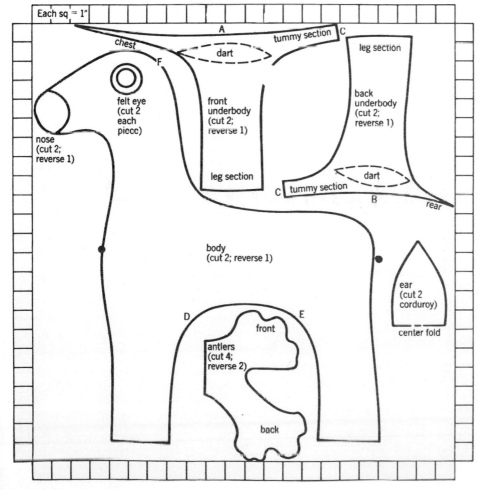

Each sq = 1″

A
chest
tummy section
C
dart
F
leg section
felt eye (cut 2 each piece)
nose (cut 2; reverse 1)
front underbody (cut 2; reverse 1)
back underbody (cut 2; reverse 1)
leg section
C
tummy section
dart
B
rear
body (cut 2; reverse 1)
ear (cut 2 corduroy)
center fold
D
E
front
antlers (cut 4; reverse 2)
back

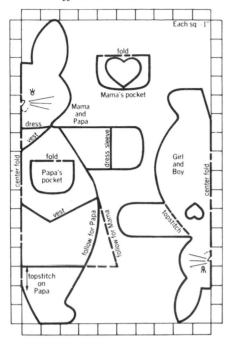

Honey bunnies

This adorable, quick-to-make foursome is all ready to hop right down the bunny trail and into a youngster's heart. To make the whole family — Mama, Papa, Baby Girl and Boy Bunny — all it takes is 1¼ yards of 45" fabric.

HOW TO ENLARGE PATTERNS

You will need brown wrapping paper (pieced if necessary to make a sheet large enough for a pattern), a felt-tipped marker, pencil and ruler. (When pattern you are enlarging has a grid around it, you must first connect lines across pattern with a colored pencil to form a grid over the picture.) Mark paper with grid as follows: First cut paper into a true square or rectangle. Then mark dots around edges, 1" or 2" apart or whatever is indicated on pattern, making same number of spaces as there are squares around the edges of pattern diagram. Form a grid by joining the dots across opposite sides of paper. Check to make sure you have the same number of squares as diagram. With marker, draw in each square the same pattern lines you see in corresponding squares on diagram.

SIZES Mama and Papa are about 15" tall; Girl and Boy are about 12" tall.

MATERIALS 45"-wide white cotton-blend fabric for bodies, 1¼ yds. will make whole family; small pieces of printed fabrics for appliquéd clothes (for fronts of bunnies only); scraps of eyelet lace and ⅝"-wide ribbon for trims; 6-strand embroidery floss in tan, brown and pink; pink crayon; polyester fiberfill stuffing.

CUTTING Enlarge diagram according to adjacent instructions, and cut out paper patterns for body (follow broken lines for Mama's skirt extension at sides). Make separate patterns for dress, vest, pockets and hearts.

Cut out fabric pieces, adding ¼" to all body edges for seam allowance. Add seam allowance to dress and vest only at sides and shoulders where edges will fit into body seams. Do not add seam allowance to hearts or pockets. Cut pockets double.

FEATURES Using 2 strands floss, embroider whiskers in tan outline stitch, mouth in tan backstitch, nose in pink satin stitch and eyes in brown satin and straight stitches. For help with stitches, see stitch diagrams, page 184.

ASSEMBLING Mama and Papa Fold pockets in half and appliqué heart to Mama's pocket in narrow machine zigzag stitch. (**Note** *Work all appliqué in this manner.*) Appliqué pockets to dress and vest. Topstitch row of lace to dress neck and one or two rows to skirt as shown. Turn under sleeve edges ¼" on dress, lap over edge of lace and topstitch. Pin dress and vest to bunny fronts. Appliqué vest down center front, along lower edges, armholes and neck. Appliqué dress across legs.

Girl and Boy Cut a pink felt or fabric heart for each. Work pink blanket stitch (diagram, page 184) around hearts and sew each to body front. Sew lace to neck of girl's front.

All bunnies With right sides facing, stitch together body pieces, leaving 3" open along one side for stuffing. Clip curves, turn and stuff. Close opening. Topstitch armhole line through bunny (vest armhole line on Papa and Mama and broken line on others).

FINISHING For Girl's apron, cut 4" x 23" piece fabric. Topstitch 1" hem along one long edge and ¼" hem at each end. Gather other long edge to fit around her waist. Topstitch ribbon across gathers, leaving 5" ends for ties. Tie apron around waist. Tuck folded pieces of fabric or lace in pockets. Tie bows around bunny necks; tack Mama's between ears. Tint cheeks, ears and paws with pink crayon.

SIZE Lion measures about 9½″ wide x 12″ tall.

MATERIALS 12″ x 15″ piece mono (single-mesh) needlepoint canvas with 10 meshes per inch; 12″ x 15″ piece yellow stretch knit for backing; acrylic knitting worsted, 2 ounces yellow (color Y), 10 yards each gold (G) and brown (B), 3 yards orange (O), 1 yard each rust (R) and white (W); polyester fiberfill for stuffing; tapestry needle.

To prepare canvas Fold masking tape over edges to prevent raveling.

Enlarge pattern, following adjacent instructions. Slide pattern under canvas and trace, using pencil or needlepoint marker.

Yarn Use 2 strands of yarn for bargello and satin stitches, 1 strand for all other stitches. Cut yarn in 10″ lengths. For stitching guidance, see stitch diagrams on page 184.

To work design Work satin stitch in direction of markings for eyes, nose and inner ears. Work a white French knot in each eye. Following bargello-stitch pattern, work lion's head and body.

Mane With color G and tapestry needle sew 1½″ yarn loops around lion's head. **Eyelashes** With B make three ½″ loops as for mane over each eye. Clip loops. **Tail** Cut eighteen 8″ strands Y and make braid. Cut thirty 6″ strands G. Hold together and tie around center to make fat tassel. Sew to one end of braid.

FINISHING Block needlepoint and trim canvas; leave ½″ seam allowance all around stitching. Cut backing piece to same shape as canvas. With right sides facing, stitch needlepoint and backing together, leaving lower edge (including area around dot) open. Turn and stuff. Insert end of tail in opening at dot. Sew opening, catching tail in stitching.

Lonely Leo

Lonely Leo needs a friend, and you know just the one! He's a quick bargello fellow 12″ tall.

Each square = 1″

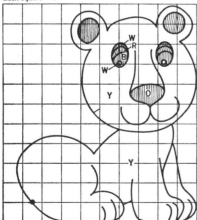

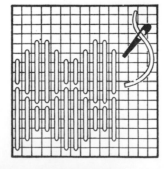

Color Key
Y—Yellow
G—Gold
B—Brown
O—Orange
R—Rust
W—White

HOW TO ENLARGE PATTERNS You need brown wrapping paper (pieced if necessary), a felt-tipped marker, pencil and ruler. When pattern you are enlarging has a grid around it, you must first connect lines across pattern to form a grid. Mark paper with grid this way: First cut paper into true square or rectangle. Mark dots around edges as pattern specifies, making same number of spaces as there are squares around diagram. Form a grid by joining dots across opposite sides of paper. Make sure you have the same number of squares as diagram. With marker, draw in each square the pattern lines in corresponding squares on diagram.

Satin-smooth teddy

A smooth and shining example of the latest style in bears, this dapper satin teddy with his crisp grosgrain jabot and velvet-ribboned neck. He stands 13" tall.

SIZE 13" tall.

MATERIALS ⅜ yd. tan satin; scrap brown satin; ¾ yd. each 1½"-wide striped grosgrain ribbon and ¼"-wide red velvet ribbon; 2 red buttons and 1 round black button (if bear is for small child, substitute felt circles for all buttons); polyester fiberfill stuffing.

Enlarge 2 pattern pieces according to directions opposite, and cut out, adding ½" to all edges for seam allowance. Cut out fabric pieces.

Bring dot X to dot Y on snout and tack to form pleat; also tack at Z. Turn under seam allowance and, following broken lines, slip-stitch to bear face, easing to fit and stuffing snout as you go. With right sides facing, stitch bear halves together, leaving opening for stuffing. Turn, stuff and close opening. Sew on red buttons for eyes and black button for nose (or felt pieces if those are used).

Fold striped ribbon in graduating loops, as shown, and sew to bear's neck. Tie velvet ribbon around neck, tack in place.

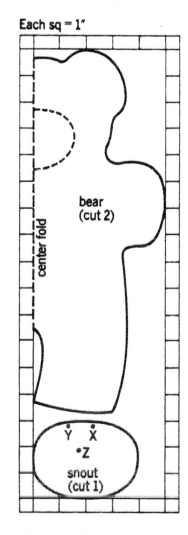

Each sq = 1"

center fold

bear
(cut 2)

Y X

•Z

snout
(cut 1)

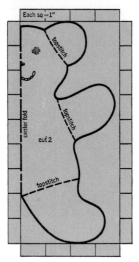

Each sq =1"

topstitch

center fold

topstitch

cut 2

topstitch

SIZE About 9" tall.

MATERIALS 48"-wide velour knit fabric, ⅝ yd. (enough for 3 bears); polyester fiberfill for stuffing; scrap of white 6-strand embroidery floss; ½ yd. ¼"-wide ribbon.

Enlarge pattern according to adjacent instructions, adding ¼" to all edges for seam allowance. Cut 2 pieces from fabric and, with right sides facing, stitch together, leaving opening at one side. Turn. Stuff ears, arms and legs, then topstitch across broken lines. Stuff body and head firmly, especially at neck; sew opening closed.

Using all 6 strands floss, embroider eyes and nose in satin stitch and mouth in chain stitch (see stitch diagrams, page 184). Tie ribbon around neck; tack securely to bear at side neck seams.

HOW TO ENLARGE PATTERNS

You will need brown wrapping paper (pieced if necessary to make a sheet large enough for a pattern), a felt-tipped marker, pencil and ruler. (When pattern you are enlarging has a grid around it, you must first connect lines across pattern with a colored pencil to form a grid over the picture.) Mark paper with grid as follows: First cut paper into a true square or rectangle. Then mark dots around edges, 1" or 2" apart or whatever is indicated on pattern, making same number of spaces as there are squares around the edges of pattern diagram. Form a grid by joining the dots across opposite sides of paper. Check to make sure you have the same number of squares as diagram. With marker, draw in each square the same pattern lines you see in corresponding squares on diagram.

VELOUR TEDDY FRIENDS

For that precious new baby,
a pair of teddy bear pals in knit velour —
pink, blue or any sweet shade you choose —
to machine-stitch and stuff.
Just 9" tall, these first "bedfellows"
are reassuringly squeezable for the smallest
hands and, with their happy
hand-embroidered faces, so comforting
to see at eye level in the crib.

shaggy sheep

A big beauty they can really snuggle up to!
This curly lambkin is made of yarn
hooked into a burlap body, stuffed with
polyester filling. Velvety face, ears
and legs are covered with felt.

SIZE 20″ x 30″.

MATERIALS Rug yarn, 3 (4-oz.) skeins eggshell or white; 1½ yds. 35″-wide white burlap; 24″ square of black felt; 2 paste-on movable eyes; polyester fiberfill for stuffing; aluminum crochet hook size H (or Canadian hook No. 8) for hooking; large-toothed comb.

CUTTING Enlarge diagram following the instructions opposite, adding ½″ seam allowance to all edges. From burlap, cut body and snout in one piece; also cut under panel and leg sections. Cut ears from felt; also cut snout and leg sections of felt.

From burlap, cut 45″-long rectangle, tapering from 6″ wide (end B) to 3¾″ wide (end A) for upper panel and two 6″ x 3¾″ rectangles for tail. From felt, cut one 10″ x 3¾″ rectangle for snout gusset. Measurements for all pieces include ½″ seam allowance.

STITCHING Stitch upper and lower panels together along ends A. Matching seam A to dot on one body section, with right sides together, pin continuous strip around body, matching raw edges; ease to fit. Stitch ends B of panels together. Stitch strip to body. Stitch other body section to free edge of strip, leaving 8″ opening. Clip curves; turn.

Leaving one end open, stitch tailpieces, rounding corners on other end. Clip curves; turn. Stitch tail to body.

HOOKING COAT Wrap yarn around a 5″ cardboard strip. Cut strands at both edges (5″ lengths of yarn). Following hooking diagram, fold 1 strand in half and, starting at top of head, hook yarn into burlap body. Omitting snout area, work knots over entire body and tail, leaving ½″ space between rows of knots. Stuff body; sew opening closed.

FINISHING Stitch 2 burlap leg sections together, leaving top edge open. Clip curves and turn; stuff. Stitch 2 felt leg sections together. Clip curves and turn; slip over burlap leg. Turn felt raw edge under around top; stitch to burlap. Make 3 more legs; sew to body. Matching raw edges, stitch felt snout gusset between felt snout sections. Clip curves and turn; slip over burlap snout. Turn raw edge under; slipstitch in place. Paste on eyes.

Sew running stitches ¼″ from lower edge of ears; gather edge to ½″. Sew ears in place. For shaggy effect, comb sheep lightly.

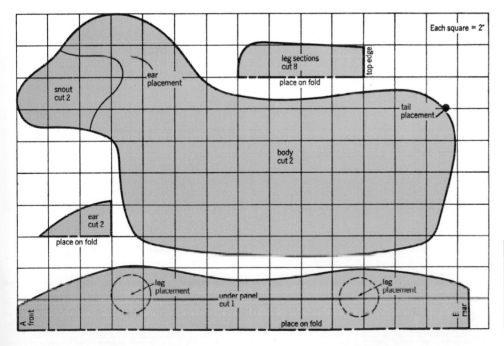

Each square = 2″

snout cut 2

ear placement

leg sections cut 8

place on fold

top edge

tail placement

body cut 2

ear cut 2

place on fold

leg placement

under panel cut 1

leg placement

A front

E rear

place on fold

Step 1

Step 2

Step 3

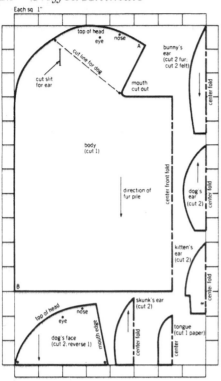

fake-fur
HAND PUPPETS

*Fuzzy Bunny, Purry Kitten,
Rascal Skunk and Curly Dog — a fleecy
handful all made from the same easy,
basic puppet pattern.
Use fake-fur fabric as suggested
or substitute textured scraps
of your own choice.*

HOW TO ENLARGE PATTERNS

You will need brown wrapping paper (pieced if necessary to make a sheet large enough for a pattern), a felt-tipped marker, pencil and ruler. (When pattern you are enlarging has a grid around it, you must first connect lines across pattern with a colored pencil to form a grid over the picture.) Mark paper with grid as follows: First cut paper into a true square or rectangle. Then mark dots around edges, 1″ or 2″ apart or whatever is indicated on pattern, making same number of spaces as there are squares around the edges of pattern diagram. Form a grid by joining the dots across opposite sides of paper. Check to make sure you have the same number of squares as diagram. With marker, draw in each square the same pattern lines you see in corresponding squares on diagram.

SIZE About 11″ tall.

MATERIALS 60″-wide fake-fur fabric (see photograph for types): ⅜ yd. for 4 puppets or 12″ x 14″ piece for each one; 2″ x 9″ strip long-haired white fur fabric for skunk's stripe; scrap contrasting fur fabric for dog's face and ears; scrap felt, 3½″ x 6½″ piece for each mouth, 5″ square for bunny's inner ears, 4″ square for kitten's ears; piece of cardboard for mouth stiffening; pink or red construction paper for tongues (optional); sew-on movable eyes (or cat's eyes for kitten); assorted pompons, ¾″-diam. for nose and bunny's tail, 1″-diam. for kitten's cheeks; white glue; compass.

PATTERNS Enlarge patterns following adjacent instructions, adding ¼″ seam allowance to all edges of body, dog's face and bunny's ears. Cut pieces from fabrics (see cut line on head for dog), following arrows for direction of fur pile.

  Body: Dog's face With right sides facing, stitch side edge of each face piece to body between dots. **For all puppets except skunk** Fold body piece in half wrong side out; stitch along top of head and back from A to B. **For skunk** With right sides facing and fur pile on stripe running downward, match one end of white fur stripe to A on body and stitch stripe to body with ½″ seam allowance. Stitch other edge of stripe to opposite edge of body in same manner. Bring remainder of body edges together and stitch from end of stripe to bottom of body with ¼″ seam allowance.

  Mouth Cut 2⅝″-diam. circle from cardboard and two 3¼″-diam. circles from felt. Glue felt circle to each side of cardboard. Flatten with book. When dry, gently fold mouth in half. With right sides facing, line up and pin corners of mouth to corners of mouth opening on body. Pin mouth around opening; stitch. Turn, then push mouth into puppet.

  Ears: For bunny ears Stitch felt inner ears to right side of fur-fabric ears, leaving lower ends open; turn. **For all ears** Cut slits in body where indicated. Insert ends of ears about ¾″, pleating bunny ears and kitten ears so they cup forward slightly and rolling edges of dog's and skunk's ears toward wrong side with right (nap) side facing forward. Turn in edges of slit and hand-sew ears in place. Tack bunny ears together so they stand up.

  Features Following photograph for placement, sew eyes to face. Sew on pompon nose (also sew cheeks on kitten and tail on bunny). If desired, cut tongues from construction paper and glue into mouths. Hem bottom of bodies.

CHAPTER 2

Adorable Dolls

Children find dolls endlessly fascinating — at first just to look at, and later as playmates in their fantasy games. To a child, a doll is a person in miniature, a special companion who is not only great fun to be with, but a great help in mastering complicated social skills. With a doll, a child is free to practice and experiment, to act out all sorts of behavior and dialogue — on his or her own terms. Young children love to play together with dolls, imitating the doings of grown-ups. And there's no ally like a doll for learning how to fasten snaps and hooks, open and close zippers, take clothes off and put them on — lessons practiced with patience because the child is in charge. Older children prize favorite dolls as room decorations — to add color and individuality and, in no small way, to keep alive the unique joy that dolls contribute as the childhood they were part of slips away.

From the jolly Family of elves to child-sized Big Girl and Big Boy, from endearing Country cousin to the appealing Heartthrobs, the spectacular dolls on the pages that follow are bursting with personality and charm. They're original in design, remarkably easy to make and destined to be the darlings of happy children everywhere.

Contents

Family of elves   **36**

The knitted family   **48**

Sweet Sue   **50**

Country-Cousin doll   **52**

Big Girl & Big Boy   **54**

Heartthrobs   **55**

A family of elves

*From their pointy ears to their
chubby feet, these merry little elves are so
full of character that children will take to
them instantly. Made with fabric snippets
and odds and ends, they are impish
creatures who dine at toadstool tables,
sit on toadstool chairs, have bugs, frogs
and bunnies for pets. Mom and Dad Elf
and their three elfin kiddies
range in size from 6" to 8"
(just the right size for made-up games).
You can make all of them, plus
everything they're shown with, using
the same-size patterns and
instructions that follow.*

Basic Doll

SIZES Dad and Mom, 9½" high; **Boy and Girl,** 8" high; **Baby,** 6" high; **Frog,** 3¾" x 7"; **Bunny,** 1⅜" x 3"; **Large toadstool,** 6" diam. x 5½" high; **Small toadstool,** 2¾" diam. x 3¼" high.

MATERIALS Peach-colored knit fabric for heads, ears and hands (a white T-shirt may be dipped in peach or orange-pink dye); polyester fiberfill for stuffing; craft fur for hair (available in craft stores or mail order catalogs such as Lee Wards); 6-strand cotton embroidery floss for features; woven or knit fabrics (see note below) for bodies in colors given in individual directions; matching sewing thread; red and white water colors or acrylic paint; small paint brush. **Note** *Buy ¼ yd. fabric unless otherwise specified, or use scraps you have on hand. Small circles of snag-loop fasteners (such as Velcro) can be sewn to small dolls' hands so they can hold hands or small objects.*

PATTERNS The cutting diagrams (the first is on page 40) are actual size and do *not* include seam allowances except where noted. Mom and Dad are made from one pattern, Boy and Girl from a second and Baby from a third, but all are assembled in the same manner. Trace patterns for each doll on tracing paper and then cut out, *adding ¼" seam allowance.* Pin to wrong side of fabric and cut out. When two corresponding pieces are called for, reverse pattern for second piece. Arrows on patterns show grain of fabric.

SEWING Pin the pieces together first, then baste, if necessary. Stitch all seams carefully, reinforcing by stitching twice where indicated. Trim seam allowances slightly after stitching and make tiny clips at curves.

Body Stitch two front pieces together, right sides facing, along front seam from A to neck, reinforcing front neck. This prevents seam from coming apart as you stuff body. Repeat with center back seam. (**Note** Front and back are identical.)

Legs: For Mom and Dad only With right sides facing, stitch upper edge of foot to lower edge of leg. **For all dolls** Fold legs along original fold line, wrong side out, and stitch around foot and front of leg, leaving top open. Turn right side out. Stuff firmly, leaving about ¾" at top unstuffed for ease in movement. Fold tops flat so toes face forward. Pin legs to right side of one body piece along

bottom seam line (see drawing); stitch. Lay other body piece, wrong side up, over legs and pin along side seam lines to B (legs are inside body pieces). Stitch side seams to B and again along bottom seam line. Turn right side out. Turn in raw side edges above B and slipstitch. Stuff body firmly. Set aside.

Head Stitch two front pieces together, right sides together, along center front seam, then stitch again along front neck area. Repeat with center back seam. Stitch head front to head back, right sides together, and reinforce at side neck. Turn right side out. Stuff firmly. Turn under raw neck edges of stuffed head and slip over body neck. Pin in place, adding bits of stuffing to make neck strong enough to keep head from wobbling. Sew with double thread and tiny stitches around neck.

Ears With right sides facing, stitch pieces together for each ear, leaving straight edge

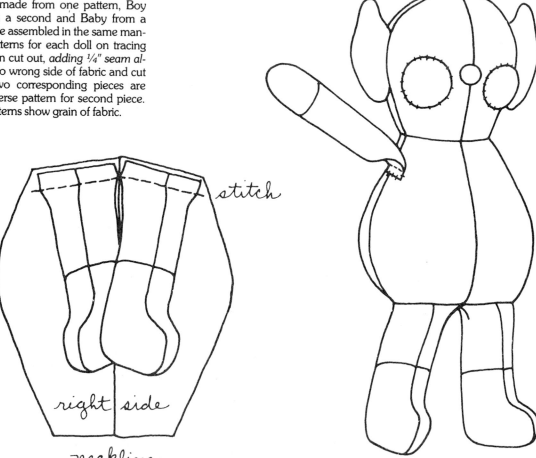

open. Turn right side out. Turn under raw edges and sew opening closed. Sew ears to sides of head with tiny stitches.

Nose Cut out a ¾" circle of knit fabric. Hand-sew line of running stitches around edge. Put a puff of stuffing in center and pull stitches tight to make small, round nose. Sew gathers tightly together; sew nose to face with tiny stitches.

Cheeks Cut out two 1" circles of knit fabric. Turn raw edges under and pin to face. Push bits of stuffing underneath edge until cheeks look full enough. Sew in place with tiny stitches.

Arms With right sides facing, stitch upper edge of hands to lower edge of arms. Fold arms along original fold line, wrong side out. Stitch along hand and back of arm, leaving top open. Turn right side out. Stuff firmly, leaving about ¾" at top unstuffed. Fold flat, placing arm seam opposite fold. Turn under all raw edges and sew opening closed. Placing arm seams toward back, sew arms to body (see drawing), about ¾" below neck seam on Mom and Dad, ½" on Boy and Girl and ⅜" on Baby.

Features Following photograph, lightly pencil outlines for eyes and mouth on face. With 2 strands black floss, embroider satin stitch eyes. With 2 strands orange floss, embroider outline stitch mouth and on Dad only, add green eyebrows. (For both stitches, see stitch diagrams on page 184.) Mix red and white paint to form pink blush. Brush on nose, cheeks and ears.

Hair See individual directions.

Dad

MATERIALS For doll See Basic Doll. Yellow fabric for body and arms; print fabric for legs; green fabric for boots; green craft fur for beard and hair. **Other clothes** Small child's yellow sock for hat; bird feather; light orange felt for vest; dark orange felt for belt; buckle from watch strap.

DOLL See Basic Doll to stitch, stuff and assemble Dad.

Hair and beard Make a paper pattern to fit Dad's face and another to fit the back of his head (see drawings). Trace patterns on wrong side of craft fur. Cut out, keeping points of scissors close to the backing so as not to cut off any fur. Pin pieces to head and sew with green thread. Trim fur.

Hat Cut 5" foot section from sock and discard heel and leg section. Fold in about 2" at cut end of foot. Tack feather in place.

Vest Using pattern, cut out vest from light orange felt, adding seam allowance to shoulders only. Machine-stitch ⅛" from cut edges, except shoulders. Stitch shoulder seams.

Belt Cut out two 11" strips from dark orange felt the width of your buckle. Cut one end to form point. Stitch strips together ⅛" from cut edges. Cut hole for prong ¾" from straight end. Insert prong and sew ¾" lap to back of strip. Cut ¼"-wide strip for belt loop long enough to wrap around belt. Sew ⅛" from cut edges. Wrap around belt just beyond buckle and sew ends to back of belt.

Put vest on. Buckle belt over vest. Put hat on; tack, if necessary.

Mom

MATERIALS For doll See Basic Doll. Light purple fabric for body, arms and turtleneck; red fabric for legs; purple velveteen for boots; yellow craft fur for hair. **Other clothes** Magenta fabric for skirt; yellow striped fabric for apron; scrap dark orange felt for purse; small silver bead; magenta felt and sheer fabric for hat; white glue.

DOLL See Basic Doll to stitch, stuff and assemble Mom.

Hair Make a paper pattern to fit front and back of Mom's head (see drawings). Trace patterns on wrong side of craft fur. Cut out as for Dad's hair. Pin and sew with yellow thread. Part hair at center, separate each section over ears and sew just in front and back of ears (see drawing on page 40).

Turtleneck From light purple body fabric, cut a 1¼"-wide bias strip long enough to fit around neck plus ½" overlap. Fold in half

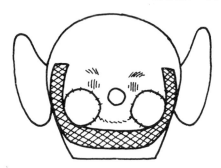

beard pattern

hair pattern

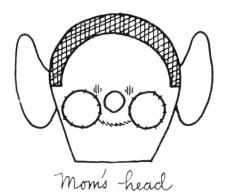

Mom's head

hair pattern

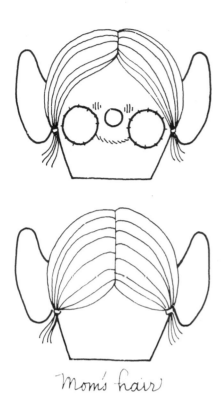

Mom's hair

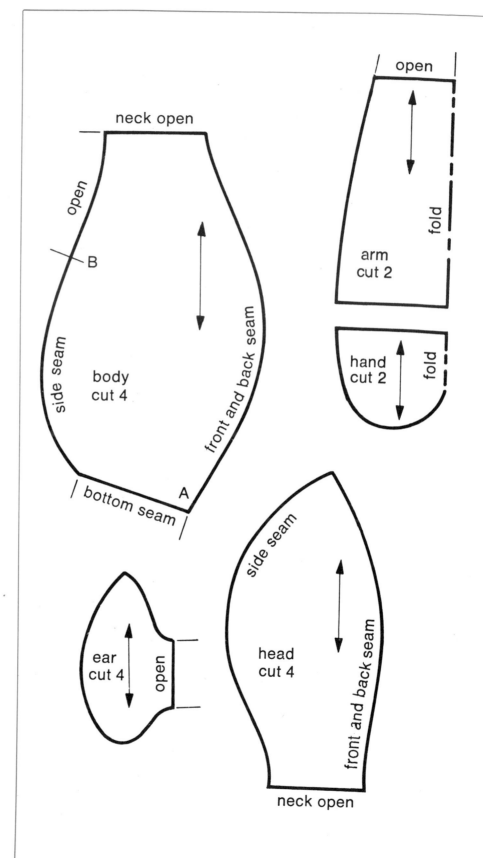

lengthwise, right side out, and stitch raw edges together. Fold so that raw edges are at center of band. Pin around neck, seam to inside, turning under raw edges at center back. Sew in place.

Skirt Cut 14″-wide x 5″-deep piece of fabric. Turn up and zigzag 1″ hem on one long edge. Hem sides of skirt. For apron, cut a 3½″-deep x 4″-wide piece of striped fabric. Turn up and zigzag-stitch ½″ hem on one long edge. Hem sides of apron. Matching raw edges, center and pin apron to skirt. Gather top edges of skirt and apron, pull up to fit doll's waist. For waistband and ties, cut 1¼″ x 18″ strip. Matching edges, center strip on wrong side of gathered edge of skirt; stitch. Fold strip over gathers to right side, turn under all raw edges along strip and topstitch.

Purse Using pattern, cut out purse from felt (do not add seam allowance). Fold at A to form elongated oval; cut fold. Stitch ⅛″ from edge, forming pocket. Lap at B to form flap. Sew bead to flap. Attach to belt with orange embroidery floss.

Hat Using pattern, cut hat from felt. Sew side seams, leaving small opening at top. Turn hat right side out. Turn lower edge under and glue. Cut 7″ square of sheer fabric. Poke center of square through hole and sew in place.

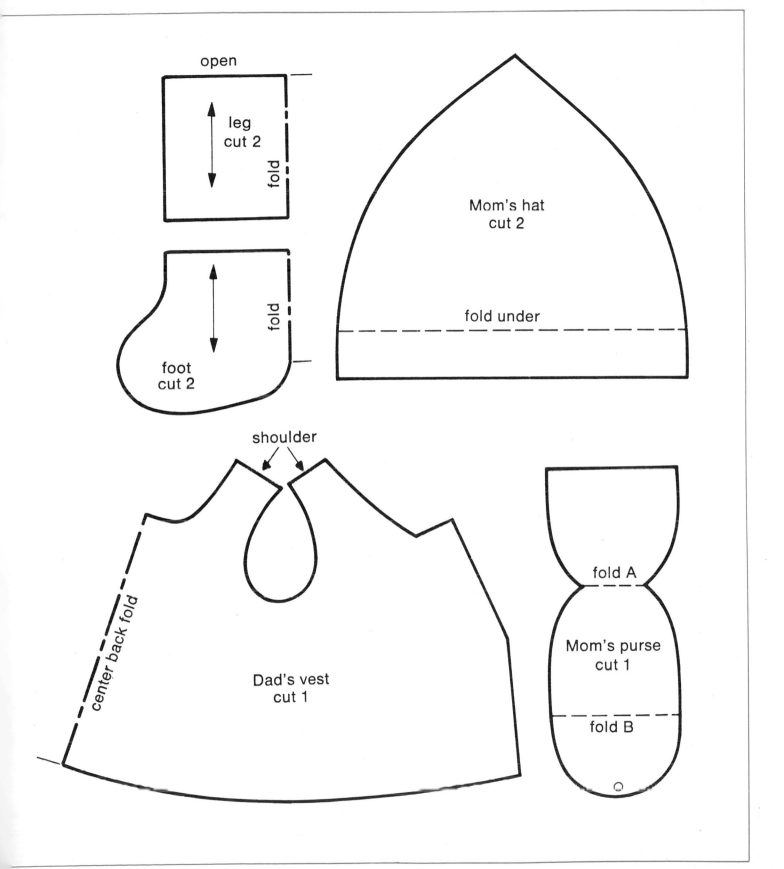

Boy

MATERIALS For doll See Basic Doll. Green fabric for body, arms and legs; orange craft fur for hair. **Other clothes** Small child's green sock and 1"-diam. blue yarn pompon for hat; dark blue felt for collar.

DOLL See Basic Doll to stitch, stuff and assemble Boy.

Hair Make pattern, cut out and sew to head as for Mom. Trim hair as shown in photograph.

Collar Cut out felt collar from pattern (no seam allowance necessary). Wrap around neck and tack at center back.

Hat Cut 4" tubular section from foot of sock, discarding toe, heel and leg. Gather one end of tube for top of hat and attach pompon. Fold other edge up ½", then fold again to form brim. Put on head; tack, if necessary.

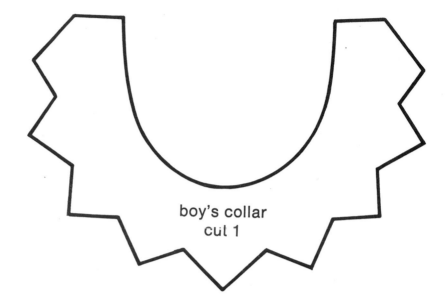

boy's collar
cut 1

Girl

MATERIALS For doll See Basic Doll. Turquoise fabric for body, arms and legs; yellow craft fur for hair. **Other clothes** Turquoise and green felt for collar; light turquoise and light green felt for hat.

DOLL See Basic Doll to stitch, stuff and assemble Girl.

Hair Make pattern, cut and sew to head as for Mom.

Collar Using pattern (no seam allowance necessary), cut out smooth-edged collar from green felt. Cut scallops from paper pattern, then cut out scalloped collar from turquoise felt. Wrap around neck as shown in photograph and tack at center back.

Hat Using patterns, cut out 5 petals from light turquoise felt and 5 leaves from green felt (⅛" seam allowance included). Sew side seams of petals together to form ring. Turn right side out. Repeat for leaves, leaving one seam open. Pin leaves to flower. Sew last seam closed, stitching leaves to petals at the same time.

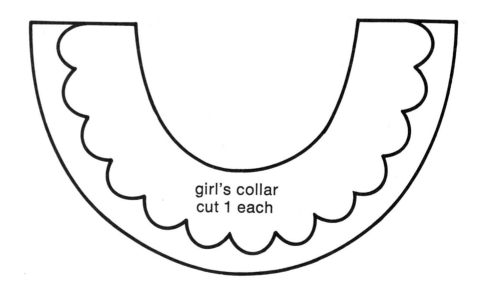

girl's collar
cut 1 each

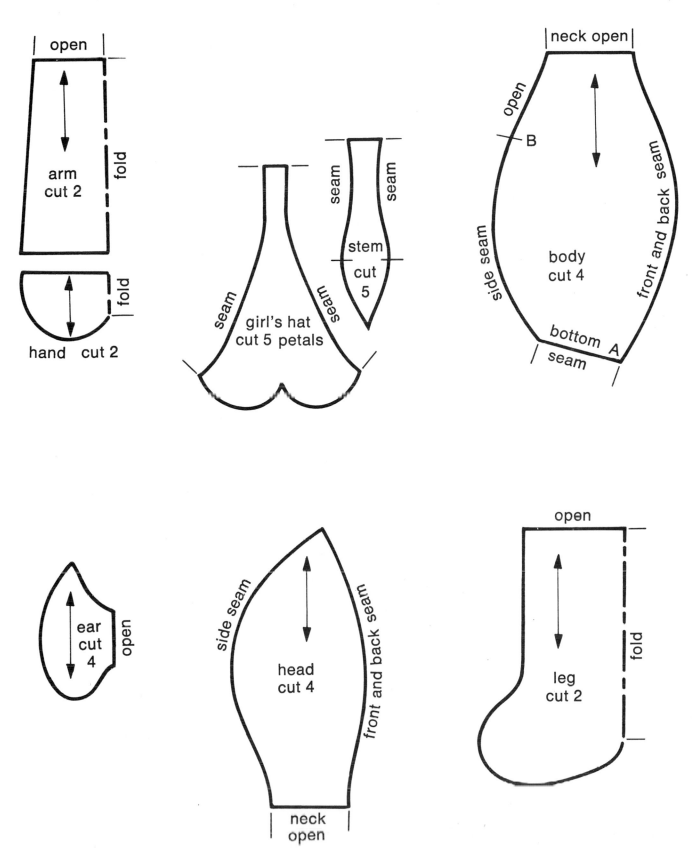

open

arm
cut 2

fold

fold

hand   cut 2

seam

seam

girl's hat
cut 5 petals

seam

stem
cut
5

seam

neck open

open

B

side seam

body
cut 4

front and back seam

bottom   A

seam

ear
cut
4

open

side seam

head
cut 4

front and back seam

neck
open

open

leg
cut 2

fold

Baby

MATERIALS For doll See Basic Doll. Bright pink fabric for body, arms and legs; yellow craft fur for hair. **Other clothes** Gold felt and small gold sleigh bell for collar; bright pink and light green felt for hat.

DOLL See Basic Doll to stitch, stuff and assemble Baby.

 Hair Make pattern, cut and sew to head as for Mom, but trim hair in shaggy cut as shown in photograph.

 Collar Cut from pattern and make as for Boy's collar. Sew bell through center front scallop to body.

 Hat Using patterns, make as for Girl's hat.

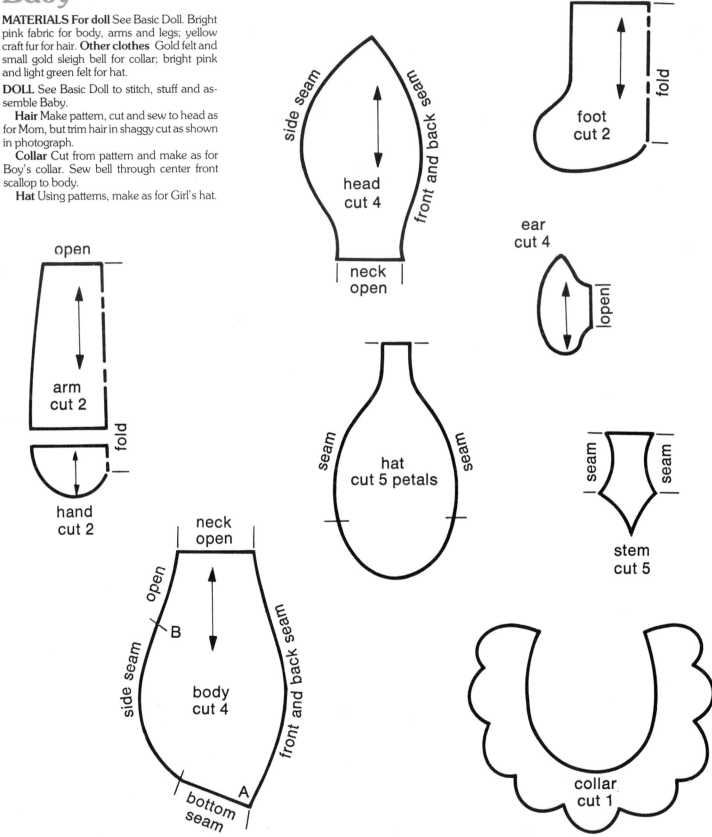

Frog

MATERIALS Green fabric with white polka dots for upper body, arms and legs; yellow fabric for under body; 2 round buttons; orange embroidery floss; green, yellow and black acrylic paint; small brush.

Using patterns, cut out upper and under body pieces, arms and legs. Make dart at hind end of each body piece. With right sides facing, stitch pairs of arms and legs together, leaving straight ends open. Turn right side out. Stuff arms firmly, leaving about ½″ at open ends unstuffed. Lay arms across right side of upper body (see dotted line on pattern) and pin ends. With right sides facing, pin under body piece to upper body piece with arms inside; stitch, catching arm ends in stitching and leaving opening for turning. Turn right side out, stuff and sew opening closed.

Stuff legs lightly. Turn in raw top edges and sew. Sew top edges to A and B on body. Bend legs as shown in photograph and tack to hold shape. Sew button eyes in place; paint carefully (see photograph). Make outline stitch mouth (see stitch diagram, page 184) with 6 strands orange floss.

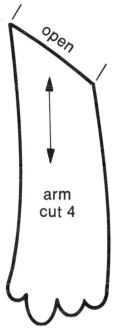

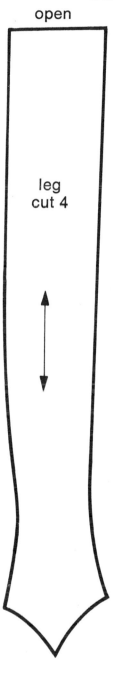

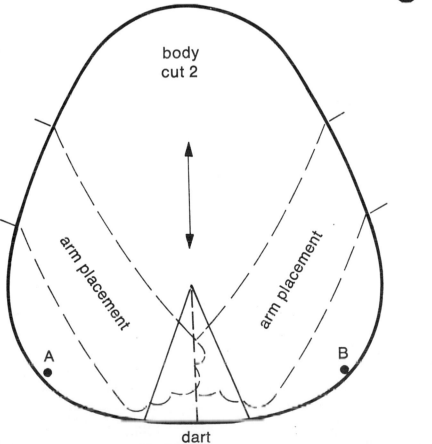

Bunny

MATERIALS Light yellow baby sock; scraps light yellow, bright pink, gold and light pink felt; cotton ball for tail; brown, gold, pink and orange embroidery floss; white glue.

Cut two 2″ x 3″ ovals from sock. Following photograph, shape at center of sides. With right sides facing, stitch pieces together with ¼″ seam, leaving small opening. Turn right side out, stuff and sew opening closed. Cut ½″ x 1″ outer ears from light yellow felt and slightly smaller inner ears from light pink felt. Glue inner ears to outer ears. Sew to top of head. Cut round gold eyes and bright pink heart-shaped nose. Cross stitch eyes in place with 2 strands brown floss and sew on nose. Using single strand floss, embroider 2 pink straight stitches for mouth, make orange straight-stitch whiskers and outline-stitch paws with gold. (For stitching guidance, see stitch diagrams on page 184.) Glue cotton puff to back for tail.

Dishes, Bowl, Spoon & Placemats

MATERIALS Flour (unsifted); salt; water; brown acrylic paint; skewer or blunt needle; small paint brush; about 1½″-diam. cookie cutter.

Combine 2 cups flour and 1 cup salt. Add 1 cup water, a little at a time, kneading with hands for 7 to 10 minutes until dough is smooth and firm. Place dough in plastic bag to prevent drying.

To make plates, roll dough to ¼″ thickness. Cut out circles with cookie cutters. With skewer or blunt needle, draw rings to simulate wood grain. Mold bowl and spoon with fingers. Make acorn-cap-textured lines on sides of bowl with skewer or needle.

Bake dishes at 325° for about 30 minutes until golden brown. Watch carefully because the thinner pieces will be done first. Let cool. Paint dishes tan with brown edges.

Note If desired, plates can be made by sawing rounds from 1½″-diam. branch and acorn caps can be used for cups.

For placemats, cut leaf shapes from green crepe paper. Mark veins with black marker.

Spider & Ladybug

MATERIALS For spider Orange and yellow yarn; blue pipe cleaners; 2 small movable animal eyes; bits of green, orange and blue felt; small white feather; silver cord for hanging; large needle; white glue. **For ladybug** Black and red yarn; white artificial flower stamen; 2 small movable animal eyes; bits of orange and black felt; small snag-loop fastener circle; white glue.

Spider From yarn, make 1½″-diam. orange pompon for body and 1″-diam. yellow pompon for head. With needle and double thread, sew head to body, leaving thread and needle dangling from bottom of body pompon. Glue to secure. Twist 3 pipe cleaners together at center and fasten to body with thread; glue to secure. Bend pipe cleaners as shown to form legs. Glue eyes to head. Cut small orange felt nose and tongue; glue in place. Cut green felt triangle for hat. Cut 2 slits in center and slip feather through. Cut small strip blue felt for hatband and glue in place. Glue hat to head pompon. Thread silver cord on needle. Make several stitches through center of body pompon to secure. Make loop at opposite end for hanging (see color photograph).

Ladybug From yarn, make ¾″-diam. black pompon for head and 1″-diam. red pompon for body. Fold flower stamen in half for antennae. Glue pompons together, sandwiching fold of stamen between. Glue animal eyes and small orange felt oval on black pompon for facial features. Glue 2 small black felt circles to red pompon. Glue small red felt circle to bottom of red pompon. Attach to girl's collar with snag-loop fastener circle glued in place (see color photograph).

Toadstools

MATERIALS ⅜ yd. beige double-knit fabric (will make 1 large and 2 small toadstools); about 1¾″-diam. and 2¾″-diam. jar lids to fit bottoms; small stones for weights; polyester fiberfill for stuffing.

Cut 11″-diam. circle for top of large toadstool and 5½″-diam. circle for top of small toadstool (¼″ seam allowance included). Use patterns to cut other pieces, adding ¼″ seam allowance.

With double strand of thread, hand-sew a row of running stitches ¼″ from edge of top circle. Place some stuffing in center, pull threads to form cup, stuff firmly, then pull threads tightly but do not close entirely; fasten securely. Stitch side seams on stem. With right sides together, stitch bottom circle to lower edge of stem. Turn right side out. Place jar lid in bottom, add a few stones, then stuff firmly. Pin top to stem, turning under raw edges on stem. Sew in place with double strand of thread.

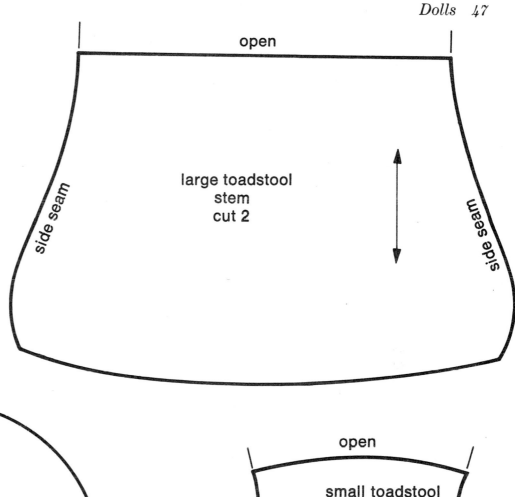

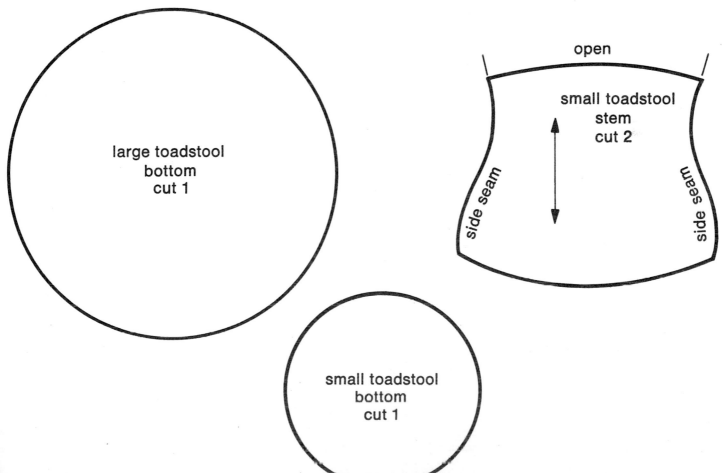

GENERAL DIRECTIONS

SIZES From about 10″ to 14″ tall.

MATERIALS (for set of 4 dolls) Lightweight knitting-worsted-weight yarn: 1 (2-oz.) skein each red (color A), black (B), blue (C), white (D), yellow (E) and green (F); 1 pair knitting needles No. 3 (or English needles No. 10) **or the size that will give you the correct gauge;** steel crochet hook No. 0; tapestry needle; polyester fiberfill stuffing. (For knitting refresher course, see Chapter 6.)

GAUGE 5 sts = 1″; 6 rows = 1″.

FINISHING After knitting each doll (see below), sew side edges of piece together to form cylinder (seam is at center back). Stuff head section. Form brim on man's blue hat as follows: Fold so 1st and 9th rows of hat section meet (see photograph); sew rows together to form brim.

On all dolls, sew running stitch around neck with matching yarn and draw together slightly. Complete stuffing. Draw cast-on sts at bottom tightly closed for man and two boys; for woman, draw slightly closed, then sew remaining opening closed.

On man and boys, with matching yarn, sew a tight running stitch up center of body from feet to within 1¼″ of trouser top, sewing through stuffing from front to back to form trouser legs.

For arms on all dolls, sew running stitch in same manner from bottom of sweater to about 1½″ from top of sweater at each side (see photograph). Embroider all features with 2 or 3 straight stitches (diagram, page 184).

On woman, tie bow of double color F strand at neck. On man, with double B strand crochet 12″ chain; tie in bow at neck.

the knitted family

Big Boy, Small Boy, Mom and Dad — these jaunty knitted tube dolls have arms and legs stitched in, knitted headgear added on and features embroidered with a few straight stitches. The knitting is simple stockinette.

Big Boy

Body Starting at feet with color B, cast on 40 sts. Work in stockinette st for 8 rows. Break off B; attach F. With F, k 2 rows, then work in reverse stockinette st (p 1 row on right side, k 1 row) for 30 F rows. Break off. With A, k 1 row (right side), p 1 row. Attach E and, continuing in stockinette st, work 2 rows E, 2 rows A until there are 6 A stripes. Mark last row. Break off E. With A only, work in k 1, p 1 ribbing for 8 rows. Bind off in ribbing.

Fold ribbing down on right side of work for collar.

Head Attach D and, with right side of work facing you, pick up and k 1 st in each st of marked E row (40 sts). Continue in stockinette st for 13 more rows. Break off D. With B, work 7 more rows. Now shape crown same as for man (see below). See General Directions to finish.

Hat With A, cast on 40 sts. Work in k 1, p 1 ribbing for 2½″. Shape crown same as for head.

Small Boy

Body Starting at feet with color B, cast on 30 sts. Work in stockinette st for 6 rows. Break off B; attach C. With C, work in k 1, p 1 ribbing for 10 rows. Break off. Working in

stockinette st, work 6 rows D, 10 rows A, (2 rows C, 2 rows E) 4 times. With C, k 1 row. Mark last row. Break off. With C, work in k 1, p 1 ribbing for 6 rows. Bind off in ribbing. Fold ribbing down on right side of work for collar.

Head Attach D and, with right side of work facing you, pick up and k 1 st in each st of marked C row (30 sts). Continue in stockinette st for 10 more rows. Now shape crown same as for man (see below). See General Directions to finish.

Hat With C, cast on 30 sts. Work in k 1, p 1 ribbing for 2″. Shape crown same as for head.

Woman

Body Starting at skirt bottom with color C, cast on 40 sts. Work in stockinette st for 4 rows. Drop C; attach F. Now work stripe pattern as follows: * With F, k 2 rows. Break off. With C (k 1 row, p 1 row) twice. Drop C; attach A. With A, k 1 row, p 1 row. Break off A; attach F. Repeat from * 3 times more. With F, k 2 rows, p 1 row, k 1 row. Break off F; attach A. **Note** *When changing colors in a row, twist new yarn under old to prevent holes in work.*

Next row With A, k 6; attach D and k 8; attach 2nd ball A and k 12; attach 2nd ball D and k 8; attach 3rd ball A and k 6. **Following**

row P 6 A, 8 D, 12 A, 8 D, 6 A. Repeat these 2 rows 5 times more. Break off both D balls and last 2 A balls. With remaining A only, work in stockinette st for 10 more rows. Break off.

Head With D, work 4 rows. Break off. **5th row (right side)** With E, k 13; attach D and k 14; attach 2nd ball E and k 13. **6th row** K 13 E, p 14 D, k 13 E. **7th row** P 13 E, k 14 D, p 13 E. Repeat last 2 rows twice more, then 6th row once again. Break off D and 2nd ball E. With E only (p 1 row, k 1 row) 3 times, then p 1 row. **20th row** K 2 tog across (20 sts). **21st row** P 2 tog across (10 sts). **22nd row** K 2 tog across (5 sts). Break off, leaving sewing end; with tapestry needle draw sts tightly to-

gether. Fasten off. See General Directions to finish.

Cap With D, cast on 3 sts. Work in stockinette st for 15 rows. K 1 row on wrong side for ridge. Continue in stockinette st for 6 rows. Bind off. Sew side edges together from ridge to bound-off edge. Gather bound-off sts together, leaving ¾″ circle open at center back of cap. Roll front edge.

Man

Body Starting at feet with color A, cast on 40 sts. Work in stockinette st throughout (unless otherwise specified). Work 8 rows. Break off A; attach B. With B, work 30 rows. Break off.

With C, k 2 rows, p 2 rows. Now work pattern st on sweater as follows: **Next row (right side)** K 3, * p 2, k 2. Repeat from * across, ending k 3. P 1 row, k 1 row. **Next row** P 1, * k 2, p 2. Repeat from * across, ending p 1. K 1 row, p 1 row. Repeat these 6 rows for pattern st 3 times more (end of sweater pattern). Break off.

Head With D, work 12 rows. Break off. With E, work 2 rows. Break off.

Hat With C, work 23 rows. To shape crown: **Next row** P 2 tog across (20 sts). K 1 row. Repeat these 2 rows twice more (5 sts). Break off, leaving sewing end; with tapestry needle draw sts tightly together. Fasten off. See General Directions to finish.

SIZE About 52″ tall.

MATERIALS ¾ yd. 45″-wide unbleached muslin for body; ⅜ yd. red-and-white striped cotton for stockings and apron waistband; ¼ yd. black cotton for shoes; ¾ yd. cotton print for dress; 1⅛ yd. white muslin for bloomers and apron; scraps eyelet ruffling for dress and bloomers; 2¼ yd. striped ribbon to trim apron; 1 yd. ¼″-wide elastic; 4 oz. yellow yarn and 1 yd. red ribbon for hair; red, white and black cotton embroidery floss for features; wooden paint-mixer paddle to support neck; polyester fiberfill; 2 snap fasteners.

Doll Enlarge diagram following adjacent instructions, and cut out patterns, adding ½″ to all edges for seam allowance. Cut head from muslin. Also cut 2 body pieces 10″ x 11″, 2 legs 6½″ x 24″ and 2 arms 5½″ x 20½″. Shape ends of arms slightly to form rounded hands as shown in photograph.

Cut 2 stockings 6½″ x 14″ with the stripes crosswise. Using pattern, cut black shoes.

Following pattern and photograph, embroider features on 1 head piece, working satin stitch for eyes and nose, chain stitch for eye and nose outlines and mouth, French knots for freckles (see stitch diagrams, page 184, for guidance). With right sides facing, stitch head pieces together, leaving neck end open. Clip seams; turn and stuff. Stitch body pieces together, leaving opening at center of one 10″ edge for neck; turn and stuff. Insert half of paddle into head through neck and other half into body. Insert neck edge into body opening and sew securely.

Fold arms in half lengthwise and stitch side and hand; turn and stuff. Fold in seam allowance at open end, stitch edges together and sew arms near upper corners at sides of body.

Stitch a stocking end to each leg. Fold legs and stockings in half lengthwise; stitch and turn to form tubes. Stitch pairs of shoes together, leaving tops open. Stuff all pieces. Turn in open ends of shoes; insert ends of stockings into shoes and slipstitch. Stitch legs to body in same manner as arms.

For hair, cut 4-oz. skein of yarn into 2-yd. strands. Reserve 1 strand for bangs. Tie hank of strands together in center. Starting about 3″ from tie, braid half of hank to form pigtail. Tie with ribbon. Make second pigtail. Cut reserved strand into 4″ lengths and, following photograph, sew braids and bangs to head (back of head is bare).

Dress Following dimensions in diagram, cut front and back of dress. Cut slit in back piece. Stitch side seams from lower edge to dots. Stitch shoulder seams to dots. Cut sleeves 10½″ x 14″. Fold in half crosswise and seam to form tubes. Stitch into armholes, gathering to fit. Turn in wrist edge ½″, then again 2″. Starting 1¼″ from edge, topstitch 2 lines ⅜″ apart to form casing, leaving opening for elastic. Cut elastic to fit around arm; run it

through casing and sew the ends together.

Hem neck and slit. Cut two 1″ x 13″ neck ties. Fold in half lengthwise and topstitch; sew ends at neck edge. Cut eyelet ruffle to fit around neck; sew in place.

Bloomers Cut 2 pieces 22″ x 26½″. Fold each lengthwise around half of body and 1 leg of doll. Pin inseam of each leg to crotch. Pin front and back seam from crotch to waist. Remove bloomers and stitch seams; turn. Stitch 1″-wide waist casing; cut and insert elastic. Stitch ½″-wide casings at leg edges; cut and insert elastic. Trim with eyelet ruffling.

Apron Cut apron skirt 19½″ x 12½″ and bib 6½″ x 7½″. Cut waistband 3″ x 30″, piecing where necessary. Fold in and press both sides and bottom long edge of skirt. Cut lengths of ribbon to fit; topstitch. Repeat with both 6½″ sides and top 7½″ edge of bib. Fold waistband in half lengthwise, right side out, and cut ends on diagonal. Turn in all edges and baste. Gather top of skirt to 9½″. Center and stitch bib to skirt. Center and pin waistband to apron. Topstitch around all edges of waistband. Cut two 10″ pieces ribbon for shoulder straps. Sew end of each to top of bib, cross over back and sew snaps to other ends and to waistband.

SWEET SUE

Our Susie is well over four feet tall — big enough to dance with! Beginning with a muslin body, she's completely outfitted with fetching dress, apron, bloomers, shoes and socks. Basic shapes for all are easy to cut out and sew; a wooden paint-mixer paddle supports her neck.

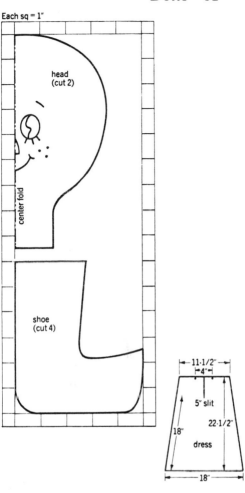

Each sq = 1"

head
(cut 2)

center fold

shoe
(cut 4)

11-1/2"
4"
5" slit
22-1/2"
18"
dress
18"

HOW TO ENLARGE PATTERNS

You will need brown wrapping paper (pieced if necessary to make a sheet large enough for a pattern), a felt-tipped marker, pencil and ruler. (When pattern you are enlarging has a grid around it, you must first connect lines across pattern with a colored pencil to form a grid over the picture.) Mark paper with grid as follows: First cut paper into a true square or rectangle. Then mark dots around edges, 1" or 2" apart or whatever is indicated on pattern, making same number of spaces as there are squares around the edges of pattern diagram. Form a grid by joining the dots across opposite sides of paper. Check to make sure you have the same number of squares as diagram. With marker, draw in each square the same pattern lines you see in corresponding squares on diagram.

SIZE About 19″ tall.

MATERIALS 45″-wide cotton-blend fabric, ½ yd. for body, ¼ yd. calico for dress, ¼ yd. solid color for collar and panties; felt scraps for shoes; matching sewing thread; pair of baby socks; 3½- or 4-oz. skein sport-weight or knitting-worsted-weight yarn for hair; 1 yd. ½″-wide hair ribbon; 1¼ yd. each baby rick-rack and ½″-wide lace ruffling; 3 small snap fasteners; ⅜ yd. ⅛″-wide elastic; scraps red, white, green, black and brown 6-strand embroidery floss for features; polyester fiberfill; brown marker for freckles (optional).

PATTERNS Enlarge patterns following adjacent instructions, adding ⅜″ seam allowance to all except shoe edges (to shoes, add ⅛″ seam allowance to outer edge, nothing to top edge X or to U-shaped edge Y). Cut out pieces from fabric (on bodice, cut one front on fold; cut 2 backs, adding seam allowance to center back edges). From calico, also cut 6½″ x 27″ strip for skirt and two 2½″ x 10½″ strips for sleeves. Cut 1″-diam. circle from body fabric for nose.

DOLL With right sides facing, stitch one long shaped edge of front/back head around a side head piece, then stitch opposite shaped edge to other side head piece (unit resembles deflated ball, open at neck). Clip curves and turn.

Embroider face as follows: Using all 6 strands floss, embroider red mouth in backstitch, white and green eyes in satin stitch, black French knot for each pupil, brown lashes in straight stitch, brown eyebrows in backstitch (see stitch diagrams, page 184). Run basting thread around nose circle ⅛″ in from edge. Stuff and draw closed. Sew nose to face. Stuff head firmly. Add freckles with felt-tip marker if desired.

Stitch body pieces together at shoulders and at sides below dots (leave armholes, neck and lower edge open). Turn and stuff. Stitch arms and legs; turn and stuff. Pinch tops of arms together with seams at center of each side. Insert in armholes, turn in armhole edges and slipstitch securely. Pinch tops of legs together as for arms (toes point forward). Insert in bottom of body and join as for arms.

Insert body neck into head neck, turn head neck edges in and slipstitch, adding bits of stuffing to firm neck and easing edges to fit.

Hair For bangs cut enough 2½″-long strands yarn to spread across 3″ of top of head. Sew firmly across center of head, making 2 rows of stitches ¼″ apart. For braids cut from 99 to 120 strands yarn (depending on thickness) about 28″ long. Center and spread on head horizontally across bangs, starting 1″ behind front of bangs and ending 1″ above back neck. Sew along center to simulate part. Gather bunches of yarn at each side of face in line with nose; sew to head. Braid ends.

Country-Cousin Doll

With her sunny embroidered smile and quaint calico dress, here's a little charmer to win the heart of any little girl. Country Cousin is about 19″ tall.

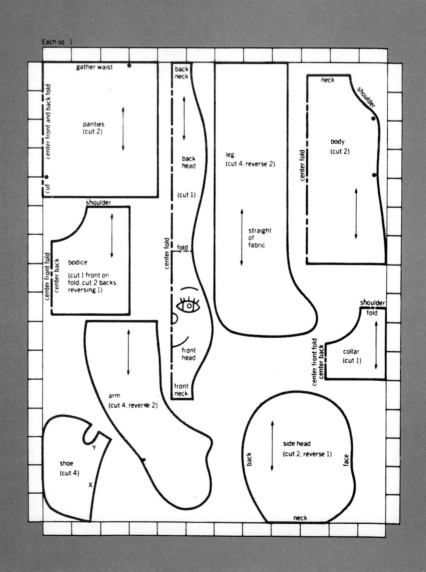

Cut ribbon in half and tie around braids.

Clothes Cut collar open at center back. Turn under all except neck edges ⅜″ and baste. Pin edge of lace behind basted edge and topstitch. Trim one long edge of each sleeve with lace in same manner.

With right sides facing, stitch bodice front and backs together at shoulders; turn. Clip and turn neck edge of bodice to right side, then clip and turn neck edge of collar to wrong side; pin the two together, right sides up, and topstitch ⅛″ from edge.

Gather raw edge of sleeve to fit bodice armhole between dots, drawing most of gathers along 2½″ center of piece. With right sides facing, stitch sleeve to bodice, centering gathered section at shoulder seam. Stitch side and sleeve seams.

Gather one long edge of skirt to fit bodice; stitch to bodice. Turn up ¾″ hem and topstitch ¼″ from fold. Topstitch rickrack ¾″ from lower edge of skirt and to bodice just above waistline. Turn in back edge of dress; topstitch. Add snaps at neck, waist and halfway down skirt.

Stitch pantie pieces together along sides. Make cut at center front and back from lower edge to dot to form crotch. Seam crotch edges to form legs. Topstitch hems at leg and waist edges. Cut elastic to fit snugly around doll's waist. Stretch and topstitch elastic around inside of waist edge of panties.

Stitch shoe halves together with ⅛″ seam allowance; turn. Put socks, wrong side out, on doll. Pin any adjustment on socks to make them fit. Remove socks and stitch; trim seams and turn.

HOW TO ENLARGE PATTERNS

You will need brown wrapping paper (pieced if necessary to make a sheet large enough for a pattern), a felt-tipped marker, pencil and ruler. (When pattern you are enlarging has a grid around it, you must first connect lines across pattern with a colored pencil to form a grid over the picture.) Mark paper with grid as follows: First cut paper into a true square or rectangle. Then mark dots around edges, 1″ or 2″ apart or whatever is indicated on pattern, making same number of spaces as there are squares around the edges of pattern diagram. Form a grid by joining the dots across opposite sides of paper. Check to make sure you have the same number of squares as diagram. With marker, draw in each square the same pattern lines you see in corresponding squares on diagram.

SIZE About 50" tall.

MATERIALS For both Solid-color tights for each head (includes girl's arms); knit shirt (short sleeves for girl, long for boy); mittens; 2 oz. knitting worsted for girl's hair, rug yarn for boy's; scraps fabric and felt for features; white or fabric glue. **For girl** Pair of tights; scrap ribbon. **For boy** Colorful pants; striped socks.

Head Cut legs from tights, just below crotch, and save for girl's arms. Using body of tights for head, turn inside out, pin edges of each leg opening together and sew. Turn right side out. Stuff head softly. Opening at waist is neck edge of head. Cut out features from fabrics or felt and glue to one side of head.

Girl's hair For each ponytail, cut about 55 lengths yarn 15" long. Hold together, fold in half and sew fold to side of head near top. Tie ponytail with ribbon. Make and sew ponytail to other side of head. Cut 5" lengths of yarn and sew bunches of them through center across top of head for shaggy bangs.

Boy's hair Cut 6" lengths yarn. Sew shaggy bunches through center and across top of head.

Girl's body Cut feet off leftover legs of tights and use legs for arms. Cut legs off tights. Softly stuff shirt, arms, legs and mittens. Baste tops and bottoms of arms closed, insert one end into arms of shirt, other into mittens; topstitch. Insert tops of legs into bottom of shirt and topstitch across. Topstitch across ankle area of legs. Insert neck of head into neck of shirt and hand-sew securely.

Boy's body Softly stuff arms, mittens, shirt, pants and socks. Baste wrists of sleeves closed, insert into mittens 1½" and topstitch 1" from tops of mittens. Fold mitten cuff down. Insert bottom of shirt into pants top and hand-sew around securely. Insert tops of socks into pants bottoms and topstitch across.

HOW TO ENLARGE PATTERNS

You will need brown wrapping paper (pieced if necessary), a felt-tipped marker, pencil and ruler. Pattern you are enlarging has a grid around it; first connect lines across pattern to form a grid over the picture. Mark paper with grid as follows: First cut paper into a true square or rectangle. Then mark dots around edges, 1" apart as pattern indicates, making same number of spaces as there are squares around the edges of diagram. Form a grid by joining the dots across opposite sides of paper. Make sure you have the same number of squares as diagram. With marker, draw in each square the pattern lines you see in corresponding squares on diagram.

Big Girl and Big Boy

Talk about good company! To make your version of these long, lanky dolls, save outgrown kids' clothes — stitch them — sew together and stuff with batting.

Heartthrobs

*Here's an engaging duo —
boy-meets-girl pillow dolls to give to
anyone whose heart needs melting*

TO MAKE EACH DOLL Enlarge patterns following instructions. Add ¼" for seam allowance. From pink cotton, cut 2 head, 4 hand and 4 leg pieces for boy (for girl, cut the 4 legs from dotted Swiss). Cut 2 body pieces, blue gingham for boy and calico for girl.

Following stitch diagrams, page 184, embroider features on one head piece (satin stitch lips and nose, outline stitch mouth, straight stitches for eyes). Tint cheeks with crayon. Place other head piece on top, right sides facing, and stitch around curve, leaving bottom open. Turn; stuff. Repeat for hand and leg pieces. Topstitch fingers.

Pin red piping for boy or eyelet for girl around right side of one body piece, edges matching. Slip hand pieces between fabric and edging; stitch edging and hands to body; remove pins. Place second body piece on top, right sides facing, and stitch sides from X to Y; turn. Tack hands to front body piece at fingers only. Insert legs and head and sew by hand, closing openings. Sew yarn loops for hair, using 2 strands to cover back.

For boy, sew buttons to front. Cut paper flowers, tape to florist's wire; tie on satin bow; insert in hand. Tie shoelaces around feet. Make red gingham bow tie; sew in place.

For girl, with pinking shears cut white paper heart to fit on doily; cut smaller pink paper heart to fit on white. Write words with marker. Rubber-cement pieces together; attach to doll with double-stick tape. Tie ribbon bow in hair; tie ribbons on feet.

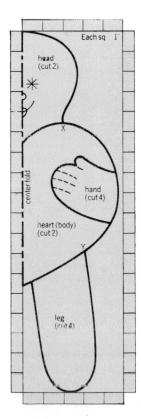

SIZE Each doll is about 17" tall.

MATERIALS For boy ¼ yd. each blue gingham and pink cotton; ⅛ yd. red gingham; 1 pkg. red welted piping; three ½" heart buttons; two 26" blue shoelaces; ½ yd. ⅛"-wide pink satin ribbon; construction paper, florist's wire; 1 oz. orange yarn. **For girl** ¼ yd. each calico print and pink cotton; ⅛ yd. pink dotted Swiss; ¾ yd. pleated ¾"-wide eyelet; 1 yd. ¼"-wide blue satin ribbon; 1 oz. yellow yarn; 4" gold heart doily; pink and white construction paper; pinking shears; rubber cement; double-stick tape; marker. **For both** Polyester fiberfill; red, pink and blue embroidery floss; crewel and embroidery needles, pink crayon.

CHAPTER

3

Just-for-fun Activity Toys

While store-bought toys can be wonderful, homemade activity toys are better by far. The proof is in the playing: Because you know the children best, inside and out, the toys you make are geared to their preferences, and thus more stimulating and appealing than anything you can buy. And though the display of toy store items is vast and impressive, some quality and individuality must be sacrificed to mass production. Even that vastness has its drawbacks: It's a challenge to make a suitable choice, and you might, in the confusion, spend more than you'd planned.

With something that is handmade, *you* choose the materials, the colors, the textures of a toy tailored specifically to the interests of the little boy or girl you want to please.

The projects that follow share several virtues. As a group, they are "mixed materials" toys—some of fabric but most of "found objects" readily available in every household. This toy group, too, tends elsewhere (and on toy store shelves) to be categorized by age level, but not very precisely by skill or preference. One six-month-old may find it satisfying to squeeze a toss toy; another wants no part of it, and would rather kick his feet in time with a moving mobile. That children cannot be categorized is what makes them so individual, and their diversity so remarkable. So browse through the projects with some unique little person in mind. You are sure to find any number of toys just right for him or her.

One final characteristic worth mentioning: Children do *outgrow* activity toys, sometimes at an astonishing rate, so we've seen to it that nothing here requires too much time or effort. A couple of evening hours or a few during the day is all it takes to complete a toy, and have it ready *then and there* for those eager little hands.

Contents

Bath splashers **58**

Music-box crib pillow **59**

Balloon mobile **60**

Clown mobile **60**

Airmobile **61**

Throwaway Quartet **62**

   Cradle twins **62**

   Clown marionette **63**

   Shoe bank **64**

   Pup & piggy pull toys **65**

Panda pendant **66**

Whirligig on wheels **67**

Bean-bag toss toys **68**

Teaching board **70**

Foam-ball finger puppets **71**

Squeezable foam blocks **72**

Creature kites **74**

Football & basketball pillows **76**

Owlish pencil caddy **77**

Socko the Hobbyhorse **78**

Canny pig **79**

SIZE Fish measures 4″ x 9½″; the duckling, 5″ x 6″.

MATERIALS For fish 1½″ x 4½″ x 8″ heavy-duty sponge; ¾″ x 3½″ x 5″ oval orange sponge; ½″ x 3½″ x 4″ oval green sponge; scrap 1¾″-wide blue sponge. **For duckling** 1½″ x 4½″ x 8″ heavy-duty sponge; ¾″ x 3½″ x 5″ oval orange sponge; scrap 1½″-wide red sponge; scrap 1¾″-wide blue sponge. **For both toys** Serrated kitchen knife.

PATTERNS Enlarge diagrams, following adjacent instructions. Cut out shapes with serrated knife. Whenever possible, use edge of sponge for edge of toy.

FISH

Cut heavy-duty sponge body, orange mouth, green fins and blue eye (use eye-hole pattern). Cut out eye and fin holes crosswise completely through body. Cut 1″ mouth hole lengthwise into body between dots. Insert pieces as shown.

DUCKLING

Cut heavy-duty sponge body, red bill, orange feet and blue eye (use eye-hole pattern). Cut eye and feet holes crosswise completely through body. Cut 1½″ bill hole lengthwise into body between dots. Insert pieces as shown.

Bath splashers

Standard household sponges are snipped and trimmed with a serrated knife to shape these bathtime playmates.

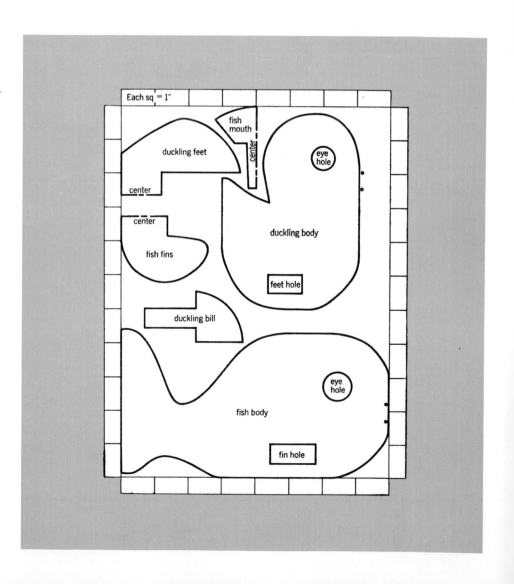

Each sq = 1″

fish mouth

duckling feet

center

center

center

fish fins

eye hole

duckling body

feet hole

duckling bill

eye hole

fish body

fin hole

Music-box crib pillow

The tinkling sounds of a music box are a soothing sensory experience for an infant. Here's an original way to supply them — a music box mechanism nestled in a small, plump tea-towel-covered pillow.

SIZE About 5½" x 7½".

MATERIALS Linen tea towel with embroidered motif; 1 yd. green single-fold bias tape; ¾ yd. each 1"-wide ruffled eyelet trim and pink fabric-covered cord; green and white sewing threads; polyester fiberfill stuffing; music-box mechanism (see note below).

Note *You can order a small music-box mechanism from Lightsaround Inc., 855 Conklin St., Farmingdale, New York 11735. Write for price and mailing information.*

PILLOW From towel, cut two 5½" x 7½" pieces with embroidered motif centered on one piece. With edges matching, pin bias tape around embroidered piece, mitering corners. Topstitch close to inner folded edge of tape. With edges matching, pin cord on tape, then ruffle on cord.

Near center of back piece make ¾" buttonhole for music-box winder. With right sides facing and tape, cord and ruffle sandwiched between, stitch towel pieces together, leaving 4" opening at top edge for hanger loop. Turn right side out. Insert music box in case, poking winder through buttonhole; stuff generously, making sure stuffing is packed well around box. Gather buttonhole edges tightly with hand stitches. Cut 5" length bias tape. Fold in half, insert ends in pillow opening and sew opening closed.

HOW TO ENLARGE PATTERNS

You will need brown wrapping paper (pieced if necessary to make a sheet large enough for a pattern), a felt-tipped marker, pencil and ruler. (When pattern you are enlarging has a grid around it, you must first connect lines across pattern with a colored pencil to form a grid over the picture.) Mark paper with grid as follows: First cut paper into a true square or rectangle. Then mark dots around edges, 1" or 2" apart or whatever is indicated on pattern, making same number of spaces as there are squares around the edges of pattern diagram. Form a grid by joining the dots across opposite sides of paper. Check to make sure you have the same number of squares as diagram. With marker, draw in each square the same pattern lines you see in corresponding squares on diagram.

Balloon mobile

*Presenting a cinch-to-assemble
skyriding home for a stuffed animal pet.*

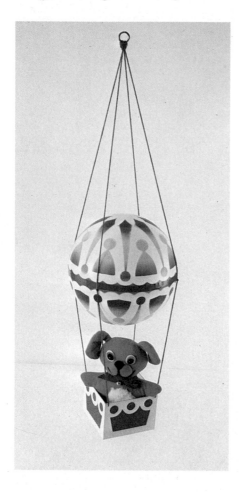

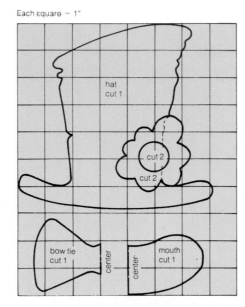

Each square — 1″

hat
cut 1

cut 2

cut 2

bow tie
cut 1

center

center

mouth
cut 1

SIZE 9″ x 33″.

MATERIALS 9″-diam. beach ball; box big enough to hold your stuffed animal (our box measures 3½″ deep x 5″ square); vinyl self-adhesive tape; 3½ yd. cord; red and white paper; white glue; ¾″-diam. metal ring.

If necessary, cover box with white paper; decorate with red paper as desired. Punch small hole in opposite upper corners of 2 facing sides of box. Cut four 30″ lengths cord. Thread end of each through a hole; knot on inside. Make single knot in each cord 10″ above box. Place ball in box and wrap tape once around center of ball, taping each cord to ball just above knot. Gather 4 cords together above ball, run through ring and tie to secure.

Clown mobile

*Guaranteed to attract the roving
eyes — and joyful smiles — of an infant or
toddler, this goggle-eyed clown mobile is
made of shirt cardboard and
table-tennis balls.*

HOW TO ENLARGE PATTERNS

You will need brown wrapping paper (pieced if necessary), a felt-tipped marker, pencil and ruler. Mark paper with grid as follows: First cut paper into a true square or rectangle. Then mark dots around edges as indicated on pattern, making same number of spaces as there are squares around edges of diagram. Form a grid by joining the dots across opposite sides of paper. Make sure you have the same number of squares as diagram. With marker, draw in each square the pattern lines in corresponding squares on diagram.

MATERIALS Scraps of medium-weight cardboard; blue, yellow, white and red acrylic paints; felt scraps; white glue; pins; black cotton thread; 3 table-tennis balls; needle.

Enlarge diagram, following adjacent instructions, for hat, daisy, mouth and bow tie on cardboard. Cut out pieces with sharp scissors. Brush a sealer coat of white glue on all surfaces; let dry. Following photograph, paint cardboard pieces, front and back, with slightly thinned acrylic paints; let dry thoroughly. Pierce one table-tennis ball with needle and stick impaled ball in work surface; paint red for nose; let dry. When bow tie dries, add polka dots. Glue daisies on hat as indicated. Also cut out two black felt strips for mouth; glue a strip to each side as in photograph.

Refer to photograph to assemble mobile. With pin, punch three centered holes along bottom edge of hat to suspend the eyes and the centered nose, mouth and bow-tie pieces. Pierce remaining balls with needle. Wrap, knot and glue a piece of black thread to a straight pin. Snip off head of pin with knotted thread attached to it and push pin and knot into one uncolored ball; dab with glue and let dry. Repeat with second uncolored ball. Thread loose end of black thread in needle and push through one of the outermost holes along bottom edge of hat, adjust length of eye (should hang 1¼" down from hat edge) and tie off. Repeat for second eye. To hang red nose, push a threaded needle through ball and out the other side; remove needle and pull thread so a single strand runs through ball. Attach one end of thread through middle hole in bottom edge of hat and adjust length of nose between eyes (about 2½" down). Dab glue in top hole of nose; let dry. Punch hole in center of top edge of mouth and bow tie. Connect mouth to loose end of thread coming out bottom of nose; tie off. Punch last hole in bottom edge of mouth. Cut another piece of thread to connect mouth to bow tie. Hold mobile loosely at top of hat to find balance, make hole and add thread with loop at top through top edge of hat. Hang mobile and let it come to a standstill. Cut out felt disks for eyes as shown; glue to the back and front of white balls.

Airmobile

This ingenious, five-plane airmobile is put together of clothespins, dowels, ice cream sticks, toothpicks and snaps.

MATERIALS 3' of ³⁄₁₆"-diam. dowel; 5 wooden clothespins; 1' of ½"-diam. dowel; 4"-long wooden ice cream sticks; wooden toothpicks; ¼"-diam. snaps; 20-lb.-test nylon monofilament; white glue.

Assemble following for each airplane: clothespin for body, two ice cream sticks for wings, two ½"-thick slices of ½"-diam. dowel for wheels, 1½" pieces of toothpick for propeller with snap centered for knob, and one each ¾", 1½" and 2" pieces of ice cream sticks, ends rounded, for tail assembly. Glue wings side by side inside top leg of clothespin body by crotch. Glue wheels butted against wings and body near head of clothespin. Add toothpick across head with snap.

To assemble tail, attach 1½" piece to end of top leg of clothespin, glue 2" crosspiece centered and butted against end of top leg, then add ¾" upright piece (this should be done on 2 planes only).

Cut ³⁄₁₆" dowel into two 18" pieces; notch ends of each with sharp knife. Center dowels to form cross; cut a shallow notch for each. Glue for hanger. Suspend each plane from a 3½" double loop of monofilament and slip monofilament into notched end of hanger. (Hang planes with 3-piece tail assembly from opposite arms.) Loop and tie fifth plane at crossed center. Tie long length of monofilament around center to suspend mobile. Adjust balance.

Throwaway Quartet

You'll enjoy concocting this collection of amusing toys from throwaways you rescue and transform. Read the general directions first, then scout around for the easy-to-find materials.

cradle twins

This time a cutaway plastic bottle is covered with fabric and furnished with tiny bedclothes, just right for two snug-as-a-bug clothespin babies.

GENERAL DIRECTIONS

MATERIALS For clown 5"-high plastic shampoo bottle (excluding cap); 6 plastic pill containers; 2"-diam. plastic foam ball. **For pull toys** Plastic dish-detergent bottle for dog, large round plastic shampoo bottle for pig; 4" length of ¼" dowel for each toy; 3 wooden beads for each toy; compass. **For cradle twins** Round plastic shampoo bottle; 2 wooden clothespins (without metal springs); scraps each of calico, cotton batting, ¾"-wide eyelet ruffle and ½"-wide bias tape. **For clown and pull toys** 6" x 36" sheet ¼"-thick balsa wood (will make control bars for clown and wheels on pull toys); fine sandpaper; 1 yd. braided cord for each pull toy, and 1½ yd. each of 3 colors for clown; scraps felt in assorted colors. **For all the toys** Acrylic paint, sponge and brush; Krylon® Crystal Clear spray; Slomon's Quik Glue®; X-acto® knife.

To make holes To cut holes specified in plastic bottles and pill containers, punch or hammer first hole with thick nail, then enlarge hole with X-acto knife. Or you can hold a large nail with pliers over flame on gas stove, then insert hot nail into plastic. Remove immediately or it will adhere. Continue to heat nail and rub it back and forth to enlarge hole.

To paint bottle Soak and peel paper labels from bottle. (Discard bottle cap for clown.) Using sponge, pat and smooth one or two thick layers acrylic paint on bottle, then brush on final coat. When dry, apply coat of clear spray.

To cut balsa wood You can cut very soft balsa wood with X-acto knife. For clown, cut two 1" x 8½" bars; sand. For each pull toy, mark two 3½"-diam. wheels with compass; cut out and sand edges smooth. Cut hole in center of each to fit dowel snugly.

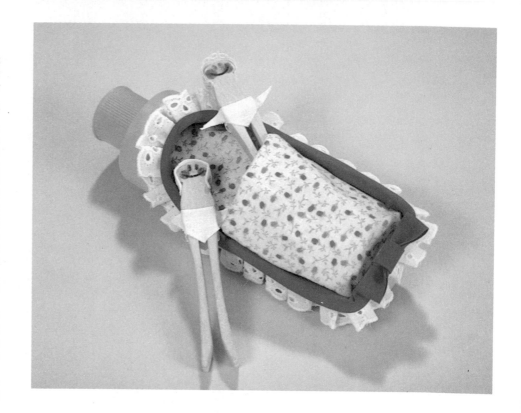

See General Directions, left, for materials and basic instructions. Following photograph for shape, cut out opening in side of bottle with X-acto knife so piece resembles cradle. Following General Directions, paint outside of cradle. Cut eyelet ruffle and bias tape to fit around cradle opening. Sew tape to edge of ruffle; glue ruffle around opening, starting and ending at foot of cradle. Make small bow from tape and glue over joining.

Make mattress by wrapping calico around batting; place in cradle. Double another piece of calico and tuck in for coverlet. Paint faces on clothespins, then cut tiny fabric triangles for diapers and glue to "babies" (or paint on diapers).

Clown marionette

*The perky little puppet has a
plastic shampoo-bottle body and pill-bottle
arms and legs. Thread them
all together and watch him roll and tumble,
dance and play.*

See General Directions, p. 62, for materials and basic instructions. Following photograph for placement of holes to admit cords, cut hole on each side of shampoo bottle for arms and 3 holes evenly spaced at bottom. Cut hole in bottom of each pill container and in center of lid. For arm, thread a cord through a lid and make knot on outside of lid 18″ from one end of cord. Thread other end through container and out through bottom; make knot, thread through lid and another container; make knot; thread through one arm-hole on bottle and out through other arm-hole; make knot; thread another arm onto same cord. Glue lids to containers.

For legs, make tight knot at end of one cord, cover with glue and force into a hole (not center hole) at bottom of bottle. Thread cord through a pill container and lid; make knot; thread through another container and lid; make knot and cut cord. Make other leg in same manner; glue lids to containers.

Knot end of 19″ length of cord to cord between the two containers of each leg. Thread a cord up through body from bottom center hole and out through neck. Knot and glue end of cord at bottom.

For head, cut hole through center of plastic-foam ball. Cut out and glue on felt features as shown. Then cut out 2¼″-diam. felt circle for cap. Make cut to center, then cut ¼″ center hole. Fold piece into cone shape to fit ball and trim excess; glue and decorate. Thread body cord up through ball and cap, slide cap down onto head with cord extending through top of cap; glue cap to head.

To decorate body, cut three ¾″-diam. felt dots and glue to body. For ruff, cut 1¼″ x 13″ felt strip. Run basting thread through one long edge, pull up to fit bottle neck and fasten. Glue ruff around neck. Slide head down onto bottle neck and glue.

Pull all cords up so clown hangs properly. Trim ends to same length (body cord should extend about 8″ above cap). Cut hole to admit cord through each end and center of balsa control bars. Cross bars, matching center holes. Draw body cord through center holes and knot. Draw ends of arm and leg cords through end holes and knot.

See General Directions, p. 62, for comments about materials.

MATERIALS High-top sneaker in good condition; new, colorful shoelace; sport sock; round potato-chip can; acrylic paint and brush; white glue (optional).

Wash sneaker in washer and allow to dry thoroughly. Paint as shown. Insert sock foot in sneaker and stuff sneaker foot with paper. Lace sneaker. Cut slot for coins in plastic lid of potato-chip can. Slide into sock and pull up sock to top of can. Glue if necessary.

Shoe bank

The shoe bank is nothing but an old sneaker, spiffed up with acrylic paint. A slotted can takes pennies.

See General Directions, p. 62, for materials and basic instructions. Cut 2 holes directly opposite each other in bottle about 2″ from bottom. Paint dowel and sides of balsa wheels. Insert dowel into a wheel, through holes in bottle and through other wheel, allowing enough space for wheels to turn freely. Glue wheels to dowels.

Following photograph for shapes, cut out felt ears and eyes and glue to bottle. For dog's tail, cut 1⅛″ x 4½″ felt oval and point ends. Fold and glue sides to center for half of oval and glue that end to bottom of bottle, allowing open end to stick up. For pig's tail, cut 3″ x 4″ piece of felt. Fringe one 4″ edge, making 1½″-deep cuts ¼″ apart. Roll piece tightly and glue to resemble tassel; glue unfringed end to bottom of bottle. Tighten cap on bottle and glue one end of cord around it. Slide beads on other end and knot.

Pup & piggy pull toys

Empty plastic bottles (from dish detergent or shampoo) become comical animals when they are decorated with acrylic paint and given the added attractions of eyes, wheels and a pull cord.

Panda pendant

It's easy, easy as can be, to turn out this teensy animal made from ball fringe and worn with proud pleasure.

MATERIALS 2 white and 4 black 1"-diam. pompons from ball-fringe trim; scraps black and white felt; 2 white seed beads; bit of red yarn; pin-back finding or ¾ yd. red rattail cord and small jewelry ring; white glue; black felt-tip marker; sewing thread.

Use one 1"-diam. white pompon for body and trim other white pompon to ¾"-diam. for head. Trim the 4 black pompons to ½"-diam. for arms and legs. Double and knot sewing thread on needle and run through one black pompon (arm), through body and through other arm. Fasten and break off. In same manner, join legs and head to body.

Cut tiny white felt circle paws and glue to arms and legs. For face, cut ½"-diam. white felt circle, cut to center and overlap cut edges to form slight cone shape; glue to head. With marker, make black dot on point of cone for nose. For eye patches, cut 2 tiny black felt circles and sew on seed-bead eyes; glue to head. For ears, cut 2 black felt ovals and 2 smaller white felt circles. Glue circles to ovals and ears to head. Make yarn bow and glue to body.

For pendant, sew ring to back of head and run cord through it; for pin, glue pin back to back.

SIZE About 14″ long.

MATERIALS 4′ of 2 x 2 pine; 2′ of 1 x 6 pine; 1 yd. silver self-adhesive plastic; 4 pinwheels; four 1½″ x No. 8 roundhead wood screws; eight ⅝″-diam. washers; two 3½″ bolts with nuts to fit; two ½″ screw eyes; 1 yd. silver braided cord; 2″-diam. circular key ring.

From 2 x 2, cut 13¾″-long body piece and two 7″-long axles. In body piece drill centered ⅜″-diam. bolt hole ⅝″ in from each end, all the way through the wood. Starting ¾″ in from bolt holes, drill three ¼″-diam. (or to fit pinwheel sticks) holes ½″ deep into top of body piece, spacing them equally.

Drill centered bolt hole into one side of each axle. Centered into ends, drill pilot hole for wheel screws.

From 1 x 6 cut four 4¼″-diam. wheel pieces. Drill centered ¼″-diam. hole in each.

Cut 2 pinwheel sticks to 6¾″ and one to 9½″. Take apart fourth pinwheel and cut out four 1¾″-diam. circles with centered ¼″-diam. holes to decorate wheels.

Cover all wood parts with self-adhesive plastic, cut to fit. Cut out small openings over holes so that they are accessible.

Bolt axles beneath body piece, leaving loose enough to turn (holes for pinwheels are on top of body). Screw on wheels as follows: Place washer between axle and wheel, then wheel, then circle cut from pinwheel, then another washer and the screw.

Set pinwheels in holes with tallest in center.

Screw screw eyes into front axle about 3″ apart. Fold silver braid in half and bring folded center through key ring, then draw ends through fold and tighten on ring. Tie other ends to screw eyes.

Whirligig on wheels

A toy beloved at the turn of the century, this updated whirligig features four glittering pinwheels set into a pine base that rolls on wheels.

SIZES Gum machine 3½″ x 4¾″. **Santa** 4″ x 5½″. **Ice cream cone** 1¾″ x 5¼″. **Christmas tree** 3½″ x 5″. **Heart** 4¼″ x 4¾″.

MATERIALS Gum machine Scraps of clear vinyl fabric and red, blue, yellow and black felt; 2 oz. assorted colored plastic beads; matching sewing threads. **Santa** Scraps of light-green, hot-pink, white and turquoise felt and clear vinyl fabric; 3 oz. dried white navy beans; white fabric glue. **Ice cream cone** Scraps of mustard and red felt and clear vinyl fabric; 3 oz. assorted white pearl beads; matching sewing threads. **Christmas tree** Scraps of clear vinyl fabric and hot-pink felt; 2 oz. dried split green peas; ½ oz. each sequins and colored beads; matching sewing thread; white fabric glue. **Heart** Scraps of clear vinyl fabric and light-green felt; 1½′ each of ⅜″-wide hot-pink woven braid trim and ½″-wide white picot lace trim; matching sewing threads; 2 oz. red aquarium pebbles. **Note** *Use caution in making these toys for infants or toddlers. Vinyl fabric must be heavy enough so that it cannot rip or be pierced; the stitching tight and secure enough that filling materials cannot escape.* ***To enlarge patterns,*** *follow the adjacent instructions.*

Gum Machine

Enlarge patterns as instructed. Using patterns, cut 2 globe pieces from vinyl, 2 base pieces from red felt and a ¾″ x 9¼″ strip from blue felt. Overlap a red base piece along

---

Bean-bag toss toys

Infants and toddlers love toss toys, the more the merrier. It's great sport to pitch them around — and hear how they rattle! In this group there are five fun shapes: a gum machine, Santa, ice cream cone, Christmas tree and lacy heart, all fashioned from clear plastic and felt, and filled with beans, beads, dried lentils and such.

HOW TO ENLARGE PATTERNS

You will need brown wrapping paper (pieced if necessary to make a sheet large enough for a pattern), a felt-tipped marker, pencil and ruler. (When pattern you are enlarging has a grid around it, you must first connect lines across pattern with a colored pencil to form a grid over the picture.) Mark paper with grid as follows: First cut paper into a true square or rectangle. Then mark dots around edges, 1″ or 2″ apart or whatever is indicated on pattern, making same number of spaces as there are squares around the edges of pattern diagram. Form a grid by joining the dots across opposite sides of paper. Check to make sure you have the same number of squares as diagram. With marker, draw in each square the same pattern lines you see in corresponding squares on diagram.

Each square = 1/2″

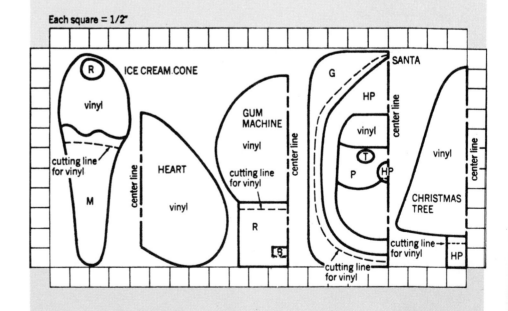

Color Key
G — Light Green
HP — Hot Pink
P — Pink
T — Turquoise
R — Red
B — Black
M — Mustard

straight edge of globe; stitch. With wrong sides together, pin blue strip around edges of globe as in photograph; topstitch. Fill gum machine with colored beads and stitch to close edges of base. Cut a tiny rectangle for slot from black felt and "10¢" from yellow felt and glue centered on base as shown in the photograph.

Santa

Enlarge patterns as instructed. Using patterns, cut 1 each full-size light-green and white felt piece for back and liner. Cut vinyl piece to dotted lines; cut 1 each light-green outer frame, hot-pink inner frame (includes crosspiece) and pink face strip. Center white liner on green back piece; dab corners with glue to hold in place. Center green outer frame on vinyl, turn and stitch in place. Glue hot-pink frame in place as indicated; add pink face strip centered on hot-pink crosspiece. Cut out turquoise eyes and hot-pink nose. Glue facial details in place. With wrong sides together, glue back and front pieces together around edges, leaving 3" opening along 1 edge. Allow glue to dry. Fill Santa with navy beans; glue opening closed.

Ice Cream Cone

Enlarge patterns as instructed. Cut 2 each ice cream pieces from clear vinyl and cone pieces from mustard felt, adding ¼" seam allowance. With right sides overlapped, stitch a cone piece to an ice cream piece. Cut 2 cherries from red felt and topstitch 1 near top edge of each ice cream as indicated. With right sides facing, stitch pieces together, leaving 3" opening along 1 side of cone. Turn cone to the right side. Fill with pearl beads and stitch opening closed.

Christmas Tree

Enlarge patterns as instructed. Using patterns, cut 2 each tree pieces from clear vinyl and trunk pieces from hot-pink felt, adding ¼" seam allowance. With right sides overlapped, stitch trunk to tree. With right sides facing, stitch pieces together, leaving 3" opening. Turn. Fill tree with peas, sequins and beads; close opening. Glue narrow strip of hot-pink felt to the stitching line between the tree and the trunk.

Heart

Enlarge patterns as instructed. Cut 1 each vinyl and green felt heart shapes, adding ¼" seam allowance. With right sides facing, stitch heart pieces together, leaving small opening. Turn. Fill heart with pebbles; close opening. Sew on picot lace and braid trim as shown in the photograph.

MATERIALS 10½" x 18" piece of ½-inch plywood, small amounts acrylic enamel or latex paints, non-toxic and in several colors; 10½" x 18" piece of colorful felt; white glue; sandpaper; 7 to 8 hardware or other screw-in devices such as latches, bolts, chain locks, eye hooks, etc., and appropriate screws. (**Note** *Screws should be flat-head type so they screw in flush.*)

Sand plywood front and edges. Glue felt piece to back of wood. Using photograph for reference, position hardware on front of board; pencil in background areas behind each piece. Paint backgrounds in contrasting colors and let dry thoroughly. Screw in objects in appropriate areas.

Teaching board

This teach-yourself activity board is backed with felt so it can rest harmlessly on any surface. Kids will turn to it again and again to practice skills and experiment with abilities.

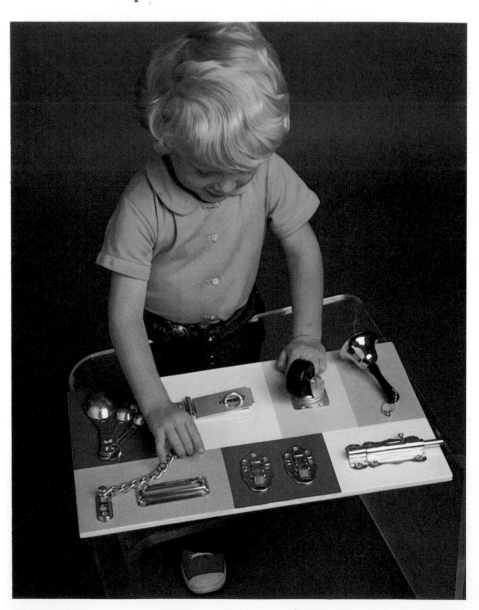

FOAM-BALL finger puppets

Felt scraps, yarn and movable eyes are the simple magic that turns plastic foam balls into these wacky and wonderful puppets, a snap for the smallest fingers to manipulate.

MATERIALS For each puppet 3"-diam. plastic-foam ball; ¾"-diam. movable glue-on eyes; several colors felt scraps; white glue; yarn scraps; serrated bread knife.

Using serrated knife, slice ball in half. To mark position for finger holes on back, hold two ball halves together and mark one hole for thumb centered ½" from slice line on one half, then two holes for index and middle fingers centered ½" from slice line on other half. Bore out holes to fit fingers, using point of knife. To hinge puppet halves, use one ball half as pattern and draw circle on felt; leave ¼" space and draw a second circle aligned with first. Cut out circles as one piece, leaving ¼" strip of felt between for hinge. Glue connected circles to each ball half so that ¼" hinge is at back where finger holes are. Following photograph for features, cut out narrow strips of felt, shaped or unshaped, for lips. Glue in place as in photograph. Cut out felt eyelashes and glue in place, then glue on a pair of movable eyes. For hair, cut short lengths of yarn, tie in middle and glue to top of puppet. For shorter hair, wrap yarn around four fingers, tie off at center and glue in place.

Squeezable foam blocks

The covers of these foam-filled softies are fast-to-crochet Granny Squares; the foam is the soft kind, layered into chunky blocks. The four are made in graduated sizes, from 4½″ to 2″ square.

SIZES Finished blocks measure:
  No. 1: 4½″ square
  No. 2: 3½″ square
  No. 3: 2½″ square
  No. 4: 2″ square

MATERIALS Acrylic knitting-worsted-weight-yarn, 1 (2-oz.) skein each white, red, yellow and .blue; steel crochet hook No. 0; 18″ square of ½″-thick polyurethane foam; tapestry needle. **Note** *You can substitute yarn scraps and hook size that will give you the block measurements above.*

BLOCK NO. 1

Square Starting at center with white, ch 4. Join with sl st to form ring. **1st rnd (right side)** Ch 3, work 2 dc in ring, (ch 1, work 3 dc in ring) 3 times, ch 1; join with sl st to top of ch-3. Break off. **2nd rnd** Make lp on hook with red, yo, insert hook in any ch-1 sp and complete dc; in same sp work 2 more dc, ch 1 and 3 dc for first corner, * ch 1, in next sp work 3 dc, ch 1 and 3 dc (another corner). Repeat from * twice more, ch 1; join. Break off. **3rd rnd** Make lp on hook with yellow, work first corner in any corner sp, * ch 1, 3-dc shell in next sp, ch 1, work corner in next corner sp. Repeat from * twice more, ending ch 1, shell in next sp, ch 1; join. Break off. **4th rnd** With blue work first corner in any corner sp, * ch 1, shell in next sp. Repeat from * to next corner, ch 1, work corner in next corner sp. Continue around in pattern; join. Break off. **5th rnd** With white repeat last rnd.

Edging With right side of square facing you, working through back lps only, sc with red in each st around, working 3 sc in each corner sp; join with sl st to first sc. Break off. Unblocked square should measure about 4″.
  Work 5 more squares in same manner.
Assembling Holding two squares with right sides facing you, using matching-color yarn and tapestry needle, whipstitch squares together along one side. Join 3rd square to 2nd and 4th to 3rd so that piece forms strip, then join ends of strip to form ring. Matching corners, join 5th square around one edge of ring to form square cup shape.
Finishing Cut nine 4½″ squares of foam and fit inside block. Join remaining square to close block.

BLOCK NO. 2

To change color Work dc to point where 2 lps are on hook. With new color make lp on hook and complete dc. Break off old color, leaving a 3″ end. Crochet over ends to conceal them.
  Square No. 1 With white ch 4. Join with sl st to form ring. **1st rnd** Ch 3, work 2 dc in ring, ch 1, work 3 dc in ring, changing to blue on last dc; break off white. With blue ch 1, work 3 dc, ch 1 and 3 dc in ring, ch 1; join to top of ch-3. Break off. **2nd rnd** With white make lp on hook and work 3 dc in last ch-1 sp (half of first corner made); ch 1; in next ch-1 sp work 3 dc, ch 1 and 3 dc (2nd corner), ch 1, work 3 dc in next ch-1 sp, changing to

blue on last dc (half of 3rd corner). With blue ch 1, work 3 dc in same sp to complete 3rd corner, ch 1, in next ch-1 sp work 3 dc, ch 1 and 3 dc (4th corner), ch 1, in same sp with first 3 dc work 3 dc and ch 1, join to top of first dc (first corner completed). Break off. **3rd rnd** With white make lp on hook, work half of first corner in last ch-1 sp, ch 1, 3 dc in next sp (first shell made), ch 1, 2nd corner in next sp, ch 1, shell in next sp, ch 1, 3rd corner in next sp (half white, half blue), ch 1, shell in next sp, ch 1, 4th corner in next sp, ch 1, shell in next sp, ch 1, complete first corner. Break off. **4th rnd** Work as for 3rd rnd, working 1 more shell in each ch-1 sp between corners.

Edging Work as for Block No. 1, working in colors to match square halves. Unblocked square should measure about 3″.

Work remaining squares as for first square with the following colors:

Square No. 2 Blue and yellow
Square No. 3 Yellow and red
Square No. 4 Red and white
Square No. 5 Yellow and white
Square No. 6 Red and blue

Assembling and Finishing Work as for Block No. 1, matching colors and using seven 3½″ square pieces of foam for stuffing.

BLOCK NO. 3

Work 6 squares as for Block No. 1 through 3rd rnd, working each square in one color only as follows: Do not break off at end of rnd but sl st into first ch-1 sp, ch 3, then continue in pattern as given. Work 2 squares each red, blue and yellow.

Edging With white work as for Block No. 1. Unblocked squares should measure about 2½″.

Assembling and Finishing Work as for Block No. 1, using five 2½″ squares of foam for stuffing.

BLOCK NO. 4

Square No. 1 Work as for first and 2nd rnds of Block No. 1, working first rnd in red, 2nd rnd in blue. **Squares No. 2, 3 and 4** Work as for Square No. 1. **Squares No. 5 and 6** Work in same manner, working first rnd in blue, 2nd in red.

Edging With yellow work as for Block No. 1. Unblocked squares should measure about 1½″.

Assembling and Finishing Work as for Block No. 1, using four 2″ squares of foam for stuffing.

GENERAL DIRECTIONS

MATERIALS Large plastic garbage bags for covers; colored plastic bags in any size for design details; scraps of self-adhesive plastic; 1"-wide frosted transparent tape; rubber cement; dowels, as required for frame (see specific directions); monofilament nylon fishing line; kite string; plastic curtain rings; other materials listed under specific directions.

TO MAKE KITES Several factors determine whether a kite will fly successfully. Kite must be lightweight but strong, it must be balanced, it must have the right angle of flight (usually about 45°—determined by bridle strings), it must have "drag" and be stabilized by a tail. If kite has difficulty flying, adjust angle by changing length of bridle strings. If it flies erratically, add more pieces to the tail.

   Frame of the kite is its foundation. See directions and diagrams for specific kite to make frame required. Notch ends of frame dowels and run nylon line from tip to tip to form a square outline, which is the base for the kites' cover, shown in detail of Frog diagram, below.

   For **cover,** enlarge diagram for desired kite (see instructions opposite) and cut out cover from plastic garbage bag, adding 1" all around for hem. Place flat on work surface and tape (temporarily) to hold flat. Cut out design shapes from colored plastic. Glue to cover with one coat of rubber cement. Cement will cause plastic to wrinkle up; let dry and ease back into original flat surface. Place pieces as shown. Remove temporary tape.

   Place cover face down. For each corner cut out a 2" square of self-adhesive plastic and stick in place on cover. Place frame on cover. Fold in corners, then miter them and fold in 1" hem all around cover. Tape in place securely.

   Place piece of tape on front of cover at each bridle string location. Pierce cover through tape and tie on bridle strings. For flexibility in adjusting bridle strings while flying kites, tie their other ends to a curtain ring with half-hitch knots.

   Make and tape tail to kite as shown.

Creature kites

Making a kite and watching it climb are among childhood's great delights. But not just any kite! It has to be a fantastic frog sporting a silly grin, or the green-eyed tiger, his long whiskers waving in the breeze.

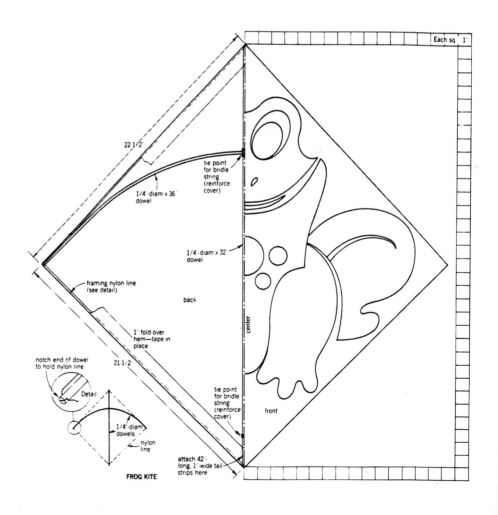

FROG KITE

Frog

MATERIALS In addition to those listed under General Directions, left, two 3' lengths of ¼"-diam. dowel. Soak 1 dowel overnight in water. Form in bow shape as shown in adjoining diagram. Tie with string and allow to dry completely. (Remove string when dry.) Make cover and decorate following diagram. Make frame from dowels following General Directions; attach cover. Attach bridle. Attach tails according to diagram.

Tiger

MATERIALS In addition to those listed under General Directions at left, 4' of ¼"-diam. dowel. Cut out and decorate cover following adjoining diagram. Make frame from dowels following General Directions and attach cover, using a curtain ring at back crossing of dowels. Attach bridle. (**Note** This is a 3-legged bridle; the two upper legs must be the same length or the kite will tend to dive.) Add tails according to diagram.

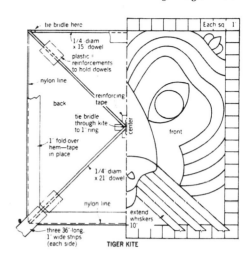

TIGER KITE

HOW TO ENLARGE PATTERNS

You will need brown wrapping paper (pieced if necessary to make a sheet large enough for a pattern), a felt-tipped marker, pencil and ruler. (When pattern you are enlarging has a grid around it, you must first connect lines across pattern with a colored pencil to form a grid over the picture.) Mark paper with grid as follows: First cut paper into a true square or rectangle. Then mark dots around edges, 1" or 2" apart or whatever is indicated on pattern, making same number of spaces as there are squares around the edges of pattern diagram. Form a grid by joining the dots across opposite sides of paper. Check to make sure you have the same number of squares as diagram. With marker, draw in each square the same pattern lines you see in corresponding squares on diagram.

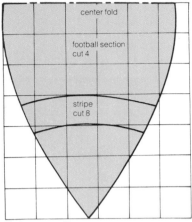

center fold

football section
cut 4

stripe
cut 8

Each square = 1"

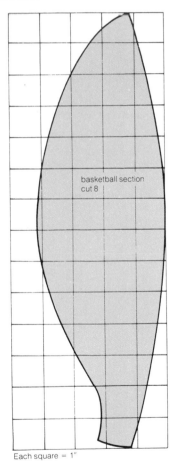

basketball section
cut 8

Each square = 1"

Football & basketball pillows

*Here are two true toss pillows
that are bound to win you extra points:
a felt football and basketball, both
regulation-size, for sports fans big
or little, girls as well as boys.*

SIZES Football 14" long. **Basketball** About 11" in diam.

MATERIALS Football ⅜ yd. 36"-wide brown felt, ⅛ yd. white felt for stripes; 16 white metal eyelets; white shoelace. **Basketball** ⅝ yd. 36" wide reddish-brown felt; 3½ yds. fine black soutache cord. Polyester fiberfill for stuffing both.

Enlarge diagrams (see adjacent instructions) and cut patterns, adding ½" for seams to all sides of football and basketball sections and to ends of stripes on football.

FOOTBALL
Cut sections and stripes from felt. Also from brown felt cut 2" x 6" rectangle. Round corners of rectangle. Following directions that come with eyelets, insert 2 rows of 8 eyelets each, ½" apart, along center of rectangle. Weave shoelace through, tacking ends on wrong side.

Topstitch stripes across ends of football sections. With right sides facing, stitch 2 sections together. Topstitch laced rectangle over seam. Join remaining seams, leaving an opening for studding. Turn and stuff. Close opening.

BASKETBALL
Cut sections from felt. Following diagram below, stitch 4 sections together so they cup.

Then stitch a section, positioned same as section 1, to section 4. Stitch remaining 3 sections in positions shown in diagram. Stitch first section to last section, leaving opening for stuffing. Turn and stuff. Close opening. Slipstitch braid around all seams.

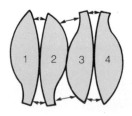

Owlish pencil caddy

Introducing a wise old bird to help with the homework — this droll pencil caddy, perfect to perch on a desk top.

SIZE 4" deep x 3" diam.

MATERIALS 4"-deep x 2½"-diam. can; ¼ yd. fake-fur fabric; 2 movable glue-on eyes; small pompon; felt scraps; cardboard; white glue; masking tape.

Cut piece of fake fur to fit around can, two 1½" x 3" pieces for ears and two 1" x 1¼" pieces for feet. From felt, cut 2½"-diam. circle, two ¾" x 1½" pieces for ears and two 1" x 3" pieces for feet. From cardboard, cut two ¾" x 3" pieces for ears and two 1" x 2½" pieces for feet.

Glue large fake-fur piece around can. Glue felt circle to bottom of can. **Ears** Fold fur ear pieces in half crosswise; insert cardboard, letting 1½" extend beyond fabric; glue. Trim edges of fur pieces to ear shape. Glue felt over extension of cardboard. Tape felt and cardboard section to inside of can. **Feet** Glue fur piece to cardboard piece, letting 1¼" cardboard extend beyond fur. Glue felt piece to bottom of cardboard, letting ½" extend beyond fur piece. Cut toes on ½" extension of felt. Glue feet to bottom of can. Glue movable eyes and pompon nose in place.

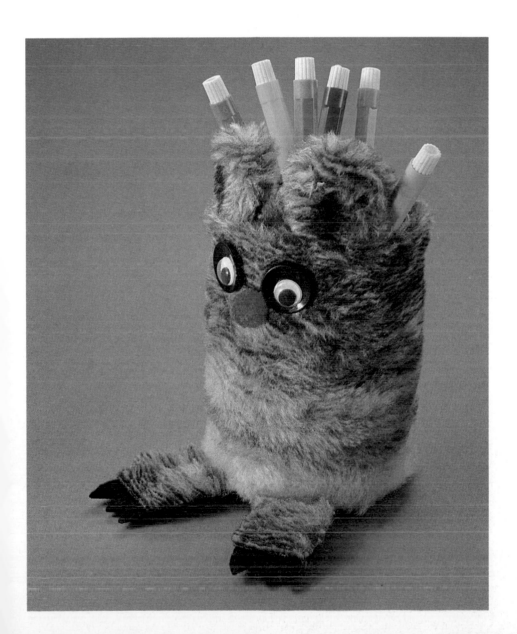

HOW TO ENLARGE PATTERNS

You will need brown wrapping paper (pieced if necessary to make a sheet large enough for a pattern), a felt tipped marker, pencil and ruler. (When pattern you are enlarging has a grid around it, you must first connect lines across pattern with a colored pencil to form a grid over the picture.) Mark paper with grid as follows: First cut paper into a true square or rectangle. Then mark dots around edges, 1" or 2" apart or whatever is indicated on pattern, making same number of spaces as there are squares around the edges of pattern diagram. Form a grid by joining the dots across opposite sides of paper. Check to make sure you have the same number of squares as diagram. With marker, draw in each square the same pattern lines you see in corresponding squares on diagram.

MATERIALS 36"-long broom handle; man's heavy wool sock; 4 colors scrap felt; 3 colors scrap yarn; polyester fiberfill stuffing; red lead-free latex paint

Paint handle red. Let dry. Cut 9½" slit around front of sock to form mouth opening. For mouth, cut two 4½" x 5" felt rectangles. Stitch two 4½" sides together. Round corners, fold in ½" around edges and sew lengthwise into mouth opening. Stuff sock and insert handle. Wrap and tie thread around neck to hold. Cut two 1¼" felt circles for nostrils and 1"-diam., 1½"-diam., and 2"-diam. felt circles for each eye. Following photograph, sew in place. Sew yarn loops for mane (5"-long at center and 2½" along each side). Cut 1½" x 2" and 2½" x 4" felt ovals for each ear. Gather ends with fingers and sew in place. Trim loops in front of ears into 2½" fringe.

For neckband, cut 1" x 7" and 1½" x 7" felt strips. Topstitch 1" strip to 1½" strip. Wrap around neck and sew ends together. For reins make two 20"-long yarn braids; knot ends. Sew one to each side of mouth.

SOCKO the
Hobbyhorse

Watch lowly materials miraculously become a child's faithful steed! The horse's head is made from a man's large woolen sock stuffed and mounted atop a 36"-long broom handle.

HOW TO ENLARGE PATTERNS

You will need brown wrapping paper (pieced if necessary to make a sheet large enough for a pattern), a felt-tipped marker, pencil and ruler. (When pattern you are enlarging has a grid around it, you must first connect lines across pattern with a colored pencil to form a grid over the picture.) Mark paper with grid as follows: First cut paper into a true square or rectangle. Then mark dots around edges, 1" or 2" apart or whatever is indicated on pattern, making same number of spaces as there are squares around the edges of pattern diagram. Form a grid by joining the dots across opposite sides of paper. Check to make sure you have the same number of squares as diagram. With marker, draw in each square the same pattern lines you see in corresponding squares on diagram.

canny pig

The perfect bank for little savers — this radiant coffee-can piggy has wooden legs, felt tail and ears, bead eyes, washer nostrils on a tuna-can snout.

holes in washers. Punch lead holes with an awl for self-tapping screws to attach ears.

Mark placement for ³⁄₁₆" x 1½" slot centered on third segment from front edge of body. Support body of can by inserting scrap 2 x 4 inside and, holding by hand or clamp, drill a ³⁄₁₆"-diam. hole at each end of slot. Cut away between holes with metal cutting blade in saber saw. File slot until smooth.

To attach snout to body, make an epoxy snake about 11" long or circumference of tuna can. Wrap snake around open rim of snout and press it onto body. Scrape away any squeezed-out epoxy with a single-edge razor blade. Attach washer nostrils in snout with tiny epoxy beds. Let set 2 hours.

Enlarge patterns on cardboard, following adjacent instructions, and cut out. Using patterns, mark 4 ears on orange felt; cut out 2. Brush a uniformly thin coat of glue on uncut ear pieces and place a piece of bent and cut wire as indicated. Press cut ears on top of wire; cut out ears. When dry, cut slit in ears as shown; overlap tabs formed and punch holes through tabs with awl. Insert ½" screws in holes. Cut pink ear liners; glue liner to each ear. Glue small pieces of orange and pink together. Mark curlicue for tail as shown. Make a slot plate from 2 pieces of pink felt glued together and mark shape as shown; cut out. Following pattern, mark 4 identical legs on pine; cut out with saber saw. Mark and drill pilot hole centered on top of each leg. Following diagram, use legs to mark and punch for leg screws. Paint legs pink; let dry. Spray body, lid and beads orange; let dry.

Begin assembling pig when paint is dry. To attach legs, insert screws in holes in bottom of body from inside and hold screws still while turning legs onto them. To cover protruding screw points inside body after attaching ears and eyes, hold a block against each screw and tighten screw into block. Glue tail to lid near rim. Glue slot plate in place. Punch out 2 tiny circles with paper punch from pink felt to cover screw heads in bead eyes; glue in place. Paint nostrils hot pink by spraying cardboard, then painting washers with small brush.

SIZE Approximately 11½" tall.

MATERIALS 2-lb. coffee can with plastic lid and 13-oz. tuna or cat-food can; thin flexible steel wire; cardboard; 1' of 1 x 4 pine; 12"-squares bright orange and bright pink felt; white glue; 2-part epoxy putty; six ¾" and two ½" No. 6 self tapping panhead screws; burnt orange and hot pink spray enamel.

Soak label and glue residue from tuna can. Wash and dry both cans thoroughly. Place cans so that both seams fall in center bottom, then, following adjoining front-view diagram, with felt-tipped marker mark placement for holes to attach ears and eyes on coffee-can body and nostrils on tuna-can snout. Drill holes for nostrils with a bit slightly larger than

attach ears with 1/2"
self-tapping screws

slot plate over
3/16" x 1-1/2" slot

ear liner

3/4"-diameter bead eyes
attached with 3/4"
self-tapping screws;
add felt pupils

3/4" o.d.
washers

5"-diameter x 6" coffee-can body

3-3/8"-diameter x 2" tuna-can snout

seam

3/4" x 2" x 2-1/4" legs
attached with 3/4"
self tapping screws

Front View

CHAPTER 4

Wooden Playthings

Wooden toys, for many reasons, well deserve a chapter of their own. First and most important, they get rave reviews from little critics. Not surprising, when you consider how pretty wood is, and how pleasing to the touch. But wood is far more than merely appealing. It is safe in young hands, and it can withstand, better than any other material, the thumps and bumps, knocks and clunks of everyday play—all of which makes it a natural for action toys of the kind collected here.

There is, it should be noted, an enormous saving in making, rather than buying, anything in this category. Woodworking can be an intricate art, with prices to match. Fortunately for the less-skilled (which means most people), the tools and skills needed for these projects are minimal. Should woodworking tools not be available to you, many lumberyards will cut wood to order, to exact specifications. These you will find in every project, in patterns and diagrams and corresponding instructions.

A glance at the group—from Squiggly dragon to the Seesaw table to Noah's Ark complete with animals—will show that these are one-of-a-kind originals, works of art in their own way, but far easier and less costly to produce. Before you proceed with any project in this chapter read the Basic Pointers on Woodworking on page 185. They will get you off to a well-informed start.

Contents

Squiggly dragon **82**

Gas station
– at your service! **84**

Dotty Dinosaur **85**

Rocking pony **86**

Pine Unicorn **87**

Giraffe toy chest **88**

Seesaw table **89**

Noah's Ark cradle
& animals **90**

MATERIALS 4′ of 1 x 8 clear pine; 3′ of ⅜″-diam. birch dowel; 6″ of ¾″-diam. dowel; 1′ of 2⅝″-diam. pole; three ¼″-diam. x 1″ coil springs; white semigloss latex enamel; ½″-diam. self-adhesive dot labels, colored if available; tubes of artists' acrylic paint in colors desired; 5′ length of leather thong; materials for woodworking listed under Basic Pointers on page 185.

Cut 1 x 8 pine in half lengthwise; glue pieces together to laminate; clamp until dry.

Enlarge pattern following adjacent instructions. Mark outline and pattern information on laminated wood. Cut outline with jigsaw, then cut away jaw and tail. Drill axle holes.

Following detail that adjoins pattern, drill centered hole as far into each end of pole as bit will go, then cut wheels, again drilling holes for center as required. Using ¾″ dowel, drill centered hole and cut 4 spacer pieces as shown. Cut ⅜″-diam. dowel axles on same angle as wheels (end cuts are not parallel).

Sand, prime and paint body, wheels and spacers white.

Hinge tail to body and jaw to head, then drill matching holes for springs as shown. Use

Squiggly dragon

Turn a sweet-tempered toddler into a dragon-tamer with this sensational wooden wonder — a new and novel pull toy with a meandering jigsaw shape, brilliant acrylic colors and bobbing tail and jaw set on springs.

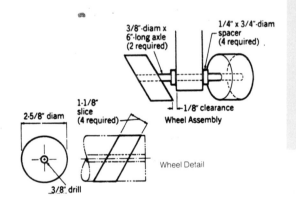

3/8″-diam x 6″-long axle (2 required)
1/4″ x 3/4″-diam spacer (4 required)
1/8″ clearance
Wheel Assembly
1-1/8″ slice (4 required)
2-5/8″ diam
3/8″ drill
Wheel Detail

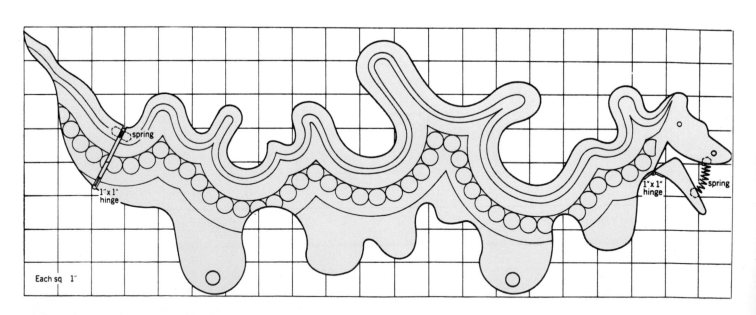

spring
1″ x 1″ hinge
1″ x 1″ hinge
spring
Each sq 1″

2 springs slipped together between body and tail; epoxy into holes. Use half a spring between jaw and head; attach in same way. Drill ⅛"-diam. hole in nose for pull cord.

Paint along center of top edge, stopping short of outer edges (blue paint used here). Cover both sides and tail of dragon with overlapping masking-tape strips; trim around edges with knife. Center ½"-wide tape on top edge over blue (or other color) painted portion. Draw guidelines for paint stripes as shown. Cut along lines; peel tape from areas to be striped. Put short strips of tape across bottom edge to mask unpainted areas that adjoin unpainted areas on sides.

Mix paints with small amounts of water. Paint stripes in desired colors (or follow our design). Remove tape when dry. Paint dot labels, if colored ones cannot be found, on their backing sheet. When dry, place as shown. Apply 1 coat polyurethane over all.

Sand axles; place in holes. Glue on spacers with 1⁄16" body clearance, then glue wheels to axles. Thread leather-thong pull through nose and knot ends.

HOW TO ENLARGE PATTERNS

You will need brown wrapping paper (pieced if necessary to make a sheet large enough for a pattern), a felt-tipped marker, pencil and ruler. (When pattern you are enlarging has a grid around it, you must first connect lines across pattern with a colored pencil to form a grid over the picture.) Mark paper with grid as follows: First cut paper into a true square or rectangle. Then mark dots around edges, 1" or 2" apart or whatever is indicated on pattern, making same number of spaces as there are squares around the edges of pattern diagram. Form a grid by joining the dots across opposite sides of paper. Check to make sure you have the same number of squares as diagram. With marker, draw in each square the same pattern lines you see in corresponding squares on diagram.

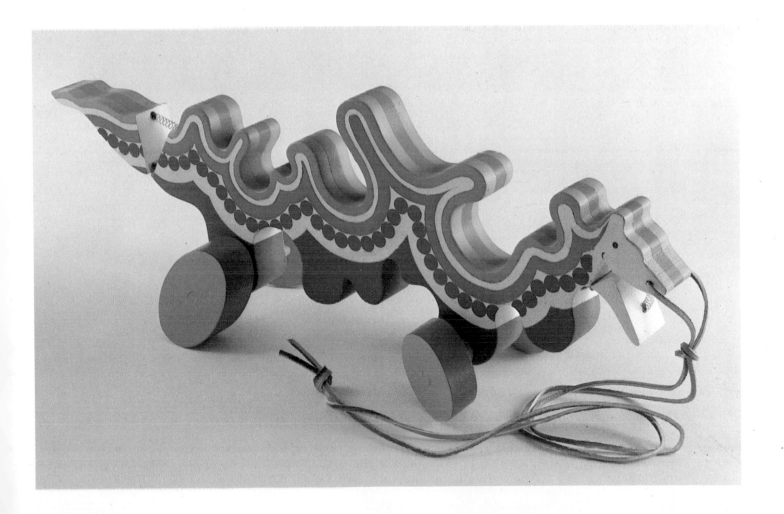

SIZE Car, about 5" long; pump base, 6" long.

MATERIALS Scrap wood; scrap dowels; scraps of self-adhesive plastic; large and small wooden beads; yellow plastic tape; red and blue plastic-covered cloth tape; artists' acrylic paints; small paintbrushes; 2 wooden Tinkertoy® wheels and 2 spools from buttonhole twist thread (or two ½"-thick pieces each of 1"- and 1⅜"-diam. pole) for wheels; thin navy-blue braided cord; wood putty; wood glue; high-gloss red, yellow and black paint; 2 screws with washers for wheels; 2 flat-head nails; 2 Phillip's-head screws.

Note *See color photograph for details.*

FOR STATION ATTENDANT

Cut 2"-long piece ⅞"-diam. dowel from scrap. Glue on 1¼"-diam. wooden bead for head. Fill bead hole with wood putty; sand smooth when dry. Paint body blue with acrylic and paint cap with high-gloss red. Paint features with acrylics.

FOR CAR

Cut 1" x 1¾" x 4⅞" piece of wood scrap for body. Cut ⅛" x 1" x 3⅜" piece of slat from scrap for decorative end and drill ¼"-diam. hole ½" in from one corner; glue slat to body. Drill ¾"-diam. hole for driver dowel (see Driver, below) ¾" from slat. Paint green. Paint wheels and 2 washers high-gloss black. Nail larger wheels on back and screw smaller wheels on front with washers. Stick on decorative yellow tape stripe.

Cut out two ¾"-diam. circles of yellow self-adhesive plastic. Cut out 2 numerals, as shown, from cloth tape. Stick circles, then numbers to sides of car as shown.

DRIVER

Cut 1½" length ¾"-diam. dowel from scrap. Glue on 1"-diam. wooden bead for head. Fill hole with wood putty. Sand and paint with high-gloss yellow for hair. Paint body red acrylic; paint features. Glue into hole drilled into car.

GAS PUMPS

Cut ½" x 1¾" x 6" base from scrap. Cut two 1⅛" x 2" x 3" pumps. Glue pumps to base.

Paint base high-gloss red; edge with black acrylic. Paint pumps white; edge with ⅛"-wide strips black self-adhesive plastic. Cut a blue plastic rectangle for each pump and yellow squares for decoration. Add small strips red cloth tape. Knot short length of braided cord to each Phillip's-head screw; screw tight into each outer side of pump. Knot small black bead on end of each cord, passing cord through bead twice to secure.

GAS STATION
— at your service!

Station attendant, gas pumps, car and driver are ready to do business in no time with scraps of wood and dowels, wooden beads and other commonplace materials. The car is about 5" long, the pump base about 6" long.

DOTTY DINOSAUR

What you see is a prehistoric monster who rolls undaunted over the roughest terrain, on twenty wooden wheels.

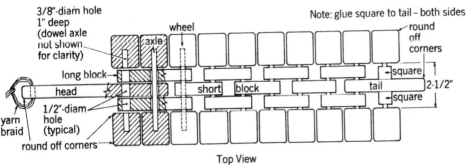

Side View

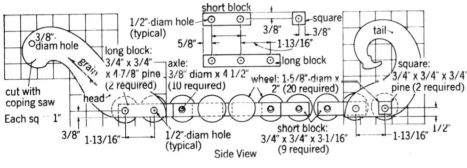

Note: glue square to tail – both sides

Top View

SIZE 26″ long fully extended; 6½″ high with head up.

MATERIALS 2′ of 1 x 6 clear pine; 4′ of 1 x 1 clear pine; two 3′ pieces of ⅜″-diam. dowel; 4′ of 1⅝″-diam. oak pole; ½″- and ⅜″-diam. spade bits; fine sandpaper; 8′ each red, white and blue knitting yarn; white shellac or clear polyurethane.

Enlarge and transfer head and tail diagram (see adjacent instructions) directly onto 1 x 6 pine. Drill two ½″-diam. axle holes in each, then cut out pieces with jigsaw or coping saw. Drill eye; cut mouth.

From 1 x 1 cut 2 squares, 2 long blocks and 9 short blocks. Drill as shown with ½″-diam. bit. From oak pole cut 20 wheels, each 2″ long. Drill ⅜″-diam. holes, 1″ deep, centered in wheels. From dowel cut 10 axles, each 4½″ long.

Test-assemble to check rolling action. Take apart and sand, rounding corners of wheels, head and tail. Dust, then coat all parts (except axles) with shellac or polyurethane. Reassemble, gluing axles into wheels.

For pull, thread 3 strands yarn through eye. Center lengths, pair strands by color and braid together; knot ends.

HOW TO ENLARGE PATTERNS

You will need brown wrapping paper (pieced if necessary to make a sheet large enough for a pattern), a felt-tipped marker, pencil and ruler. (When pattern you are enlarging has a grid around it, you must first connect lines across pattern with a colored pencil to form a grid over the picture.) Mark paper with grid as follows: First cut paper into a true square or rectangle. Then mark dots around edges, 1″ or 2″ apart or whatever is indicated on pattern, making same number of spaces as there are squares around the edges of pattern diagram. Form a grid by joining the dots across opposite sides of paper. Check to make sure you have the same number of squares as diagram. With marker, draw in each square the same pattern lines you see in corresponding squares on diagram.

SIZE 12½" x 18" x 25".

MATERIALS 2' of 1 x 10 pine; 8' of 1 x 6 pine; 1' of ¾"-diam. dowel; 1' of 1"-diam. dowel; 1¼" x No. 8 flathead wood screws; ¼" pine scrap; wood rasp; coarse, medium and fine sandpapers; wood stains (Minwax Independence Red and Liberty Blue used here).

Following instructions, page 85, enlarge head pattern (diagram on grid) and transfer directly onto 1 x 10 pine. Drill 1"-diam. eye. Cut out head shape with jigsaw or coping saw. Repeat for tail on 1 x 6 pine.

Cut out all other flat parts, including cleats, from 1 x 6 pine. Rocker is based on an 18" radius. Cut notches for rockers in front and back.

Clamp rockers together and drill for ¾"-diam. dowel footrest. Round ends with wood rasp, reducing length to 19½". Cut footrest dowel 12½" long; cut 7"-long handle from 1"-diam. dowel.

Screw cleats to front and back as shown. Attach head and tail to seat. Attach seat to front and screw from inside front into head. Add back and floor. Attach rockers with footrest dowel placed through both to be sure they are correctly aligned.

Glue handle and footrest in place. Cut ears from scrap pine and glue in place.

Sand rest of pony. Round edges of rockers and body box, particularly the seat, with wood rasp. Sand edges smooth with 3 grades of sandpaper in succession. Stain in 2 colors, following photograph.

Rocking pony

Having a pony is every child's dream, and now you can make it come true! This easy-to-manage pine rocker is just one foot tall, and ideal to take a toddler riding through to that first tricycle.

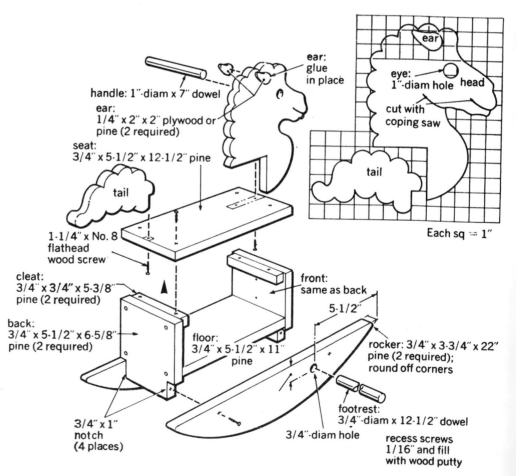

ear: glue in place

eye: 1"-diam hole   head

cut with coping saw

tail

Each sq = 1"

handle: 1"-diam x 7" dowel

ear: 1/4" x 2" x 2" plywood or pine (2 required)

seat: 3/4" x 5-1/2" x 12-1/2" pine

tail

1-1/4" x No. 8 flathead wood screw

cleat: 3/4" x 3/4" x 5-3/8" pine (2 required)

back: 3/4" x 5-1/2" x 6-5/8" pine (2 required)

front: same as back

5-1/2"

floor: 3/4" x 5-1/2" x 11" pine

rocker: 3/4" x 3-3/4" x 22" pine (2 required); round off corners

3/4" x 1" notch (4 places)

3/4"-diam hole

footrest: 3/4"-diam x 12-1/2" dowel

recess screws 1/16" and fill with wood putty

PINE
Unicorn

*This mythical visitor from a storybook
world will feel right at home with
a down-to-earth little boy or girl.
He's an especially rewarding pull toy because
his jointed legs move up
and down as he rolls along.*

MATERIALS 2' of ½ x 8 and 1' of 1 x 10 clear pine; 3' each of ⅛"- and ¼"-diam. dowel; 1 small screw eye; braided or twisted yarn for pull; small skein rust-color yarn; acrylic paints; materials for woodworking listed under Basic Pointers on page 185.

Enlarge pattern following instructions on page 85; cut wood parts accordingly. Also cut 2¼" x 9½" rectangle from 1 x 10 for platform. Drill holes as shown; sand all parts smooth.

From ¼" dowel, cut four 1½" knee joints, two 3¾" body dowels, two 3¼" axles, one 6"-long support. Sand to taper ends of body dowels and one end of each joint. From ⅛" dowel, cut eight ¾" pegs.

Drill ⅛"-diam. holes, 2 in each body dowel and 1 in each joint, all ¼" from tapered end. Drill ¼"-diam. centered hole in platform face, then two 9/32"-diam. axle holes through long edges, 2" from end.

Glue body dowels in place with equal amount extending on each side. Glue washers to inside top, then joints into outside bottom of thighs with unsanded end flush with inside thigh and tapered end extending from other side. Glue support into body.

Insert axles in platform and glue wheels flush with ends. To assemble legs: Glue pegs into ⅛"-diam. holes. Screw legs loosely to wheels, fitting support dowel into platform at same time. Adjust height as required; glue support dowel after being sure legs move well.

Paint eyes and hooves. When dry, coat with clear varnish or polyurethane. Make and glue on yarn mane and tail. To make horn, cut felt pieces, adding ¼" seam allowance to all sides. Stitch pieces together, leaving bottom open; turn right side out and stuff with excess felt or yarn. Tie off at dotted line with thread wraps; glue horn in hole. Turn screw eye into front of platform and attach pull.

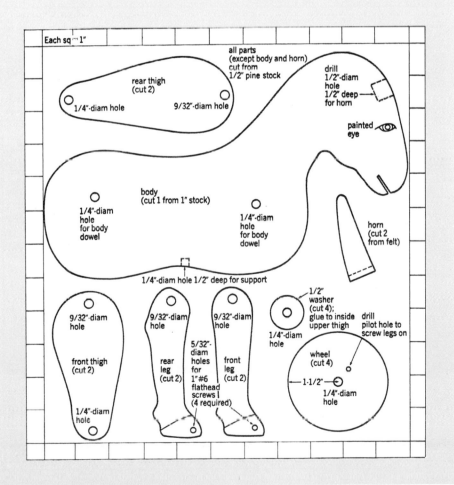

Each sq = 1"

rear thigh
(cut 2)
1/4"-diam hole
9/32"-diam hole

all parts
(except body and horn)
cut from
1/2" pine stock

drill
1/2"-diam
hole
1/2" deep
for horn

painted
eye

body
(cut 1 from 1" stock)
1/4"-diam
hole
for body
dowel
1/4"-diam
hole
for body
dowel

horn
(cut 2
from felt)

1/4"-diam hole 1/2" deep for support

9/32"-diam
hole
front thigh
(cut 2)
1/4"-diam
hole

9/32"-diam
hole
rear
leg
(cut 2)
5/32"-
diam
holes
for
1" #6
flathead
screws
(4 required)

9/32"-diam
hole
front
leg
(cut 2)

1/2"
washer
(cut 4);
glue to inside
upper thigh
1/4"-diam
hole

drill
pilot hole to
screw legs on

wheel
(cut 4)
1-1/2"
1/4"-diam
hole

SIZE 12" x 25½" x 31½".

MATERIALS 28" x 48" piece ½" plywood; 1' of 2 x 4 pine; scrap orange knitting worsted for mane and tail; scrap orange felt; four 1¼"-diam. plate-mounted casters; one 1½"-diam. plastic-foam ball; scrap ⅛"-diam. dowel; primer; white glue; 1¼" finishing nails; lime green, yellow and pink semigloss enamel.

Enlarge pattern, following adjacent instructions, for head-neck. Carefully lay out pattern on plywood and transfer shape. Cut out with saber saw. Cut long notch in neck. Also cut two 12" x 14" pieces for back-front, then two 14" x 16" pieces for sides. Mark centered 2½"-deep x 6"-long notch on bottom edge of back-front pieces. On bottom edges of sides mark a centered 2½"-deep x 10"-long notch. Cut out notches to form legs. Test-assemble side, back and front pieces and determine size to cut recessed floor. Mark and cut floor to fit from remaining plywood. Mark and drill eye in head and ¼"-diam. hole in back piece centered and 1" down from top edge. Drill eye with an adjustable bit. Also mark and cut four 2½" x 2½" mounting blocks from 2 x 4 pine. Sand all pieces.

Assemble chest with sides between back and front pieces, using glue and nails. Check that assembly is square. Add floor and head-neck pieces. Glue and nail mounting blocks in corners on underside of floor. Mark and drill holes for attaching casters to mounting blocks.

Sand giraffe smooth and dust. Apply primer; let dry. Paint all outside surfaces of giraffe yellow and inside surfaces green; let dry. Following photograph, mark random giraffe spots. Paint spots pink; let dry. Install casters.

Giraffe TOY CHEST

Set on casters, this painted plywood giraffe can stay put, or move from room to room keeping things in order as he goes.

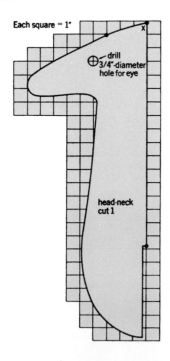

Each square = 1"

drill
3/4"-diameter
hole for eye

head-neck
cut 1

For mane, cut ½" x 21½" strip from orange felt, pieced if necessary. Cut enough 3" pieces of yarn to cover felt strip thickly. Arrange yarn fringe over felt and stitch. Glue mane between dots on head and neck as indicated. For horn, paint foam ball green and let dry. Cut 2½" piece from dowel and paint yellow. Drill ⅛" hole through mane in head at point X on diagram. Work dowel into ball and glue horn in hole.

For tail, cut eighteen 20" lengths of yarn. Divide yarn into 3 groups of 6 strands each and make 8" braid. Knot both ends. Open knot at short end and thread braid through hole in back piece. Reknot to hold tail in place. Trim unbraided strands even for tassel.

Seesaw table

Playing really has its ups and downs with this ingenious seesaw table. Turned on one side, it rocks; flipped over, it stands steady for across-the-counter give-and-take.

HOW TO ENLARGE PATTERNS

You will need brown wrapping paper (pieced if necessary to make a sheet large enough for a pattern), a felt-tipped marker, pencil and ruler. (When pattern you are enlarging has a grid around it, you must first connect lines across pattern with a colored pencil to form a grid over the picture.) Mark paper with grid as follows: First cut paper into a true square or rectangle. Then mark dots around edges, 1″ or 2″ apart or whatever is indicated on pattern, making same number of spaces as there are squares around the edges of pattern diagram. Form a grid by joining the dots across opposite sides of paper. Check to make sure you have the same number of squares as diagram. With marker, draw in each square the same pattern lines you see in corresponding squares on diagram.

MATERIALS 4′ x 8′ sheet ½″ plywood; 4½′ of 1⅛″-diam. wooden pole; scrap ½″-diam. dowel; white glue; finishing nails; spackling paste; pigmented-shellac primer; light-blue, pink and red semigloss enamel; masking tape.

Mark and cut the following from ½″ plywood: one 4′ x 4′ piece for rocker sides, two 11½″ x 23½″ seat backs, two 10″ x 23½″ seats and one 23½″ x 23½″ piece for floor. Find center of 4′ x 4′ plywood by drawing in crossed diagonal lines from opposite corners and, using a thin flexible wire, nail and pencil for compass, draw a 48″-diam. circle and a concentric 28″-diam. circle. Cut into two 2′ x 4′ pieces. Following adjoining diagram, mark seat line as indicated. Temporarily tack pieces together and, following circle guidelines, cut out two rocker sides. Check that all remaining plywood pieces are equal along 23½″ side. For handles, cut two 23½″ lengths and four ½″ pieces from 1⅛″-diam. pole. Sand all cut edges, slightly rounding them. Following handle detail, center and drill holes in each end of handles and one end of cap pieces for ½″ dowel pegs. Cut ½″ dowel pegs to length. mark and drill dowel holes on rocker sides for handles. Assemble seat backs and seats with glue and nails. When dry, position between rocker sides and glue and nail in place. Insert floor as shown. Check that seesaw table is square and use pipe clamps to hold assembled unit until dry. Assemble handles with dowel pegs and cap pieces as shown in detail.

Use spokeshave to round rocker edges. Fill all plywood edges and nail holes with spackling paste; sand smooth when dry. Apply two coats of primer, then paint entire unit pink; let dry. Following diagram, mark guidelines on rocker sides for bands of red and light blue. Put down masking tape over curve guidelines of pink borders. Cut along guideline with mat knife for a smooth paint line, sealing edge of tape with your fingernail. Spray red; let dry. Darken guideline between red and blue band with pencil, put down tape along guideline and cut away tape as described above. Spray blue band. When paint is set but not dry, remove tape and let dry.

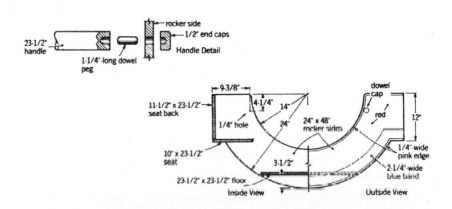

23-1/2" handle | 1-1/4"-long dowel peg | rocker side — 1/2" end caps | **Handle Detail**

9-3/8″ | 11-1/2″ x 23-1/2″ seat back | 4-1/4″ | 14″ | dowel cap | red | 12″ | 1/4″ hole | 24″ | 24″ x 48″ rocker sides | 10″ x 23-1/2″ seat | 3-1/2″ | 1/4″-wide pink edge | 2-1/4″-wide blue band | 23-1/2″ x 23-1/2″ floor | **Inside View** | **Outside View**

Noah's Ark
Cradle

*What our forefathers knew we're
discovering all over again: The gentle rocking of a cradle
soothes a restive baby. But before long the
baby outgrows his first sleeping spot, and you're left with one
cradle — to put in the attic or give away.
This one you can keep! Take off the rockers,
add casters, decks, cabin and gangplank, and
you have a toy box and Noah's Ark.
Cut out Noah's animals and imagine the games they can play!
The ark is pine with a clear, washable finish;
the animals are redwood. The decks
are removable, and the cabin
slides back and forth along the top.*

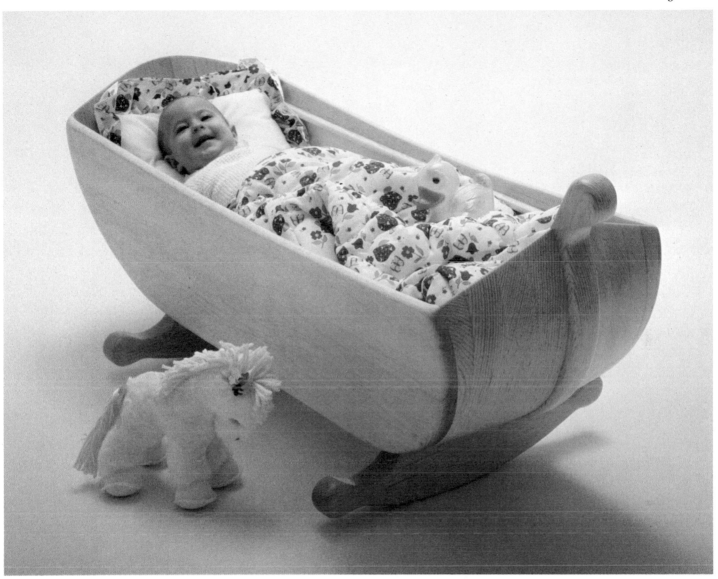

MATERIALS Wide pieces used here are pre-bonded edge-glued pine, which comes in 2" increments in width and is called 1 x in thickness—the type used has an actual thickness of $^{11}/_{16}$" (made by Potlatch, available at many lumberyards); make sure that this is the thickness because other manufacturers have the same material with an actual ¾" thickness and the same 1 x name. For the cradle, you'll need: 22' of 1 x 14 and 4' of 1 x 16 of this type of pine; 2' of 1 x 3 clear pine; 2' x 4' (¼ sheet) of cabinet grade plywood; 6' of ¹⁄₁₆" x ⅞" half round molding; 4' of ½ x 6 clear pine; 18' of 2 x 8 clear pine; ½' (scrap) of ¾" x ¾" hardwood; one 3' length of ⅜" -diam. dowel; scrap ⁹⁄₁₆" -diam. dowel; 1¼" No. 6 or 8, 1½" No. 10 and 2" No. 10 FH wood

screws; four 2½"-diam. ball casters with screws; ⅛" -diam. rope; 1" brads; wood glue; sandpaper; portable belt sander (or spokeshave, surform plane or rasp); vise or clamps; saber saw; polyurethane (clear satin).

GENERAL DIRECTIONS

Before reading specifics, we recommend a review of Basic Pointers on Woodworking, which appears on page 185. The cradle is constructed so that almost all of the joints meet at angles other than 90°. To be sure that yours do this properly, once the pieces are cut, as you assemble them, you plane them very gradually until they fit together. The three dimensional end curves are also cut and then carved to shape, as described more fully under their specific construction. It's impor-

tant to remember, when working with angles and curves such as these, that you make them to work together and to look good, rather than trying to make them geometrically perfect.

Throughout construction, the screws that hold parts together should be pre-drilled and counterbored ⅜" deep for covering plugs cut from ⅜" -diam. dowel. To cut the plugs, make them slightly longer than the bored hole, glue in place over screw and sand down to level. Don't try to cut them exactly; it won't work.

It's also helpful to sand parts smooth before assembly (such as the roof pieces in the deck house) so that they only have to be lightly sanded for finishing, since it's hard to do a complete job of sanding after assembly.

To build the cradle, start with the head and foot. First rip the required widths and lengths for pieces A, B, C, D, E and F from 2 x 8 pine as shown in diagrams. Plan the placement of pieces to be ripped carefully to avoid waste (one arrangement that will work is to put parts A and D next to each other and parts B and C next to each other on the 2 x 8; four of each are required. Then parts E and F—one only of each—can be ripped and cut separately). The remaining 2 x 8 is saved for the rockers.

Cut the pieces to the required curve, following the radius shown in the Assembly Procedure diagram. Glue up the four sets of outer pieces A, B, C and D as shown, clamping units until dry. With pieces firmly clamped, shape curve, first removing step-like corners. Use a belt sander if possible, always sanding across the grain, down the "steps". Otherwise, use a spokeshave, surform plane or rasp in the same manner. Glue two outer sets around piece E for head and the other two outer sets around piece F for foot as shown. Shape those pieces as for others. Round top edges of piece F as shown. Sand all curves smooth. Cut angled piece away from outer sides as shown.

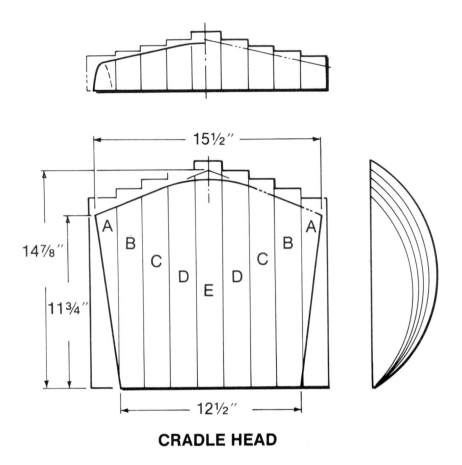

CRADLE HEAD

Step 1: Cut all pieces to size from 1¹³/₁₆″ (actual size) pine.

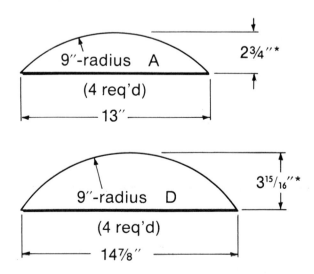

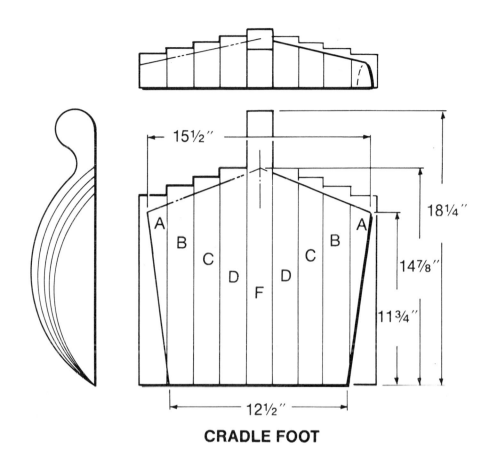

CRADLE FOOT

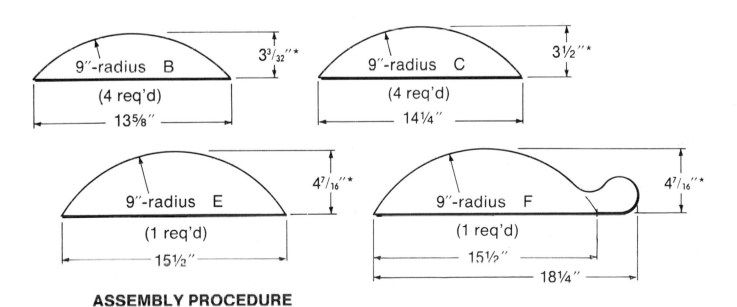

ASSEMBLY PROCEDURE

Cut two 48″ lengths from 1 x 14 pine for sides. Cut two 48″-long pine cleats for bottom as shown in Side Assembly diagram, with the 8° cut. Place one cleat along the bottom of each 48″ board. Lean the sides of head and foot on one of the boards, aligning bottom of head and foot with top of cleat and placing them at angle shown. Match up angles and mark around head and foot onto the board. Continue the curve around toward the bottom of the board (move cleat temporarily) as shown. Repeat with other sides of head and foot on other 48″ board and mark each part so that they are assembled in the same positions later on.

On each 48″ board, mark the top edge curve, which is very gradual, sloping down to a maximum of 1½″ as shown. Cut out both sides as marked. Test-assemble around head and foot. Plane sides of head and foot if required to fit; plane a little bit at a time. Sand insides. Cut the cleats to length (from their 48″ length) with angled ends to fit. Attach cleats with glue and brads.

Step 2: Assemble four sets of outer pieces A, B, C, and D, lining up backs and bottom edges.

Step 3: Shape front surfaces of all four sets.

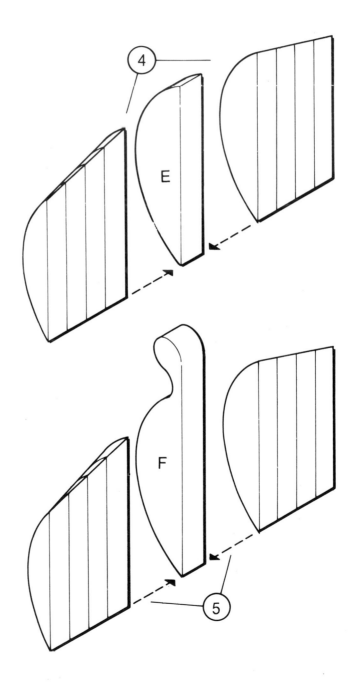

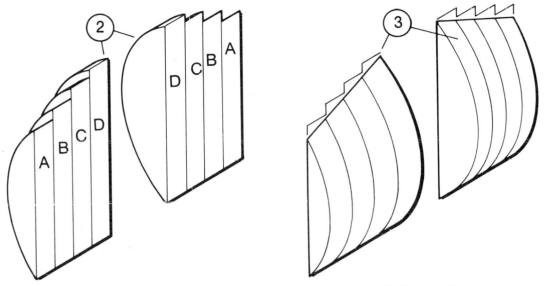

Step 4: For head assembly, glue two of the outer sets of pieces to one center piece E.

Step 5: For foot assembly, glue two of the outer sets of pieces to one center piece F.

Step 6: Shape piece E to conform to head pieces.

Step 7: Rasp ¼″ rounds on exposed edges of piece F.

Step 8: Trim outer sides of head and foot assemblies.

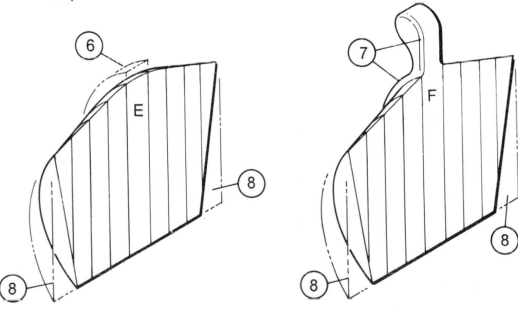

Lay out five equally spaced screw holes ¾″ from edges on center (as shown in General Arrangements—Exploded View) on sides. Drill for screws as described in General Directions and screw sides to head and foot. Plane or rasp away outer corners of sides to match curve of head and foot; sand smooth. Cut bottom from plywood as shown in Cradle Details—Bottom. Sand smooth; drill for screws and screw in place in cradle, as shown.

Make a cardboard template for the rockers as shown in Rocker diagram, page 98, enlarging the pattern as follows: First cut cardboard rectangle large enough to accommodate enlarged pattern. Mark dots around edges, 1″ apart, making same number of spaces as there are squares in the pattern. Join the dots across opposite sides to form grid. With marker, duplicate the pattern lines in corresponding squares in diagram. Cut out pattern piece, and test-fit between cleats at bottom. The rocker tops must fit snugly and slide in between cleats from either end. Cut rockers from 2 x 8 using template as a guide. Sand and round edges to ¼″-round. Screw in place.

Do a final light sanding and coat cradle with 2 to 3 coats of polyurethane, sanding lightly between coats.

Outfit with a cradle mattress or three-to four-inch-thick high-density foam cut to fit and covered with a fitted cradle sheet or a slipcover made to fit from sheeting fabric.

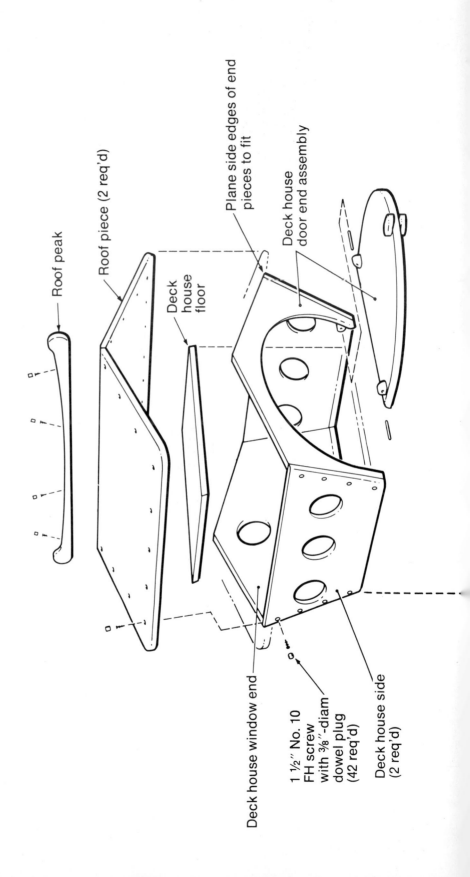

Roof peak

Roof piece (2 req'd)

Deck house floor

Plane side edges of end pieces to fit

Deck house door end assembly

Deck house window end

1 ½″ No. 10 FH screw with ⅜″-diam dowel plug (42 req'd)

Deck house side (2 req'd)

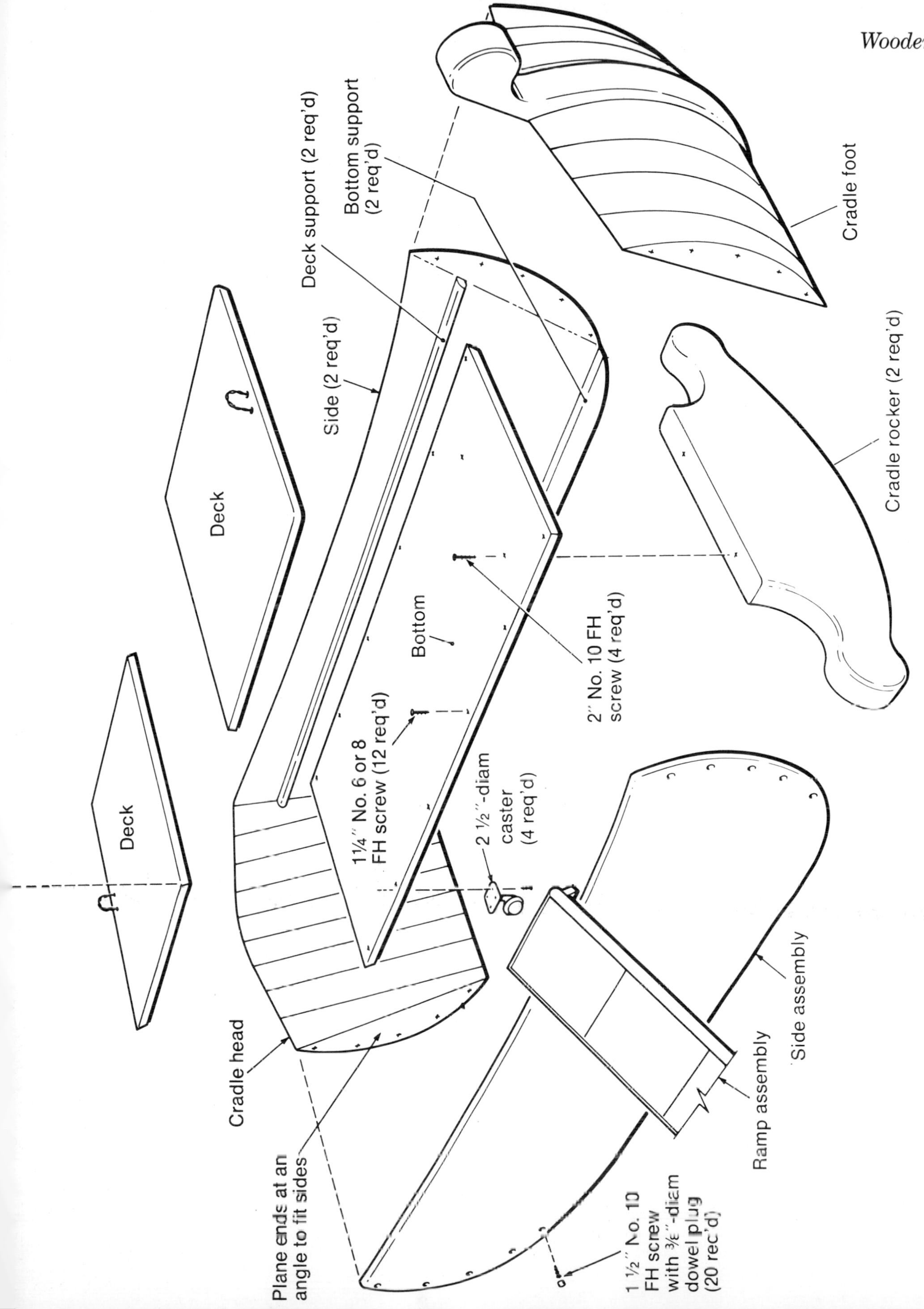

Cradle foot

Bottom support (2 req'd)

Deck support (2 req'd)

Side (2 req'd)

Cradle rocker (2 req'd)

Deck

Deck

Bottom

2'' No. 10 FH screw (4 req'd)

1¼'' No. 6 or 8 FH screw (12 req'd)

2 ½''-diam caster (4 req'd)

Cradle head

Side assembly

Ramp assembly

Plane ends at an angle to fit sides

1 ½'' No. 10 FH screw with ⅜''-diam dowel plug (20 rec'd)

GENERAL ARRANGEMENT – EXPLODED VIEW

CRADLE DETAILS

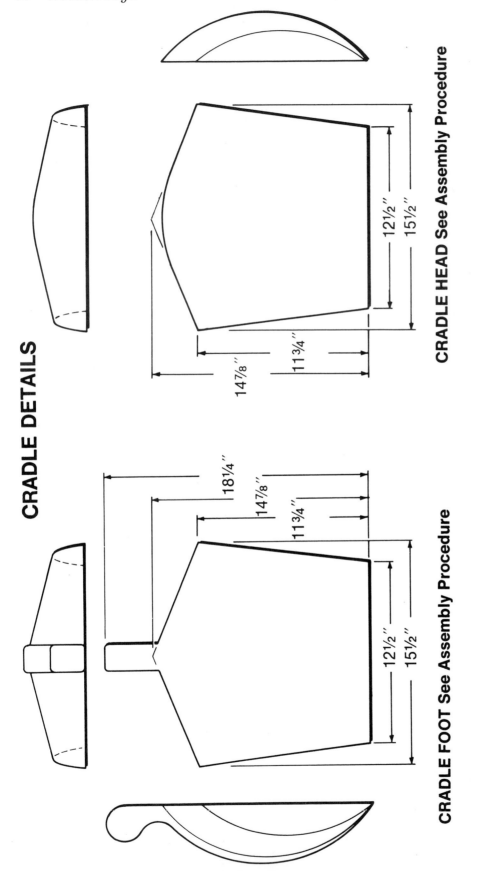

15½″
12½″
14⅞″
11¾″

CRADLE HEAD See Assembly Procedure

18¼″
14⅞″
11¾″
12½″
15½″

CRADLE FOOT See Assembly Procedure

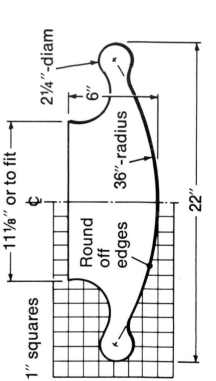

2¼″-diam
6″
36″-radius
11⅛″ or to fit
℄
Round off edges
1″ squares
22″

ROCKER (1 13/16″ pine)

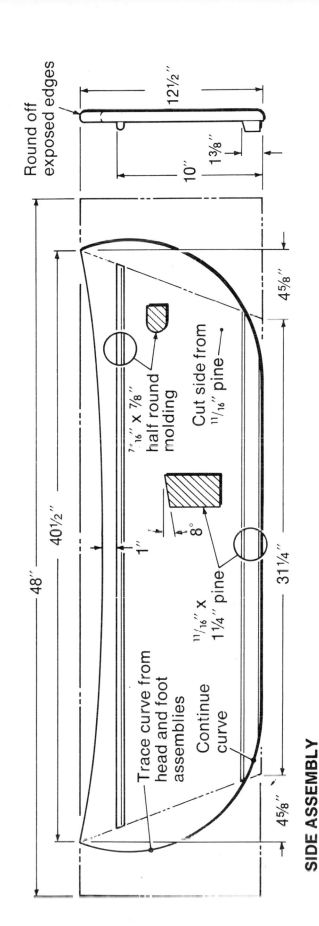

Round off exposed edges

12½"

10"

1⅜"

4⅝"

48"

40½"

31¼"

1"

8°

⁷⁄₁₆" × ⅞" half round molding

Cut side from ¹¹⁄₁₆" pine

¹¹⁄₁₆" × 1¼" pine

Trace curve from head and foot assemblies

Continue curve

4⅝"

SIDE ASSEMBLY

8°

8°

20°

20°

12¾"

2"

3"

3"

4"

32¾"

Drill and countersink 12 holes from top for No. 10 FH screws (4 additional holes for rockers)

Caster position

Rocker position

BOTTOM (¾" plywood)

The view above shows the cradle working as Noah's Ark, with redwood animals going, two by two, up the gangplank and several pairs already on board.

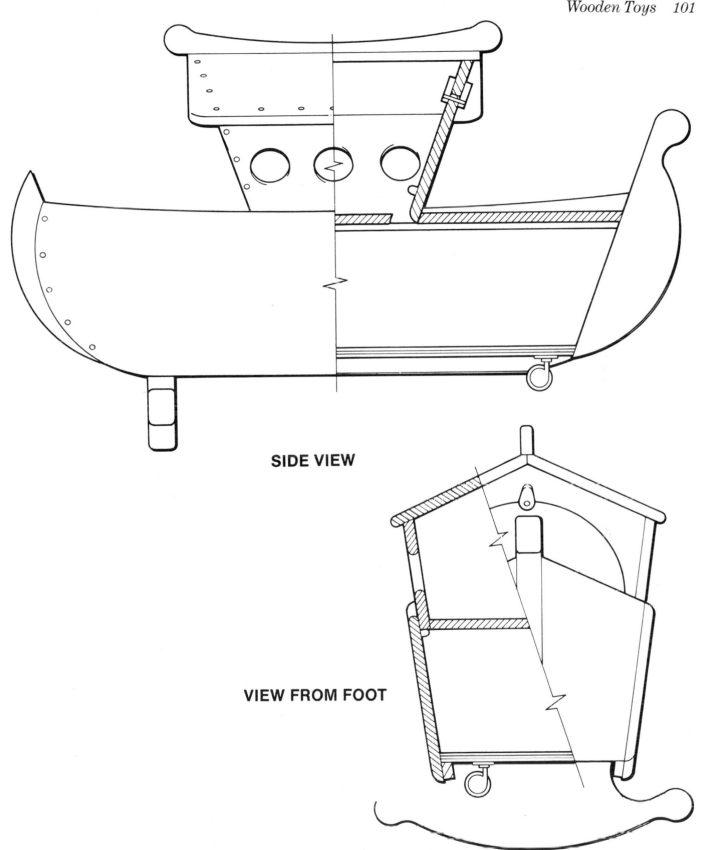

SIDE VIEW

VIEW FROM FOOT

To convert the cradle to the ark, first remove the rockers and replace them with the four casters.

Cut deck support cleats from ⁷⁄₁₆″ x ⁷⁄₈″ half round as shown on Side 1. Attach with glue and brads.

Cut out the sides, door end and window end as shown in the Deck House (Ark) Details. Plane the butted edges to fit. Cut out the door. For door pivot blocks, drill a ³⁄₁₆″-diam. hole centered in the end of the ¾″ x ¾″ hardwood. Then cut the piece to ¾″ x ¾″ x ¾″ and round ends as shown in diagram. Repeat for all blocks. Sand door and door end. Glue in place on inside of door and end as shown, leaving ½″ clearance between sets of blocks. Cut ³⁄₁₆″-diam. dowel pivots to length; sand one end of each so that it fits loosely in one of the blocks. Finish door and end. Cut the two locking cams and the ³⁄₈″-diam. dowel; drill cams and door as shown. Sand the center of the dowel so that it is slightly loose in door hole. Glue cams to dowel after inserting in door; insert dowels in pivot blocks to hold door in door end and glue the tight end of dowel in place in the block on the door. (Other end goes into block on end so that door can swing open and closed.)

Note: All parts made from ¹¹⁄₁₆″ pine unless otherwise specified. All assembled with screws and glue.

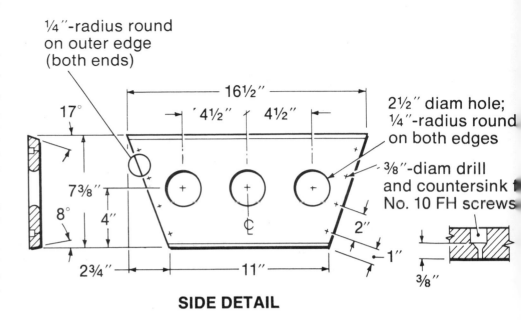

SIDE DETAIL

DECK HOUSE (ARK) DETAILS

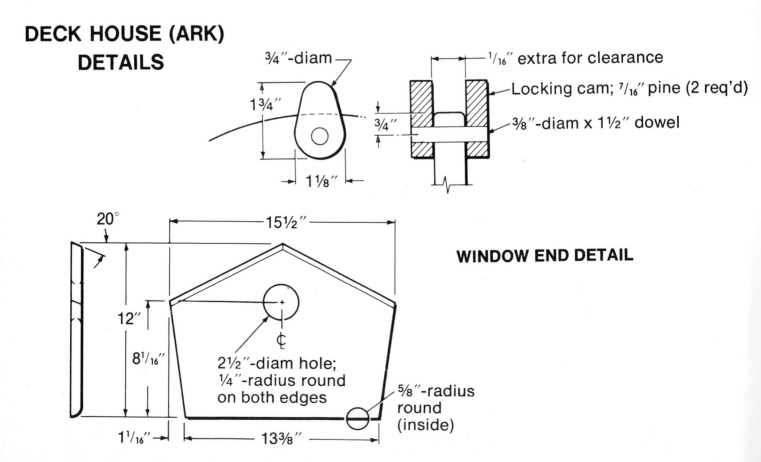

WINDOW END DETAIL

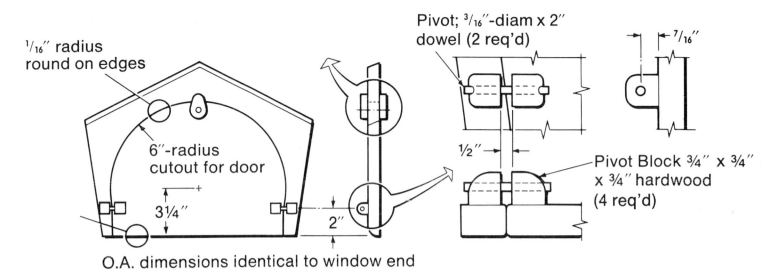

DOOR END ASSEMBLY AND DETAILS

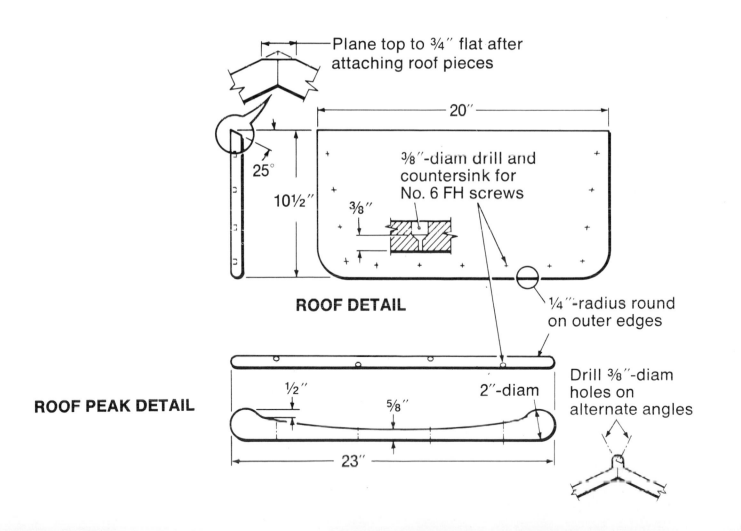

ROOF DETAIL

ROOF PEAK DETAIL

Assemble the sides as shown. Cut out the two roof pieces. Round edges and screw in place (see General Directions). Cut roof peak, round and attach with screws as shown. Cut the inner deck to fit. Finish all with polyurethane.

Cut the outer decks. Finish; add rope pull. Cut pieces for the ramp; glue and hold the steps in staggered position shown with scrap 3/8″-diam. dowel. Cut and attach molding along sides; clamp until dry. Sand and finish.

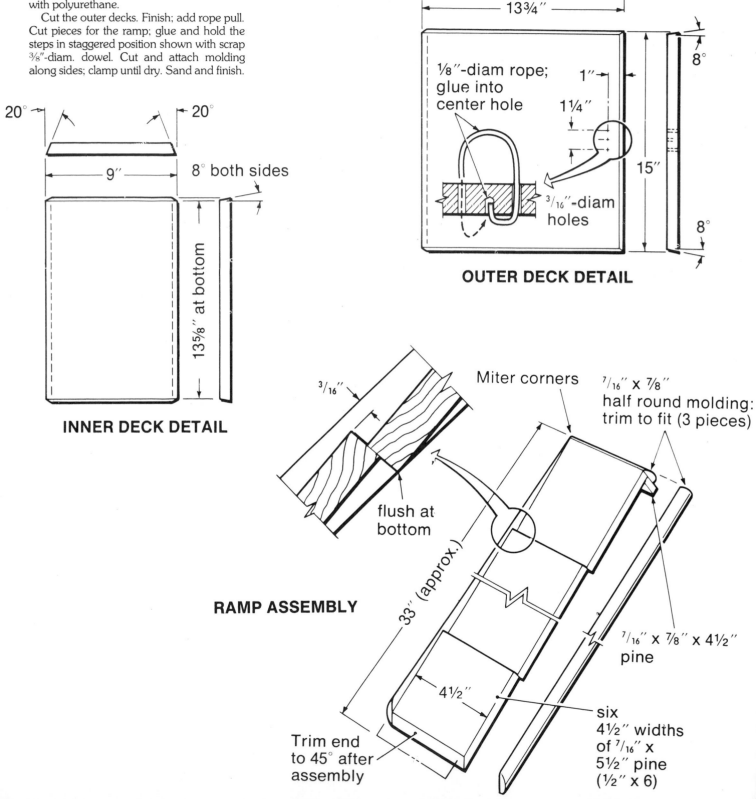

20°

9″   8° both sides

13⅝″ at bottom

INNER DECK DETAIL

20°   20°

13¾″   8°

1″   1¼″   15″

⅛″-diam rope; glue into center hole

³/₁₆″-diam holes

8°

OUTER DECK DETAIL

³/₁₆″

flush at bottom

Miter corners

⁷/₁₆″ x ⅞″ half round molding: trim to fit (3 pieces)

33″ (approx.)

4½″

⁷/₁₆″ x ⅞″ x 4½″ pine

six 4½″ widths of ⁷/₁₆″ x 5½″ pine (½″ x 6)

Trim end to 45° after assembly

RAMP ASSEMBLY

Noah's Ark
animals

*Meet Noah's famous pairs, fourteen
redwood animals in all, ready to board
the Ark. Or keep them landbound
if you'd rather. The shapes are fun to
look at and handle,
and with or without their ark, one
or two or all of them would be greeted
with glee. Such realistic touches as tails,
ears and the horse's mane
are added with rope and leather.*

MATERIALS All animals (7 pairs) can be cut from 8' of 2 x 8 redwood; details are cut from scraps of thin leather and ⅛"- and ¼" -diam. dowel; tails and manes are made from one small ball of hemp-like rope; wood glue; drill and bits; oil for finishing.

GENERAL DIRECTIONS

For animals that do not have two separate patterns for male and female, mark the full-size pattern on the wood in the same shape for each. Then, for the female, cut inside the line and for the male, cut outside the line. This slight variation will be enough to make a distinction. For pairs with separate male and female patterns, merely mark and cut out.

Sand edges smooth and slightly round. Drill holes as shown in diagram for each animal. Add trim as described under specific directions, doing the dowel parts before finishing with oil (one light coat) and the leather parts and rope trim afterward. For all dowel pieces, cut to length, round outer end, score a notch in area to be glued to let excess seep out and glue in place. Wipe away excess immediately. Finish with oil.

Then cut and apply leather and rope: for leather ears, cut one piece for both ears, about ¾" x 3" (except for elephant—see specific directions). Cut each end to a point as shown in diagrams and slip into ear hole. Insert tip of glue container and put a dab of glue inside hole on each side, being careful not to get it on ears themselves. Let dry.

Cut rope pieces (except lion) to lengths shown; glue in place. Unravel ends slightly. Compare rope piece to full-size diagram.

MAKING THE ANIMALS

Animals are made following appropriate diagrams and General Directions that appear at the beginning of the project. Special instructions, if any, are given with individual animal.

Giraffe Make two.

Bull and Cow Make one of each.

Camel Make two.

Horse Make two; lay out rope on pattern to test for right length. Cut slightly longer; glue into holes for mane as shown and trim ends. After gluing in tail, unravel completely.

Lion Make one. If a fuller mane is desired, make the loops ¾" on each side; cut open after gluing.

Lioness Make one.

Kangaroo Make two. For female only, cut out pouch as shown, making ½" tabs to glue into pre-drilled holes for pouch.

Elephant Make two as shown, except cut the ears separately, in shape shown with ½" tabs to glue into part-way holes pre-drilled for ears.

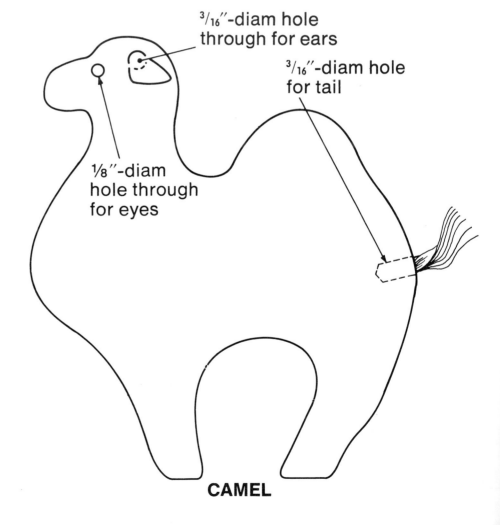

3/16"-diam hole through for ears

3/16"-diam hole for tail

⅛"-diam hole through for eyes

CAMEL

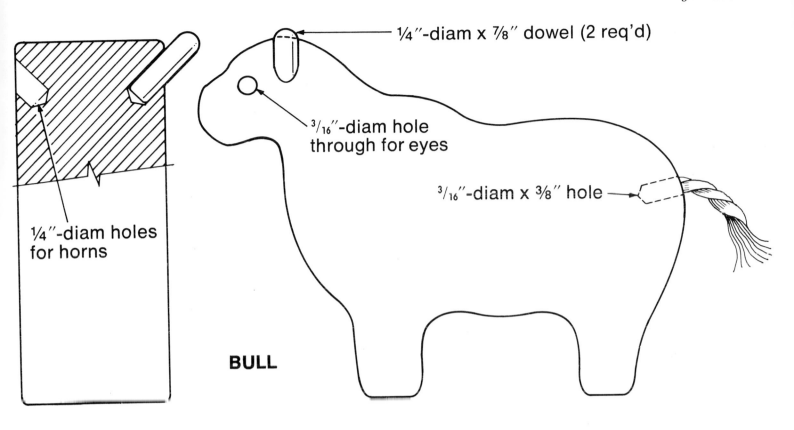

¼″-diam x ⅞″ dowel (2 req'd)

³/₁₆″-diam hole through for eyes

³/₁₆″-diam x ⅜″ hole

¼″-diam holes for horns

BULL

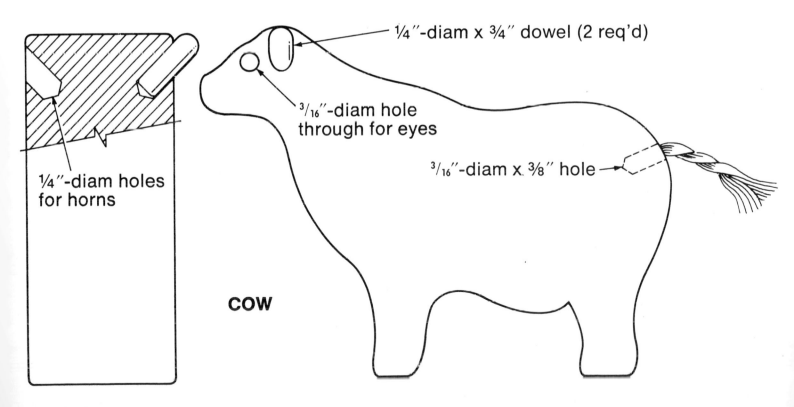

¼″-diam x ¾″ dowel (2 req'd)

³/₁₆″-diam hole through for eyes

³/₁₆″-diam x ⅜″ hole

¼″-diam holes for horns

COW

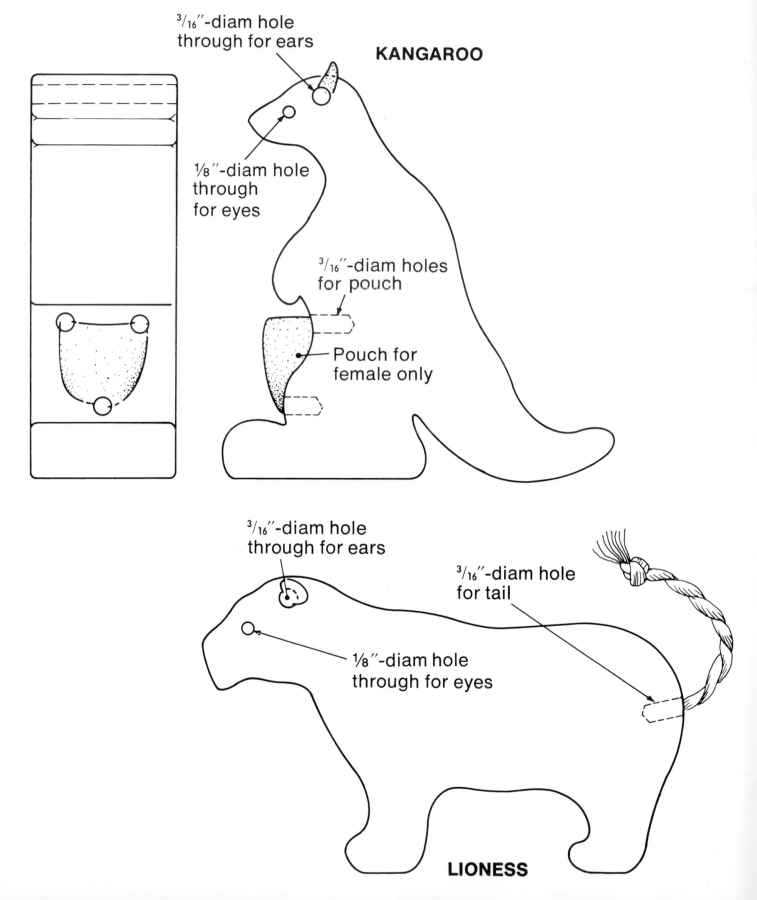

$^{3}/_{16}''$-diam hole through for ears

KANGAROO

$^{1}/_{8}''$-diam hole through for eyes

$^{3}/_{16}''$-diam holes for pouch

Pouch for female only

$^{3}/_{16}''$-diam hole through for ears

$^{3}/_{16}''$-diam hole for tail

$^{1}/_{8}''$-diam hole through for eyes

LIONESS

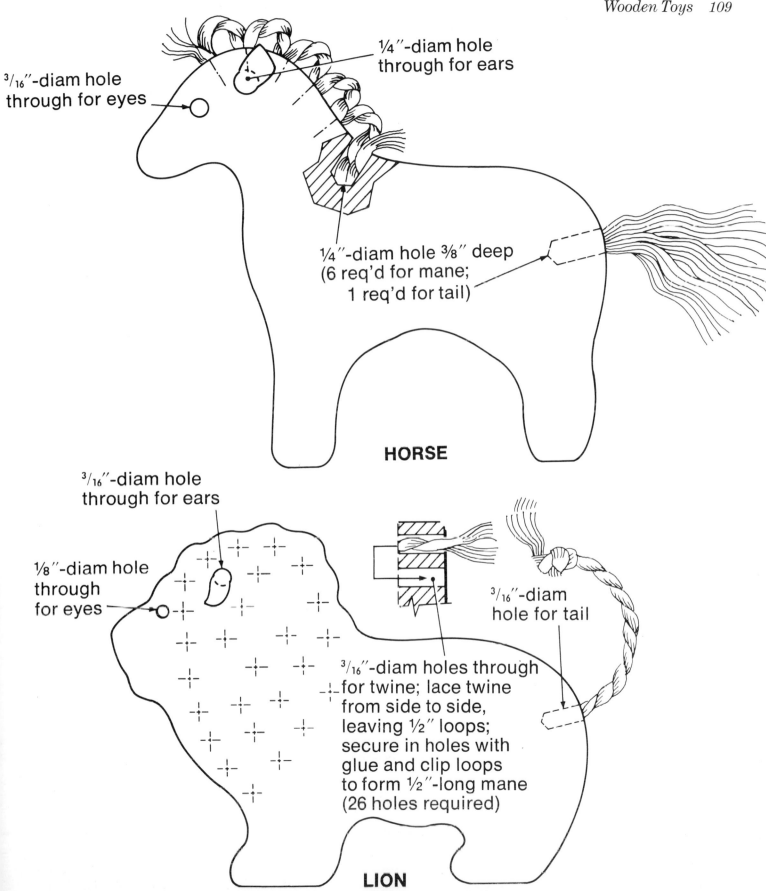

³/₁₆″-diam hole through for eyes

¼″-diam hole through for ears

¼″-diam hole ⅜″ deep (6 req'd for mane; 1 req'd for tail)

HORSE

³/₁₆″-diam hole through for ears

⅛″-diam hole through for eyes

³/₁₆″-diam holes through for twine; lace twine from side to side, leaving ½″ loops; secure in holes with glue and clip loops to form ½″-long mane (26 holes required)

³/₁₆″-diam hole for tail

LION

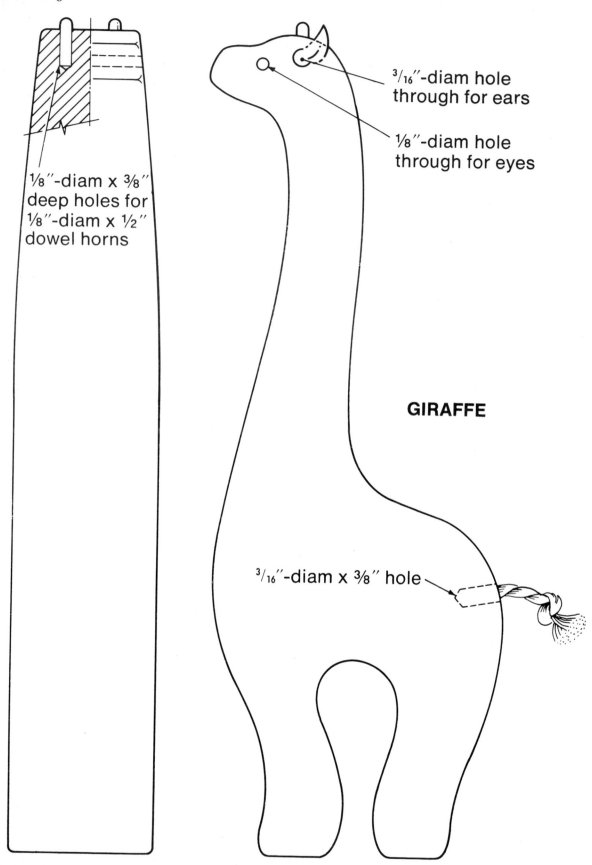

⅛″-diam x ⅜″ deep holes for ⅛″-diam x ½″ dowel horns

³/₁₆″-diam hole through for ears

⅛″-diam hole through for eyes

GIRAFFE

³/₁₆″-diam x ⅜″ hole

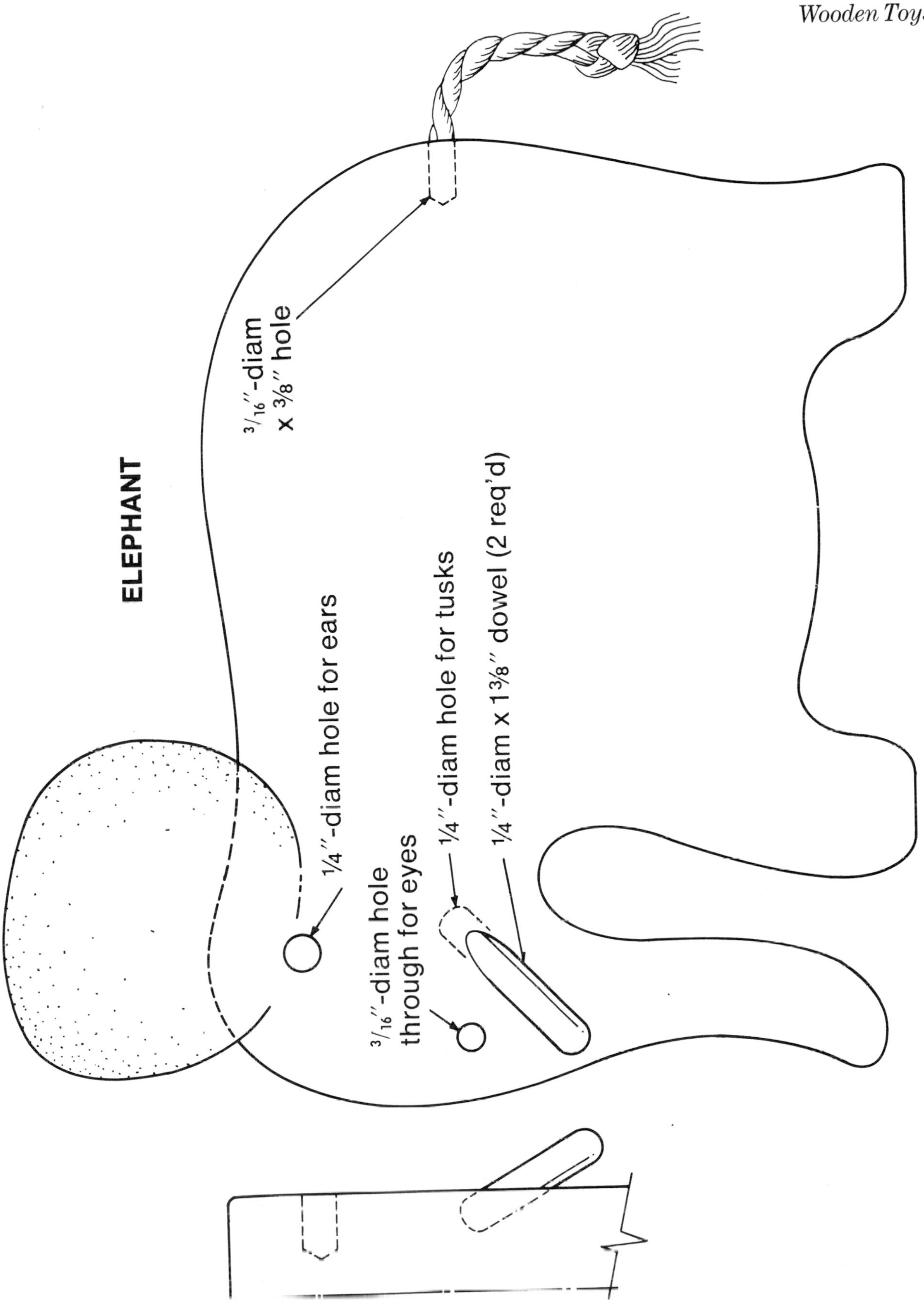

ELEPHANT

$3/_{16}$''-diam
x $3/_8$'' hole

$1/4$''-diam hole for ears

$1/4$''-diam hole for tusks

$1/4$''-diam x $1^3/_8$'' dowel (2 req'd)

$3/_{16}$''-diam hole
through for eyes

CHAPTER 5

Settings for Fantasy Play

Because children can spend hours in worlds of their own, this chapter is devoted to adventures in the realm of fantasy—to three ingenious settings designed just for the play of young imaginations.

First of the trio is Supercity!, a high-tech urban landscape where Superman and his fellow superheroes and heroines can do their thrilling deeds. Then we leap into the future and far away, to Outer-space Station, a multilevel activity center for daring interplanetary escapades. The third setting brings us back down to earth, to a dollhouse with a modern difference: it's ultra-portable. The secret is its structure, an ingenious, self-contained box (can be wood or cardboard) with a drop-down front that latches in place for convenient carrying.

These warrant being called once-in-a-lifetime toys, the kind that make memories and figure in the wishes of children everywhere. How can such settings possibly be practical? With materials so accessible, and directions so complete, they're thoroughly manageable. You'll be amazed how creative you turn out to be!

Contents

It's Supercity! **114**

Outer-space Station **144**

Portable dollhouse **173**

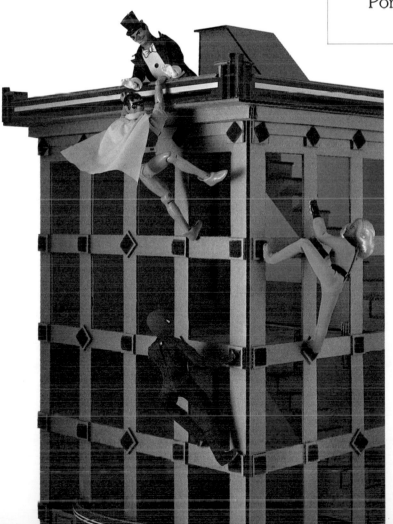

IT'S
Supercity!

Spiderman with no wall to scale?
Superman with no telephone booth to change in?
The Incredible Hulk with no place to
hulk? Isis with nowhere to land? No more! All
those superpeople who've been
cluttering up your floors and furniture can now
have their very own corrugated
cardboard Supercity, the town that has
everything, from bank to skyscraper
office building, from apartment house to garage.
It's all scaled for 8" tall figures, and
everything folds, nests or comes apart for compact
storage. The street, scored for folding,
is taped to show crosswalk, sewer grates and
manhole cover. Lampposts have
table-tennis-ball lamps. The close-up photographs
that follow make individualstructures
and their inner workings absolutely clear.

General Directions

Note *Read all instructions through thoroughly before starting project.*

Sheets of corrugated cardboard are used to build the Supercity. They can be purchased from packing material and some art supply stores. Large cardboard boxes, of the size used to ship appliances and furniture, can also be used. Ask for them at appliance, home decorating or department stores (shopping center stores are more likely to have some on hand to give you). Select clean, dry boxes in good condition, in the largest sizes you can carry.

Materials Cardboard sheets or boxes (here it is sheets of cardboard: for bank and telephone booth, one 4′ x 4′ sheet and two 3′ x 4′ sheets; for skyscraper and revolving door, three 3′ x 4′ sheets; for apartment house, two and a quarter 3′ x 4′ sheets; for garage, two 3′ x 4′ sheets; for street, amounts are given under specific directions; for accessories, excess from buildings can be used); utility knife; metal straightedge (a piece of aluminum works well; ⅛″ x ¾″ x 72″ bars are available from hardware stores); soft pencils; ruler; kneaded erasers.

CUTTING CARDBOARD

If using boxes, cut open along a seam and use the inside surface of the box for the outside surface of the building to conceal any printing. Trim pieces of boxes, reducing to the overall dimensions required for pattern pieces of building to be made. (Bends in boxes should correspond to corners of buildings but should be bent in reverse for use in buildings.) For flat sheets, score at corners of the buildings and bend away from the score. For smaller pieces of cardboard, walls can also be cut separately and joined at corners with a hot glue gun (see instructions at right).

For strength, corrugations should run vertically in the finished building. Follow patterns to lay out walls and all other pieces for each building to be made directly on cardboard with pencil, ruler and straightedge. Mark only the cutting and scoring lines, extending lines ¼″ past where they meet at corners for greater accuracy in cutting. (The extended lines will be visible when the rest of the line is covered by the straightedge, marking the starting and stopping points for each cut.) The ¼″ line can be removed later with a kneaded eraser.

Cut out parts, using utility knife and straightedge. Start with the largest cuts, such as outside walls or edges of roof and floor pieces. Always cut with knife on waste side of cutting line. Then make interior cuts. For neatness in cutting and later structural strength, try not to cut windows or other cutouts beyond the precise corners of their outlines. Check back of cardboard after making all interior cuts to be sure that they meet at corners and then push out waste. If cuts don't meet, insert knife into cut and cut just up to corner; then punch out.

To score lines for folds, and hinges, cut through just the top layer of cardboard (the side that will be the *outside* of the bend or hinge) with utility knife. If you accidentally cut all the way through, scores can be reinforced with hot glue, except when the score is a hinge. For hinges, repairs should be made with tape.

To cut arches and circle, use an X-acto® Precision Compass with a number 1 knife with a stationary blade. If this is not available, you can draw the arches and circles to be cut onto the cardboard with a pencil and compass.

When using the Precision Compass, place a small piece of heavy cardboard or a 1″ x 1″ scrap of plywood over the center pivot point to protect the cardboard and keep point from sinking into it as you cut. Use the instrument as if you were drawing a circle with a standard compass, making several passes rather than trying to cut through in one motion.

If using a utility knife on drawn circles, make a rough cut outside the marked line (from ⅛″ to ¼″ outside the line toward the waste). Then cut precisely, using a small pair of scissors. Cut small circles of cardboard with a pair of nail scissors.

DECORATING BUILDINGS

The solid color and striped areas on buildings are decorations made of self-adhesive plastic, plastic tape and automobile striping tapes in black, red, yellow, white and blue. Self-adhesive plastic can be used for all of these decorations if it is cut into strips of the appropriate widths, most often ⅛″, ¼″ and ½″.

To cut strips accurately, tape the ends of a metal straightedge to a sheet of cardboard. Do not use cardboard you'll need for one of the buildings. Mark the plastic's paper side for desired strips; then slip it under the straightedge. Line it up and cut strips with a single-edged razor or utility knife.

In some cases, you apply the plastic to separate pieces of cardboard (the bank parapet and canopy and apartment house) and attach with hot glue to building.

If you wish to make the buildings exactly as shown here, follow the colors in the photographs for all decorations.

For building signs, use felt-tipped markers. Thin tips, of the sort used for writing, are best for decorations.

USING A HOT GLUE GUN

A hot glue gun will make the construction of Supercity buildings much faster and eas-

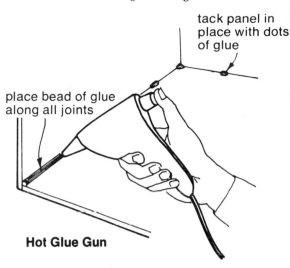

tack panel in place with dots of glue

place bead of glue along all joints

Hot Glue Gun

ier than it would be with regular glues and cements. The hot glue cools and sets rapidly, so the pieces need only be held together briefly after glue application and don't need to be weighted, clamped or taped. You can buy a hot glue gun and cartridges for under ten dollars, or you may be able to borrow one from someone you know.

Note *All references to glue throughout instructions require hot glue (unless otherwise specified).*

To glue, place each piece in intended position and lightly mark with pencil for placement. Use a dab of glue to attach small pieces to large ones (such as small cardboard squares on Supercity Bank). Use a centered, thin line of glue to attach long thin pieces to larger ones (such as decorative stripes on Skyscraper). Use diagonal crossed lines or dabs placed at corners and center of sides to attach large pieces to larger ones (such as signs on Bank and Garage). Use a bead (line) of glue to join seams (see Hot Glue Gun drawing, above). To join seams such as fixed floors or ceilings to walls, place floor or ceiling piece on work surface with walls standing around it. Hold each wall against each edge of floor or ceiling in turn, and tack with dots of glue in corners so that each dot touches both the floor and the wall. Then put down a bead of glue along all joints, making certain that it touches both parts. If desired, for additional strength, turn the assembly upside-down and place another bead of glue along the underside of each joint (this is generally not required). To reinforce scores if required, fill with a bead of glue as shown in glue gun drawing. To glue up items made of several small pieces with butted joints (such as the Bank's Staircase), place a bead of glue along the edge that will be unseen in the finished piece.

GLUING WOODEN BEADS

In the Supercity project as shown, ½"-diam. wooden beads are used as knobs to hold a looped end of monofilament cable (such as the Sky Line) or to control the direction of moving monofilament (such as in the elevator and the telephone booth). Large-eyed glass beads could also be used, but the hot glue might melt plastic beads, and very small beads would be hard to handle.

The wooden beads are attached to the surface of the cardboard when the monofilament runs parallel to that surface; they are embedded in the cardboard when the monofilament must go through the cardboard.

When attaching a wooden bead to the surface, cut a small cross where the bead is to be placed. Press the bead down into the cross to make a dent. Remove the bead and fill the depression with hot glue. Press the bead into the glue, aligning the hole as required, and allow to set.

To embed a wooden bead into cardboard, cut out a circle that is slightly smaller than the bead, using a small-blade utility knife. Circle does not have to be a perfectly cut one, since bead and glue will cover it. Line the cut-out area with hot glue. Press the bead in place in the hole, aligning its hole as required; let set. In either case if the bead seems at all wobbly, encircle it with hot glue, making sure glue touches the cardboard all around.

SEQUENCE OF ASSEMBLY FOR BUILDINGS

All buildings follow the same general sequence of assembly. First read the General Directions at the start of the project, and specific directions for the building you want to make.

1. Lay out all three walls following the pattern, directly onto the corrugated cardboard, using a ruler, pencil and straightedge.

2. Score bends for corners (see General Directions); cut out the windows and doors; hinge as required with scored lines.

3. Cut out floor (if removable, cut with ¼" clearance; if fixed, cut to fit, with less than ⅛" clearance) and ceiling/roof pieces. As required, cut stairwell or chute holes in floors and roof.

4. Attach bottom floor and roof to walls bent into shape using the glue gun as described on page 115.

5. Cut and install floor cleats for each floor as shown in diagrams.

6. Construct and attach any special features, such as revolving doors, stairs, etc.

7. Make and glue on signs, decorations cut from cardboard and covered with self-adhesive plastic or tape and any other decorations desired.

Bank Building

Note *Bank has a special material requirement—55' length (or equivalent) Velcro® self-fastening tape, at least ¾" wide and preferably black.*
Read General Directions at start of project, and then cut out all major parts for the bank. Assemble the walls and floors with their cutouts for the stairs. Add floor cleats as shown. Put roof aside until later.

Apply the three 1½"-wide notched dentil strips and three ½"-wide border strips, gluing dentils even with the three top edges of the bank walls and the borders even with the top edges of dentil strips.

Cut out 69 cardboard squares, each 1" x 1"; glue in place following bank pattern (except for the four around the portal).

Following the bank entrance diagram, cut out the portal frame. Cover it and the portals themselves with red self-adhesive plastic. Add decorative strips of black and white tape

to the frame. Glue frame in place around the doorway. Cut the panels and panel frames and glue to the portals on top of self-adhesive plastic. Just before gluing, make certain that the larger panels do not interfere with the opening of the door. If they do, make the panels slightly narrower.

Under large front windows, place centered 2" x 2" squares of black self-adhesive plastic. Cut and apply a panel and panel frame over plastic as shown. Above large front windows, decorate with frames of black and red tape.

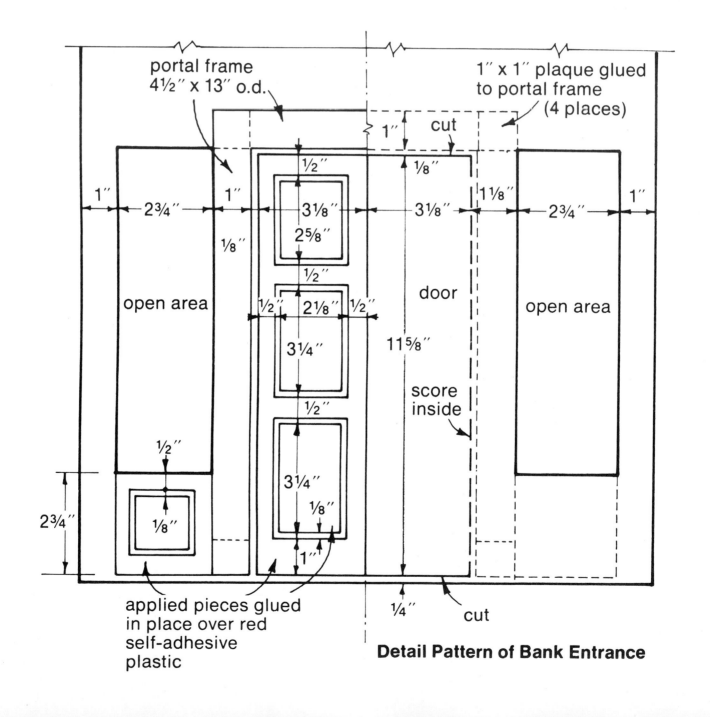

Detail Pattern of Bank Entrance

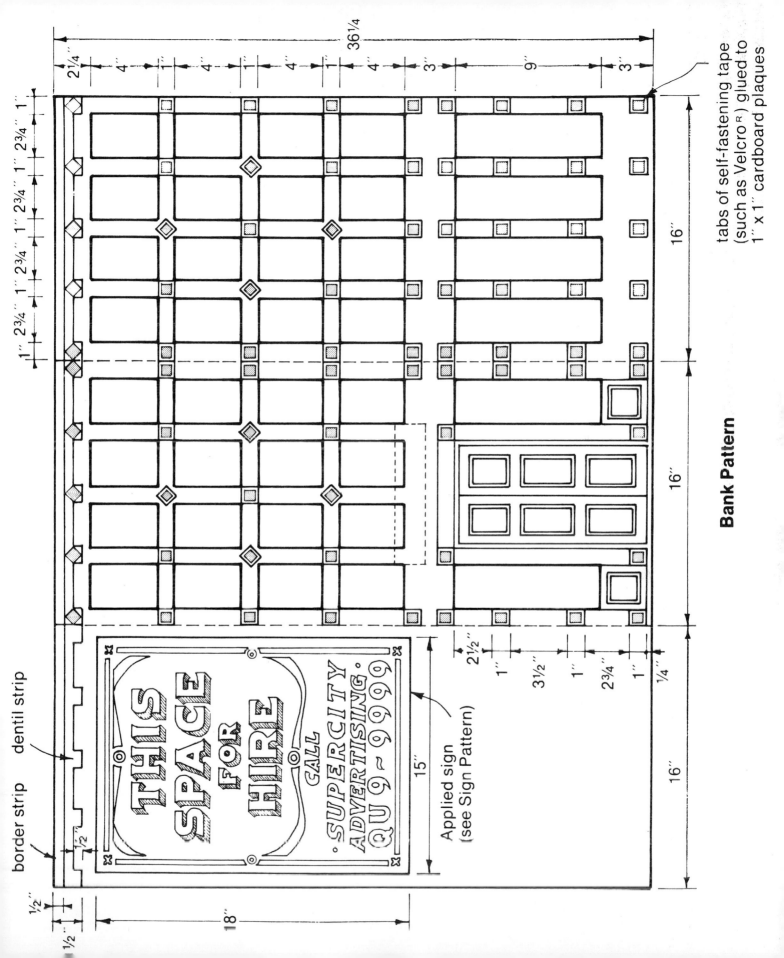

Bank Pattern

border strip   dentil strip

1/2"
1/2"
18"

1" 1/2"

THIS SPACE FOR HIRE
CALL
·SUPERCITY ADVERTISING·
QU 9 ~ 9999

15"

Applied sign
(see Sign Pattern)

2 1/2"
1"
3 1/2"
1"
2 3/4"
1"
1/4"

16"

16"

16"

16"

tabs of self-fastening tape
(such as Velcro ᴿ) glued to
1" x 1" cardboard plaques

36 1/4"

2 1/4" 4" 1" 4" 1" 4" 1" 4" 1" 3" 9" 3"

1" 2 3/4" 1" 2 3/4" 1" 2 3/4" 1" 2 3/4" 1" 2 3/4" 1" 2 3/4" 1" 2 3/4" 1"

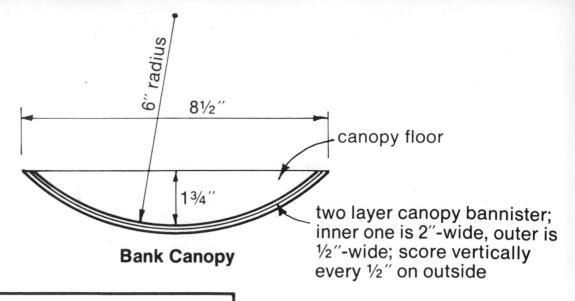

6″ radius

8½″

1¾″

canopy floor

two layer canopy bannister; inner one is 2″-wide, outer is ½″-wide; score vertically every ½″ on outside

Bank Canopy

SUPERCITY BANK

To make the canopy, first cut out its floor. Then cut a 2½″ strip for the bannister and rail to fit the length of the curve. Score it vertically every ½″. Cut off ½″ lengthwise for rail. Glue remaining 2″ bannister strip to curve of floor, flush with its bottom. Glue ½″ rail strip on, even with the top edge of the bannister. Cover the bannister and rail with separate strips of self-adhesive plastic; add black and white tape as in photograph. On plain paper with marker, trace Supercity Bank identification, cut out, rubber-cement to canopy.

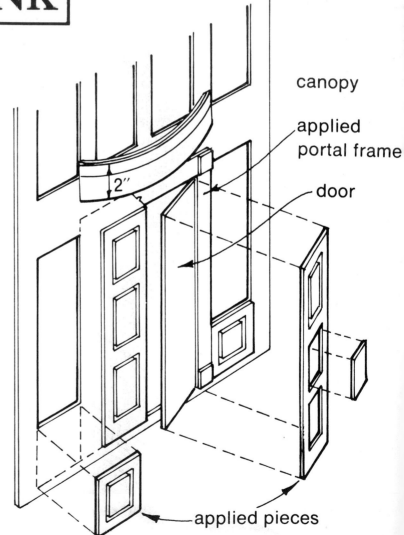

canopy

applied portal frame

door

2″

applied pieces

Construction Detail of Bank Entrance

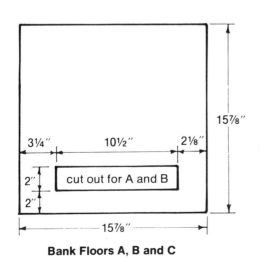

15⅞″

3¼″   10½″   2⅛″

2″

2″

cut out for A and B

15⅞″

Bank Floors A, B and C

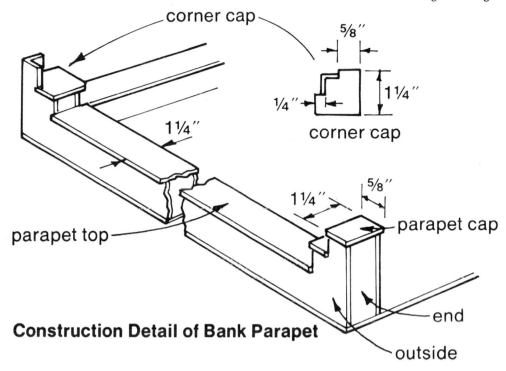

Construction Detail of Bank Parapet

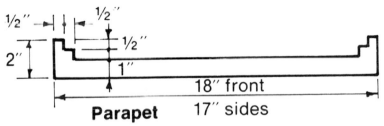

Parapet   18″ front   17″ sides

Cut out the roof with the hole in it for stairs as shown. For the outside of parapet, cut three pieces to fit edge of roof, with the pieces butted against each other at the corners. Cover with self-adhesive plastic; add black and white tape trim. Glue in place on roof. For the inside of the parapet, cut two pieces without the steps at one end for the side parapets; glue each in place parallel to each side piece, 1″ outside dimension from side pieces. Then cut a 1″ strip for the front to fit between the two pieces just placed and glue in place 1″ from the front piece. Cut 1¼″-wide parapet tops to fit and glue. Cut ends to fit and caps as shown and glue in place.

Cut out the roof stair enclosure and assemble with glue. Attach to the roof and then attach roof to bank, even with the back and centered on sides.

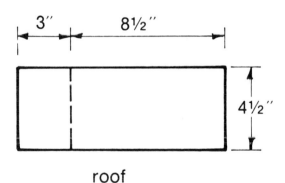

roof

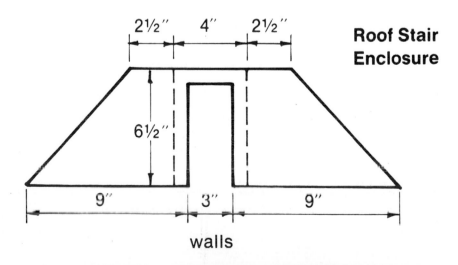

Roof Stair Enclosure

walls

In making the stairs, notice that each of the three sets of stairs has a different height and length. (Individual sets are designated A, B and C in the diagrams.) The width is constant, as are the dimensions of the risers (1″ x 2½″), treads (1⅛″ x 2½″) and landings (2¼″ x 2½″). Cut strips 2½″-wide and cut treads, risers and landings from the strips.

Draw and then cut out the stair sides following the diagram. Be sure that each pair matches. The stair back is 5⁄16″ narrower than the treads and shorter than the sides. The floor is the same length as the sides and 5⁄16″ narrower than the tread width.

When stairs are assembled, they all follow the same sequence: With glue, attach the back between pairs of sides, with one or two risers for spacing. Attach the floor and the landing. Attach all remaining risers and then all treads. Place stairs in correct places in bank.

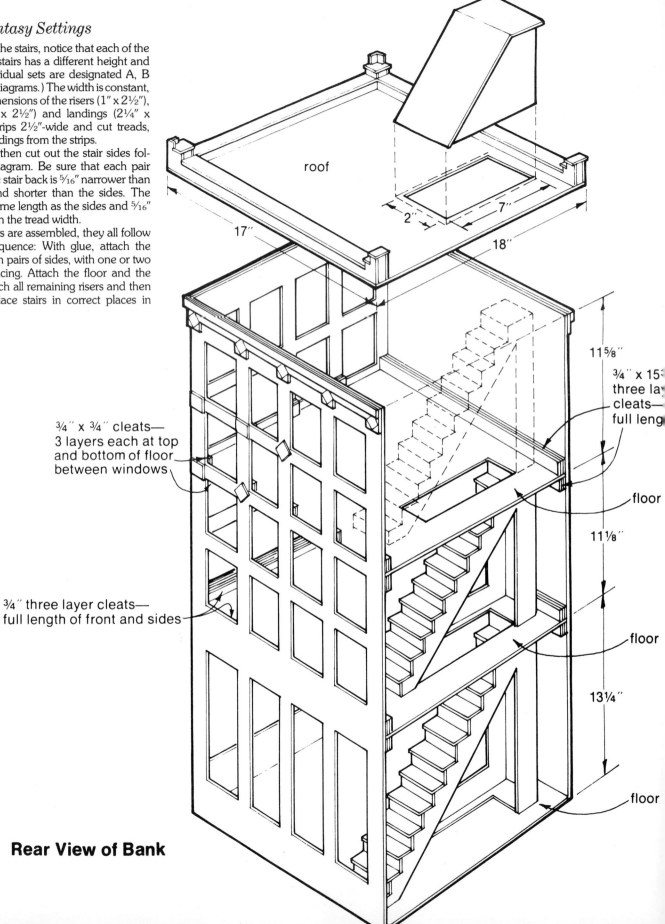

roof

2″ 7″

17″ 18″

11⅝″

¾″ x 15 three la cleats— full leng

floor

¾″ x ¾″ cleats— 3 layers each at top and bottom of floor between windows

11⅛″

floor

¾″ three layer cleats— full length of front and sides

13¼″

floor

Rear View of Bank

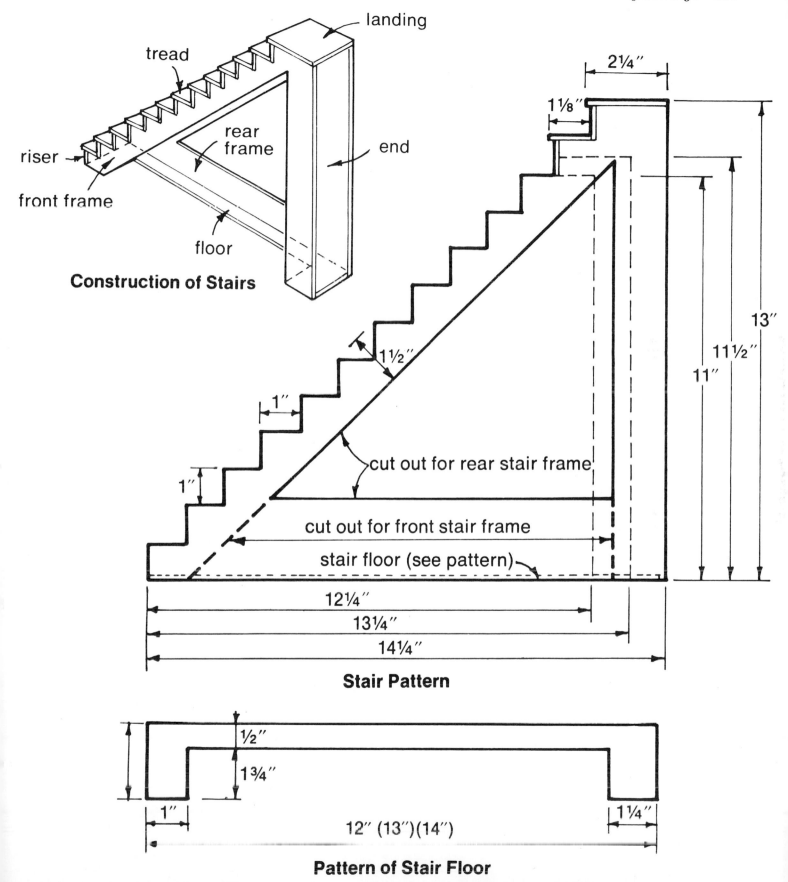

Construction of Stairs

tread

landing

riser

front frame

rear frame

end

floor

2¼″

1⅛″

13″

11½″

11″

1½″

1″

1″

cut out for rear stair frame

cut out for front stair frame

stair floor (see pattern)

12¼″

13¼″

14¼″

Stair Pattern

½″

1¾″

1″

12″ (13″)(14″)

1¼″

Pattern of Stair Floor

Each square = 1″

Bank Sign Pattern

Following adjacent instructions, first enlarge, then trace Bank Sign Pattern (advertising poster for side wall). Cut same-size piece thin cardboard; rubber-cement sign to board. Color in letters with markers. Glue sign to side of bank.

TO ENLARGE PATTERN On a photocopy (or pattern itself if you don't mind marking book), preferably with colored pencil, connect lines across pattern to form grid. On rectangle of brown wrapping paper, mark dots 1″ apart around edges, making as many spaces as pattern edges have squares; join dots to form grid. Make sure you have same number of squares as pattern, then draw in each the lines in corresponding squares on pattern.

To attach Velcro® tabs, use five-minute clear epoxy, mixed as needed in several small batches (it sets quickly). Cut ¾″ squares of Velcro and epoxy the fuzzier side of each to the cardboard plaques on building, centered on each one. The looped half of the tape can be cut into ¼″ x ½″ pieces and glued to the back of action figures' hands and feet with hot glue, even if the feet are covered with fabric. If the figures are wearing boots, however, remove them; they are too rigid for "climbing" the building. Velcro can be removed from figures without damaging them.

To hold figures on wall, self-fastening tabs are glued to building, dolls' hands and feet.

Telephone Booth

Note *In this unit, and some of those that follow, you will need varying lengths of nylon monofilament.*

Cut cardboard pieces for the telephone booth with corrugations running vertically in all panels. Laminate two pieces for panel 1. Cut panels 3 and 4; cut out windows as shown in each; laminate into panel 3-4. Cut out panels 2 and 5. Cut and score panel 5 for the bifold door. Cut out the booth floor.

Cut two platform stops; glue one each to panel 1 and panel 3-4. In panel 1, cut a centered hole for the wooden bead (see Diagram, page 126) ½" on center from the bottom edge. Embed bead (see Gluing Wooden Beads, page 117) with bead's hole centered. Glue another bead to center of booth floor as shown. Cut out the base.

Glue the floor to the base and then add panels 1, 2 and 3-4 around floor. (Panel 5 will be glued in place later on.)

Cut out parts for the roof; assemble with glue. Stand panel 5 in place and check the fit of the roof (it should be loose). Cut parts for the platform (it also should fit loosely but not be able to fit past the stops) and assemble with glue. Punch a small hole in center of platform. Cut a centered notch in the frame of platform next to panel 1 so that it will not touch the wooden bead and monofilament when completely assembled. Thread a 3' length of monofilament nylon through the bead in panel, then through the bead on the floor and hole in platform. Loop it around a toothpick placed on top of platform and then back through the platform hole. Tie off the monofilament on itself. Place dabs of glue on toothpick ends to hold it in place.

Punch holes in two diagonally opposite corners of platform and thread a rubber band through each from below (page 126). Place half toothpick through each rubber-band loop. Tack toothpick with glue to hold.

Place two pins with bead heads (or two toothpick halves with globs of glue placed at one end) into top edges of booth as shown. Pull up each rubber band. Knot band and slip around pin. The rubber bands should be tight enough to hold the platform firmly against the platform stops but loose enough so that platform can be pushed down to the booth floor.

Following page 126 diagram, glue a spring clothespin in place. Also glue a small block of wood in place to brace the clothespin. (Block here is about ¾" sawed from the thick end of another clothespin.)

Depress the platform while holding the monofilament across the clothespin to ascertain correct positions of bead and two holding knots in monofilament. While holding it down, have a helper place a small dab of hot glue (or a tab of masking tape) onto the monofilament where it crosses to the far side of the clothespin. Make a double overhand knot at that point. Thread bead onto monofilament and make a second knot to hold the bead against the first knot.

Glue the bifold door frame in place.

Decorate the booth with tape and self-adhesive plastic as desired, or follow the color photographs.

Push on clothespin (see page 126) triggers floor-raising mechanism in booth.

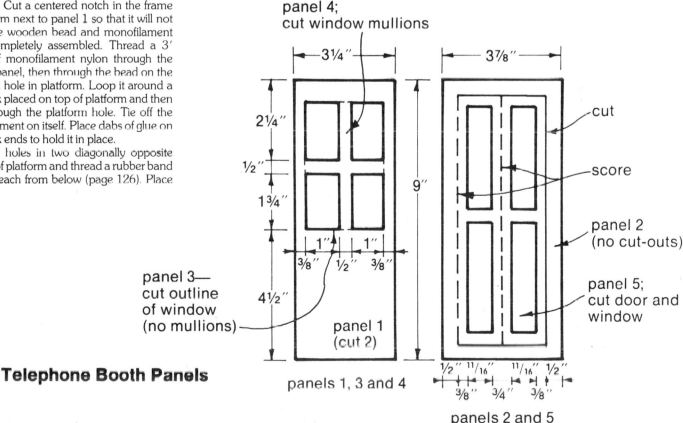

panel 4;
cut window mullions

3¼"

2¼"

½"

1¾"

9"

1"   1"

⅜" ½" ⅜"

4½"

panel 1
(cut 2)

panel 3—
cut outline
of window
(no mullions)

panels 1, 3 and 4

3⅞"

cut

score

panel 2
(no cut-outs)

panel 5;
cut door and
window

½" ¹¹⁄₁₆" ¹¹⁄₁₆" ½"

⅜" ¾" ⅜"

panels 2 and 5

Telephone Booth Panels

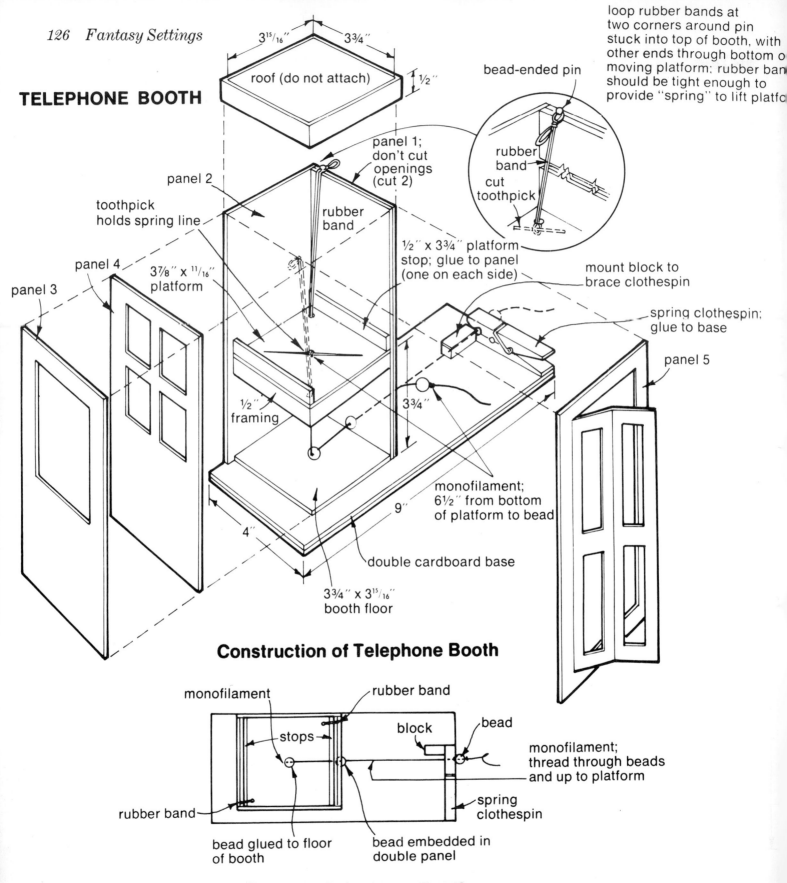

TELEPHONE BOOTH

loop rubber bands at two corners around pin stuck into top of booth, with other ends through bottom of moving platform; rubber band should be tight enough to provide "spring" to lift platform

bead-ended pin

rubber band
cut toothpick

3$^{15}/_{16}$"   3¾"

roof (do not attach)

½"

panel 1; don't cut openings (cut 2)

panel 2

rubber band

toothpick holds spring line

panel 4

3$^7/_8$" x $^{11}/_{16}$" platform

panel 3

½" x 3¾" platform stop; glue to panel (one on each side)

mount block to brace clothespin

spring clothespin; glue to base

panel 5

½" framing

3¾"

monofilament; 6½" from bottom of platform to bead

9"

double cardboard base

4"

3¾" x 3$^{15}/_{16}$" booth floor

Construction of Telephone Booth

monofilament

rubber band

stops

block

bead

monofilament; thread through beads and up to platform

rubber band

spring clothespin

bead glued to floor of booth

bead embedded in double panel

Detail of Telephone Booth

Skyscraper

Note *Instructions that follow call for table-tennis balls to decorate the skyscraper and as lights and lamps. See specific directions for number. One heavier, 4½" ball is required for the skyscraper tower — see the adjoining diagram.*

Read General Directions at start of project, and then cut out all major parts for the skyscraper. The building is composed of five separate sections. Only sections 4 and 5 (see Diagram) are attached to each other so that

section 5 with its heavy ball top doesn't topple easily. Sections 2 through 5 are four-sided; section 1 is three-sided with an open back. (The floors are removable.)

Assemble sides of section 1 around levels A and D with glue (see page 128). Then cut and laminate cleats for floors B and C. Install only the bottom cleats. Cut floors B and C with the large notch for the elevator shaft. Place floors on their cleats. While they are in place, glue on the top cleats, leaving a slight clearance so that the floor can be easily removed. Assemble all sections.

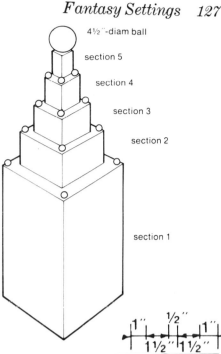

4½"-diam ball
section 5
section 4
section 3
section 2
section 1

Section Assembly

1″   ½″   1″
1½″   1½″

1″

8″

2″

8″

2″

8″

1″

30″

Score   score

9⅞″

14½″   3″   8½″   3″   14½″

Section One

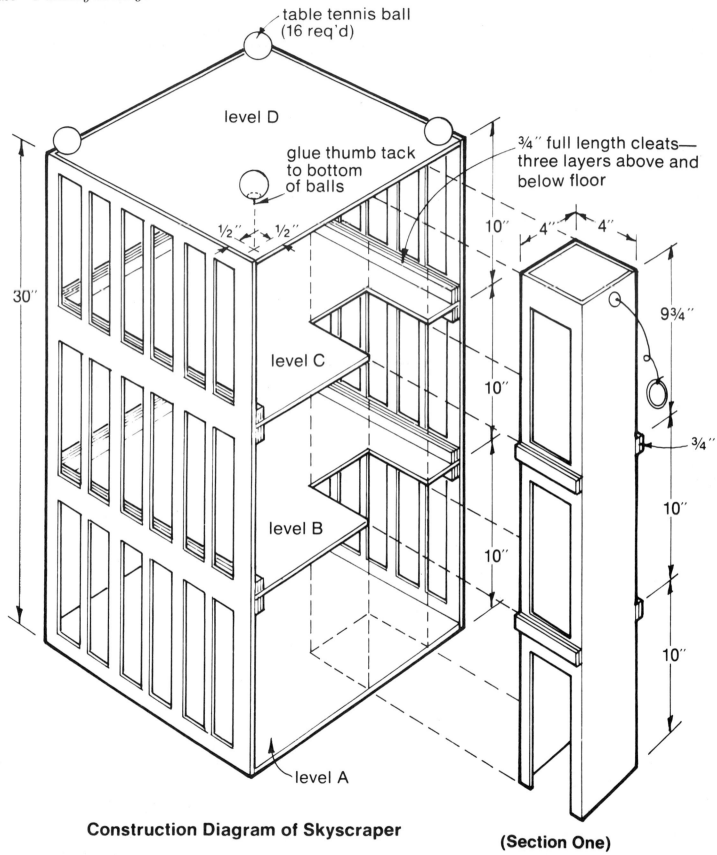

Construction Diagram of Skyscraper

(Section One)

table tennis ball
(16 req'd)

level D

glue thumb tack
to bottom
of balls

¾" full length cleats—
three layers above and
below floor

level C

level B

level A

30"

½"   ½"

10"

10"

10"

4"   4"

9¾"

¾"

10"

10"

10"

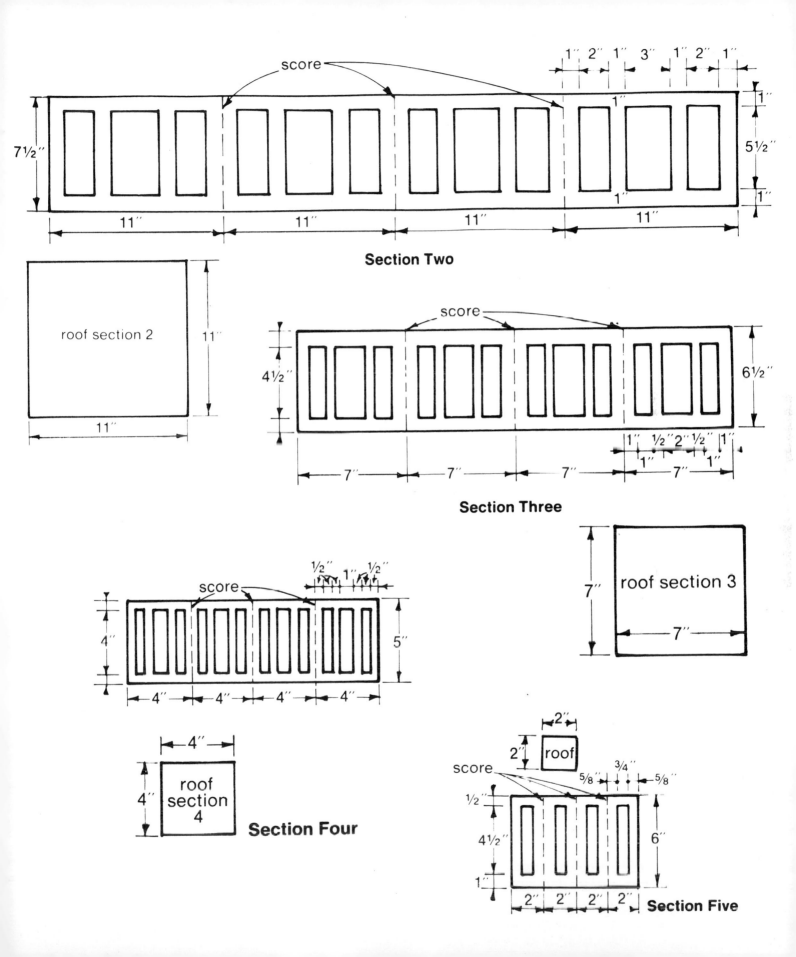

Section Two

Section Three

Section Four

Section Five

roof section 2

roof section 3

roof section 4

roof

score

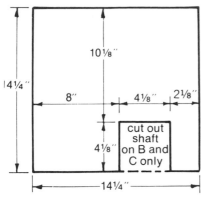

10⅛″

14¼″

8″   4⅛″   2⅛″

cut out
shaft
4⅛″ on B and
C only

14¼″

Levels A, B, C and D

Cut out and score the elevator shaft; cut its top to fit. Glue a wooden bead (*see* Gluing Wooden Beads, page 117) to center of underside of top and one into the outside wall of the shaft as shown to make a path for the monofilament. Make sure bead holes are aligned. Assemble the shaft with glue. Place shaft in section 1. Mark the shaft on each side under floors B and C for the position of two-layer ¾″ cleats. Remove shaft; cut out cleat pieces. Laminate and glue onto the shaft.

Cut out the elevator cab and assemble with glue. Place and glue a wooden bead in the center of the cab top.

Cut a 40″-length of monofilament nylon. Thread one end through the bead in the elevator cab and tie a knot that is too large to pull through the bead hole. Tack knot against the bead with a dab of glue. Thread the other end of the monofilament up inside the shaft, through the top bead and then through the wall bead. Tie the end to a 1¼″ drapery ring so that cab can reach first level of building and cut off excess.

Elevator works on pulley of monofilament threaded through beads, tied to curtain ring.

thread monofilament through bead embedded in ceiling of shaft and through second bead embedded in side of shaft

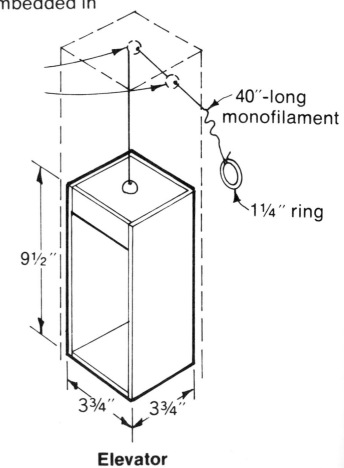

40″-long monofilament

1¼″ ring

9½″

3¾″   3¾″

Elevator

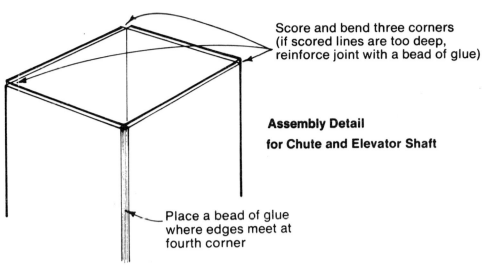

Score and bend three corners
(if scored lines are too deep,
reinforce joint with a bead of glue)

Assembly Detail

for Chute and Elevator Shaft

Place a bead of glue
where edges meet at
fourth corner

Decorate sections of skyscraper as desired.
Decorate topmost ball with strips of tape.
To attach ball to top of tower (section 5) center a glob of glue on roof; place ball on glue.
Surround the ball with a circle of glue, making
sure it touches ball and roof.

Table-tennis balls are used to further decorate the skyscraper. Paint them with acrylic
artist's paints, mixing white and burnt umber
to approximate the color of the cardboard
after gluing one thumbtack to each ball.
When dry, mark position of balls on each
section; add a dab of glue on mark and push
tack onto mark. (If young children will play
with skyscraper, omit thumbtacks and glue
on as for top ball, as described in preceding
paragraph.)

Typical Corner

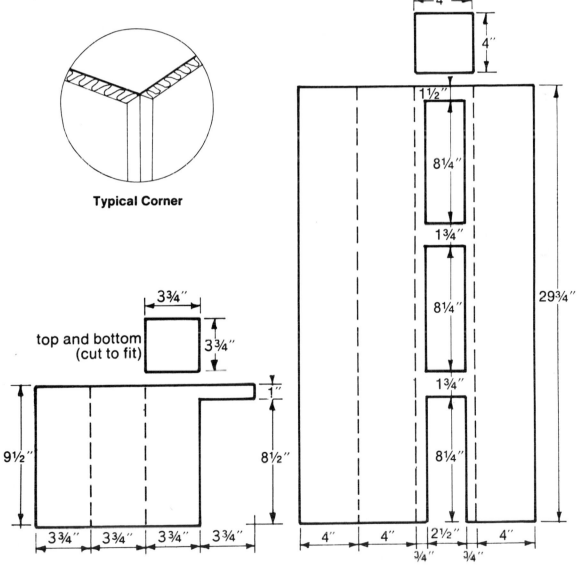

top and bottom
(cut to fit)

Cab Pattern

Shaft Pattern

Revolving Door for Skyscraper

Cut and score all parts for revolving door as required, following diagrams. Glue the enclosure floor to the enclosure, bending enclosure around to form a circular shape as shown.

Assemble the doors and glue the pins, with points directed out, in place. Glue a ¼″-diam. bead (see Gluing Wooden Beads, page 117) to the center of enclosure floor and top. Place the doors in the enclosure, with pin in center of the bead. Then glue top in place with bead on pin as shown.

Glue the entire revolving door assembly in place in the front opening in the skyscraper. Following detailed diagram, page 134, glue the semi-circular step to the floor and the three semi-circle units to the enclosure top.

Skyscraper's revolving door turns on toothpick axis; sides are scored to curve.

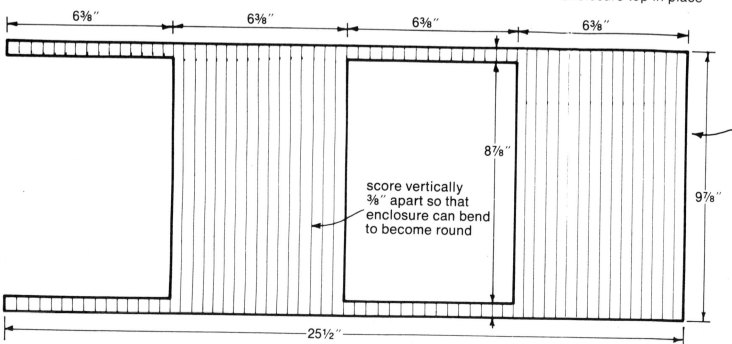

glue enclosure around its floor; place door with beads and pins, then glue enclosure top in place

6⅜″ 6⅜″ 6⅜″ 6⅜″

8⅞″

score vertically ⅜″ apart so that enclosure can bend to become round

9⅞″

25½″

Revolving Door Enclosure Pattern

Revolving Door Enclosure Assembly

center line

9⅞″

8½″

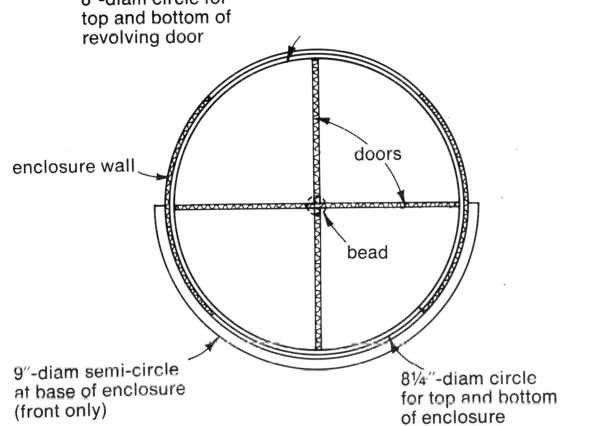

8″-diam circle for
top and bottom of
revolving door

enclosure wall

doors

bead

9″-diam semi-circle
at base of enclosure
(front only)

8¼″-diam circle
for top and bottom
of enclosure

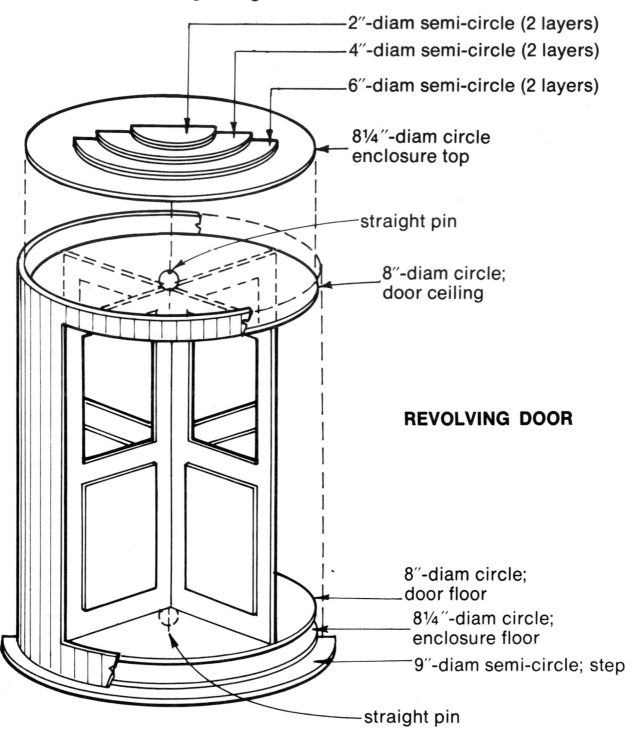

cut each as a full circle; cut in half and
glue together

2″-diam semi-circle (2 layers)

4″-diam semi-circle (2 layers)

6″-diam semi-circle (2 layers)

8¼″-diam circle
enclosure top

straight pin

8″-diam circle;
door ceiling

REVOLVING DOOR

8″-diam circle;
door floor

8¼″-diam circle;
enclosure floor

9″-diam semi-circle; step

straight pin

Construction Diagram of Revolving Door

Apartment House

The apartment house is composed of three major sections. Each has its own floor and ceiling panels, except for the top section with arches, which does not have its own floor. The sections can be attached to each other permanently with hot glue or left in separate pieces to make storage easier.

Read General Directions at start of project, and cut out all major pieces. Cut out the large notches in floor panels C and D and the trap door in floor E for the chute before assembly. Glue to assemble sections.

After assembly, cut pieces for the framing and the braces. Laminate them and install as shown on page 136.

Cut and score the chute walls to fit between floors B and E (above and below) and into the notches in floors C and D. Assemble chute around its floor and put in place in the building. (For a precise idea of chute assembly procedure, see detail on page 131.) Mark chute walls along framing on floor D for location of ¾" guides on each side of the notch. Cut out and glue the guides to the chute walls.

Cut 1" lengths of cardboard for building trim and decorate with self-adhesive plastic and tape as desired. Then glue to building, centering on top edge of each section as a low rail (to hold top sections in place) and placing one between the second row of windows and the door on the ground floor. Two additional sets of horizontal decorative panels are cut an inch narrower than the distance between rows of windows and to the same length as the total width of windows of each wall (see photograph, pages 116-117). After decorating with plastic and tape, they are glued in place, centered between windows.

Tricky getaway route for Robin: through a trapdoor and down an escape chute.

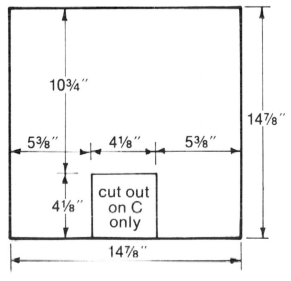

Floors D and E

5¾"
5⅜"   4⅛"   5⅝"   9½"
cut
4⅛"
hatch is on E only
14⅞"
cut out on D only

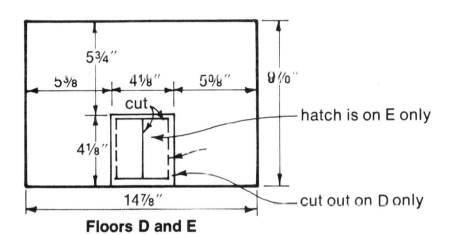

Apartment Floors A, B and C

10¾"
14⅞"
5⅜"   4⅛"   5⅜"
4⅛"
cut out on C only
14⅞"

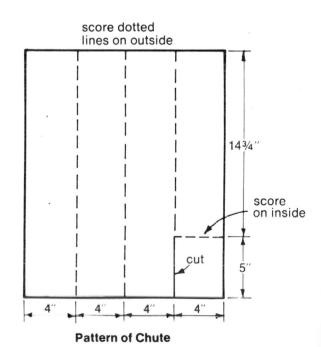

Pattern of Chute

score dotted lines on outside
14¾"
score on inside
cut
5"
4"   4"   4"   4"

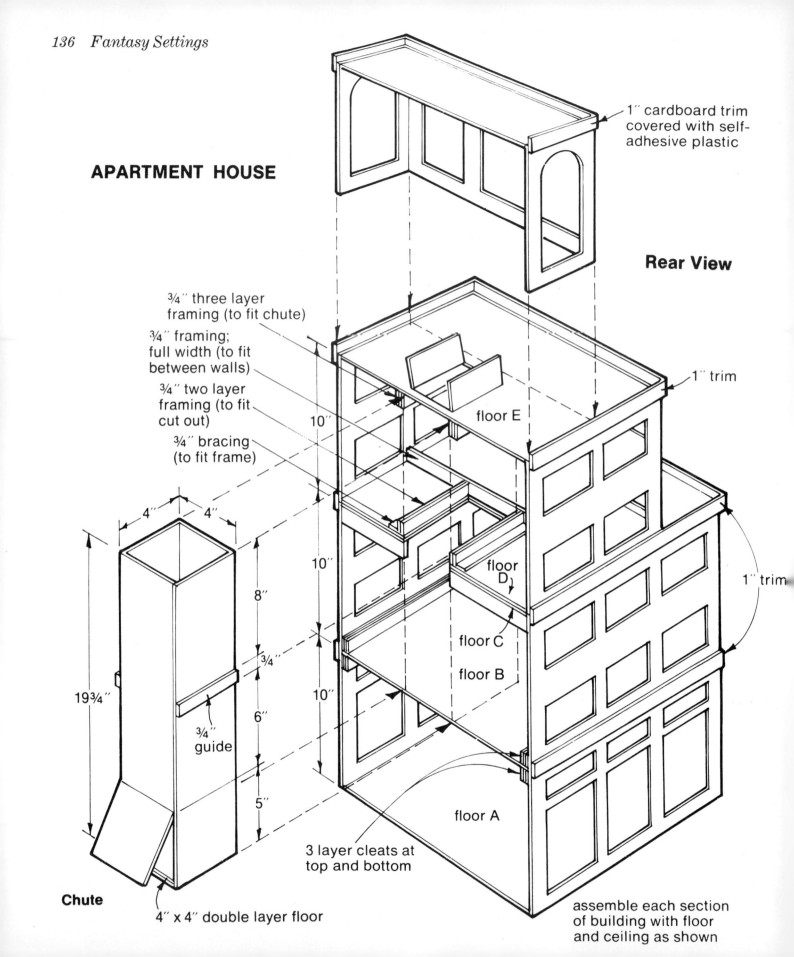

APARTMENT HOUSE

1″ cardboard trim covered with self-adhesive plastic

Rear View

¾″ three layer framing (to fit chute)

¾″ framing; full width (to fit between walls)

¾″ two layer framing (to fit cut out)

¾″ bracing (to fit frame)

1″ trim

floor E

10″

1″ trim

4″   4″

floor D

10″

floor C

floor B

19¾″

8″

¾″

6″

¾″ guide

10″

5″

floor A

Chute

3 layer cleats at top and bottom

4″ x 4″ double layer floor

assemble each section of building with floor and ceiling as shown

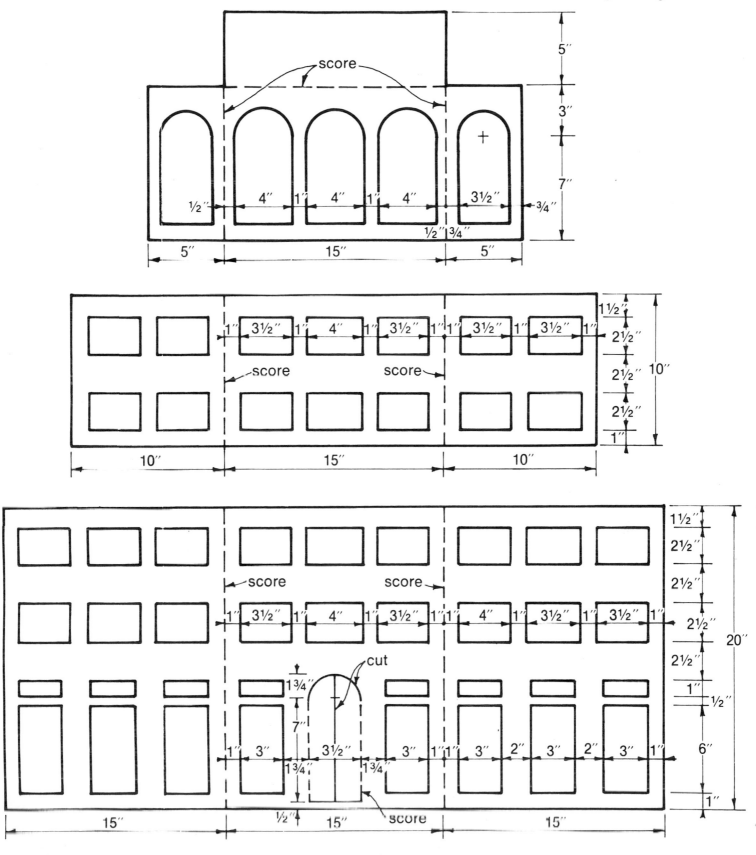

Apartment House Patterns

Garage

Read General Directions at start of project, and cut out all pieces for the garage. At the same time, cut the pieces for three-layer cleats and laminate them together.

Assemble the building around its floor and glue cleats in place. Turn building upside-down to attach the skylights and vertical roof panels. (To attach roof panels, see diagram; first glue one vertical panel, then one skylight panel, until all are used, working from the front of the building to the back.)

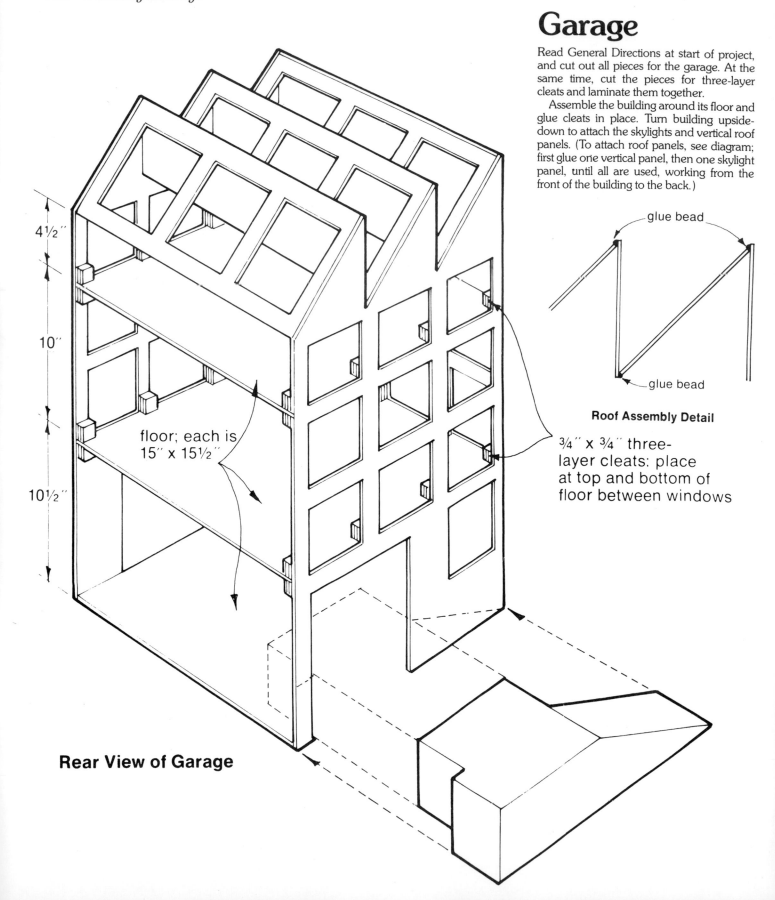

glue bead

glue bead

Roof Assembly Detail

4½″

10″

10½″

floor; each is 15″ x 15½″

¾″ x ¾″ three-layer cleats: place at top and bottom of floor between windows

Rear View of Garage

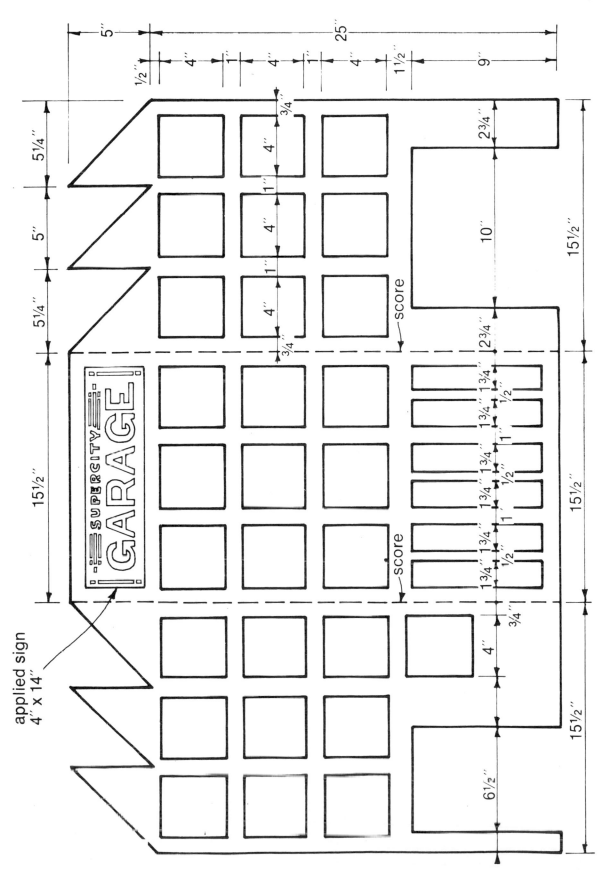

applied sign
4" x 14"

SUPERCITY GARAGE

score

score

Garage Patterns

On a 15″ x 21″ or larger piece of cardboard, lay out the pattern for the loading platform. Cut out and score on the dotted lines. Fold all parts down. Test-fit to make certain the platform fits the doorway in the garage. Secure folds and meetings with beads of glue along seams at underside. Place in garage.

Enlarge the pattern for the garage lights on lightweight cardboard (such as shirt cardboard) as follows: First connect lines across pattern to form grid over shape. Draw a true rectangle 5″ x 6″ on cardboard, then mark dots around edges, 1″ apart, as indicated on diagram. Join dots across sides of rectangle to form grid. Be sure you have the same number of squares as diagram, then draw in each square the lines in corresponding squares on the diagram. Cut out enlarged shape; use as pattern to cut pieces from corrugated cardboard. Cut two table-tennis balls in half, sand cut edges, and glue to lights as shown; glue lights to garage.

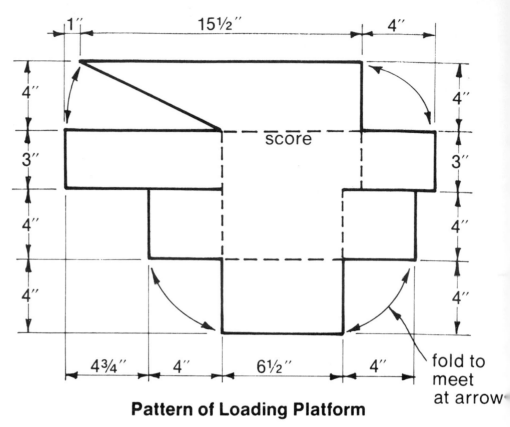

Pattern of Loading Platform

fold to meet at arrow

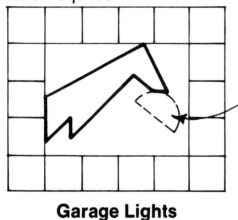

Each square = 1″

Garage Lights

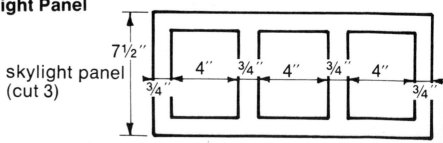

cut table-tennis ball in half with nail scissors; sand cut edge and glue to cut-out cardboard piece where indicated

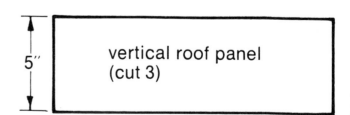

vertical roof panel (cut 3)

5″

Skylight Panel

skylight panel (cut 3)

7½″

Enlarge the garage sign as directed. Trace on plain paper. Color it with felt-tipped markers and glue to a piece of cardboard (cut to the same size) using rubber cement. Mount sign on building, where shown, with glue.

Decorate building with self-adhesive plastic applied directly to building. Make treads on ramp with ½″ blue and ¼″ yellow tape.

Each square = ½″

Garage Sign Pattern

TO ENLARGE PATTERN On a photocopy (or pattern itself if you don't mind marking book), preferably with colored pencil, connect lines across pattern to form grid. On rectangle of brown wrapping paper, mark dots ½″ apart around edges, making as many spaces as pattern edges have squares; join dots to form grid. Make sure you have same number of squares as pattern, then draw in each the lines in corresponding squares on pattern.

Lamp Posts

Enlarge the patterns on lightweight cardboard (such as shirt cardboard) as follows: First connect lines across pattern to form a grid over the pattern shapes. Draw a true rectangle 17" x 8" on cardboard (piece if necessary to get a large enough sheet), then mark dots around edge, 1" apart, as indicated on diagram. Join dots across sides of rectangle to form grid. Check to be sure you have the same numbers of squares as the diagram, then draw in each square the same pattern lines you see in corresponding squares on the diagram, and cut out the enlarged pieces. Using these as patterns, transfer lamp post diagram to corrugated cardboard, placing pieces so that the corrugations run vertically. Cut out pieces and slot in taller pieces.

Slip short piece into each slot. Test to be sure unit will stand and then run a bead of glue along the joint.

Cut a table-tennis ball in half with sharp scissors or single-edged razor blade; sand cut edges and glue to lamp post as shown.

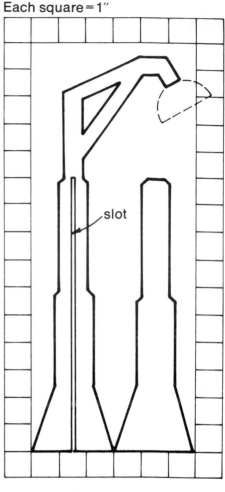

Each square = 1"

slot

Lamp Post

Street

The street can be made on one piece of cardboard, 24" x 84", scored twice on the back and once on the face so that it can be folded up for storage. To make it with smaller pieces, use three: one 19" x 24", one 24" x 39" and one 24" x 27". Score the 39" piece on the face and then join the other pieces to each end with tape hinges on the back.

Use self-adhesive plastic cut into strips (see Decorating Buildings in General Directions at start of project) or tape to make the lines as shown in the street layout. Lay out all guidelines for taped decorations with light pencil marks. Cut and place self-adhesive plastic as desired, or follow the color photographs.

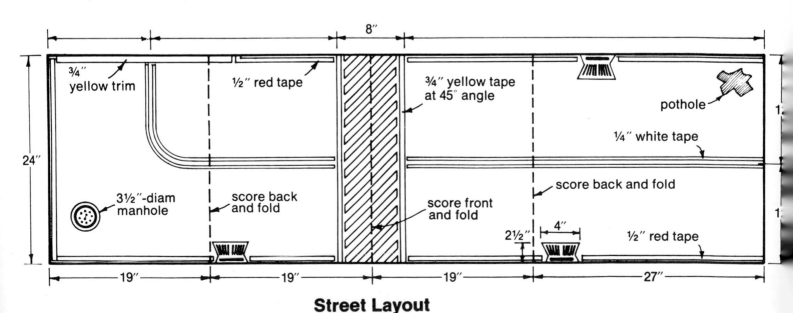

Street Layout

Skyline

Measure the distance between buildings where you want the skyline. The line in the photograph on pages 116-117 goes from the skyscraper to the garage, using a table-tennis ball at the top of one skyscraper section for one end of the line and a wooden bead attached to the garage near its bottom floor for the other. You can also use two wooden beads, attaching one near a roof of one building and the other near a bottom floor of a second. Cut monofilament nylon to the distance between buildings plus several inches at each end for attaching loops. Make skyline as shown in adjoining diagram, using plastic straws and glue. (The line must be taut to work properly.) Attach wooden bead to building (see Gluing Wooden Beads, page 117). Loop ends of line around beads (or bead and ball as was done in this project).

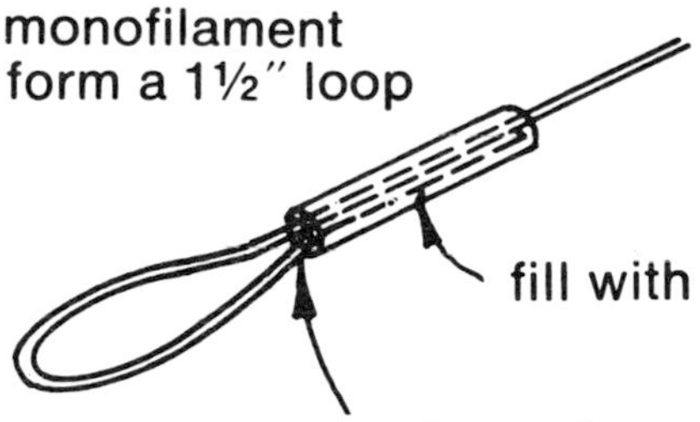
double back monofilament
into straw to form a 1½″ loop
fill with glue
¾″-long piece of
plastic straw

Trash can

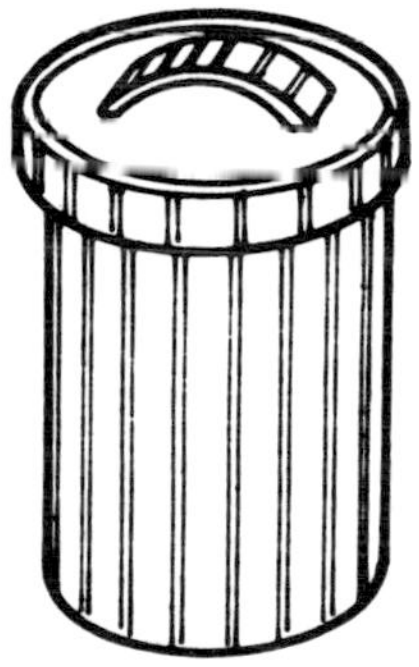

Using scraps of corrugated cardboard, cut out side and bottom as in diagram and assemble, recessing bottom slightly. Make lid to fit loosely; glue on handle as shown.

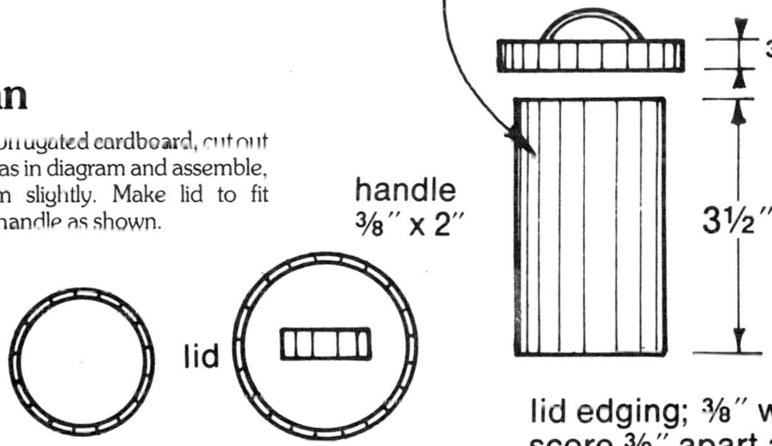
score 3½″ x 7¼″ cardboard vertically
⅜″ apart; roll into body shape
and glue seam; recess bottom
¼″ and glue in place
⅜″
handle
⅜″ x 2″
3½″
bottom
lid
lid edging; ⅜″ wide;
score ⅜″ apart and cut to fit;
glue in place around edge of
lid top circle
2″-diam (inside
measurement; trim to
fit if required)
2½″-diam
(inside
measurement)

Fire hydrant

Using scraps of corrugated cardboard, cut out side and small circles for hydrant following diagram. Assemble side on bottom, then add top and tiny side circles as shown. Cut tiny circles with nail or other small, sharp-pointed scissors.

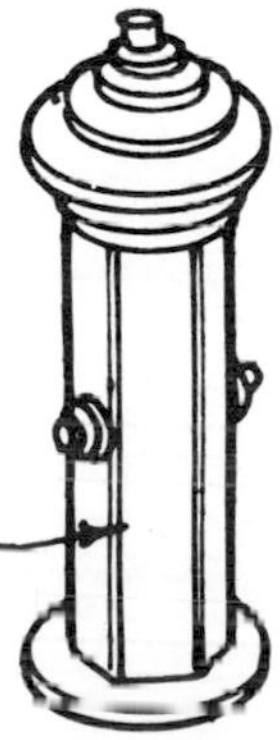
score 2⅛″ x 2¼″ cardboard
vertically ⅜″ apart;
roll into body shape and
glue seam

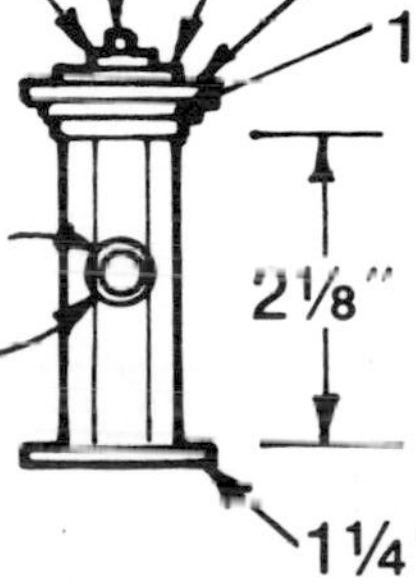
⅜″-diam
⅞″-diam
3/16″-diam
1¼″-diam
1″-diam
⅜″-diam
2⅛″
3/16″-diam
1¼″-diam

Outer-space station

*The crafty thing about this clever
layout is that you build it in sections, each one
complete in itself. Start with the rocket
takeoff site, for instance, and the kids can play
with that until you finish another
part. By the time the whole works is assembled,
you can be sure the air will be alive
with sci-fi characters, plots and ploys. For the
sake of the many families who own
sets of 3″ space-age figures but have no suitable
terrain for deploying them, the station
is built to that scale. Anticipating hard wear,
everything is covered with plastic-
laminate — even the bright, shiny decorations are
made with self-adhesive vinyl — so
this space station won't be hard to keep shipshape.
Parts that move are operated by the
simplest mechanisms — no complicated fixtures
to install or arrangements too tricky
for small hands to deal with.*

General Directions

MATERIALS AND TOOLS Table saw; saber saw; band saw or jigsaw; drill with assorted bits; awl; nail set; hammer; screwdrivers; C-clamps; vise; white wood glue; sandpaper; sanding block; carpenter's try square; ruler; pencils; paper; white decorative tape; masking tape; wood putty; white latex semigloss paint; pigmented shellac primer; wood, other building materals and special tools (if required) are given in specific directions; screws, nails and other hardware are shown in diagrams.

MARKING PATTERN PIECES Mark all pattern parts directly on the wood or other materials (such as plastic laminate) to be used, with pencil, ruler and carpenter's square. (Use a compass for any curved or rounded parts.) Be sure to mark all cuts perfectly square. On pieces cut from a continuous length, leave at least 1/8" allowance for saw cuts as you mark off the pieces.

CUTTING WOOD Cut curves with a jigsaw (or by hand with a coping saw if you don't have a jigsaw). Clamp matching parts together and cut as one with jigsaw. (Coping saw can't cut multiple thicknesses of wood; if using one, cut each part separately.) For broad curves and straight cuts, use a saber saw or table saw.

DRILLING Use an awl to mark and start holes for drilling. Clamp wood to a piece of scrap to prevent splintering as the bit comes through the bottom. Clamp and drill matching parts at one time whenever possible. Drill lead or pilot holes and then countersink for flathead wood screws.

NAILING Use finishing nails for thick wood, wire brads for thin (sizes shown on diagrams). Nails or brads should always be at least 1/8" shorter than the combined thickness of wood to be joined. For added strength, glue joints to be nailed with white glue. After nailing, drive nails slightly below surface with a nail set.

ASSEMBLY Test-assemble. Check parts that should be square with try square. Assemble when parts fit correctly, gluing then screwing or nailing (or according to specific directions). When possible, clamp glued edges until dry, placing pieces of scrap between clamp and parts and wiping away excess glue immediately with a clean, damp cloth.

SANDING AND FILLING For areas which will be painted (not those which are to be covered with plastic-laminate) and especially edges, sand smooth and fill all nail holes,
screw tops, plywood voids and defects with wood putty. Sand puttied areas smooth when putty is dry.

PAINTING After filling, as just described, apply 1 coat of primer. Let dry, sand lightly and apply 2 coats of paint, sanding lightly after first coat is dry. For added durability, a third coat can be applied after a light sanding.

APPLYING PLASTIC-LAMINATE
Materials Plastic-laminate sheet (amount given under specific directions; Formica brand was used here, in Ice White, color #953, finish #65); contact cement for plastic-laminate; router with bearing cutter or block plane or (least desirable) metal file; carbide blade or metal cutting blade for saber saw, table saw or jigsaw; roller.

To cut laminate, work with it face down and place a metal cutting, carbide blade in saber, table or jigsaw. Mark pattern on back, which is dark, with chalk, being sure to make each piece 1/8" larger all around than actual amount required to cover. For pieces which go up against an edge so that they can't be trimmed afterward, cut to fit on that side only; leave excess around rest. If you have a router, you can leave more than 1/8" around edges as router makes it easy to trim. Cut with laminate face down to avoid chipping of white on face. For pieces which must fit inside, where no trimming can be done, cut to fit.

Apply contact cement on both surfaces (one to be covered and back of laminate). Let dry until tacky, or until cement does not come off on your finger when you touch it. For a large piece, place a couple of dowels, on surface, put laminate on dowels, then position at one corner, aligning laminate with surface. Roll in place or rub down with the heel of your hand at that corner. Remove dowels as you get to them, working from first corner over toward other end. For small pieces, just press in place and roll or rub for complete adhesion.

Trim excess from edges with router, block plane, or file. To cover black edges, brush on typewriter correction fluid. (Paint visible parts aren't covered with laminate.)

Note *Standard 1/16"-thick plastic-laminate was used here. If you prefer, you can use the vertical grade, V-32, which is only 1/32" thick. Vertical grade can be cut to fit with scissors and is easier to use for that reason. It's also easier to press in place, except for the glossy type, which will show any bumps on the surface being covered. The 1/16" is slightly more durable, but black edges do show; on vertical grade, edges are not apparent and don't need covering. If you do use vertical grade, remember as you follow the diagrams that they are all keyed to use of the thicker grade and will have to be adjusted.*

DECORATING UNITS All decorations (colored bands, strips and such) are red, yellow, blue and black self-adhesive tape, or cut from sheets of self-adhesive plastic. Pressure-sensitive graphic tape, which comes in several colors and very narrow widths and is available at art supply stores, can be used to avoid cutting down larger sheets into narrow strips. Small circles of color are pressure-sensitive dot labels, but they can be punched out of the self-adhesive plastic with a hole punch.

Decorate the units following color photographs or make up your own designs.

TO POLISH ACRYLIC EDGES If any acrylic edges are exposed, or other cut surfaces can be seen in the finished unit, cut parts should be polished. To do this, you'll need very fine sandpaper and fine rubbing compound (from an auto supply store).

Sand acrylic with progressively finer sandpaper to remove saw marks from edges or other cut areas. Apply rubbing compound with a clean, dry cloth. Rub briskly until acrylic has the desired finish. For added shine, you can apply a small amount of furniture polish with a clean soft cloth after rubbing.

TO BUILD STATION with all units and platform, build in this order:

Station Platform

7 Monorail (Weather Station on upper monorail platform is optional and can be built at any time)

2 Rocket Launch Platform

3 Conveyor-belt Bridge

Trick Staircase (leads to Living Quarters)

4 Living Quarters

1 Park with Drawbridge

Numbers relate to those in large photographs. Units without numbers (Weather Station, Trick Staircase) follow, in the instructions, the units to which they relate.

No. 5 Personnel Launcher and 6 Solar Power Unit can be made at any time; they do not affect other constructions. If you need to make slight adjustments it's easier on Living Quarters and Park than on pieces with moving parts.

Note *If you are building units separately, or do not plan to make the platform, Nos. 1, 3, 4 and 6 are all shown as built to fit on platform edges. For this reason, their inner and outer walls are two different sizes. The outer wall of each is $^{13}/_{16}$" longer than inner wall as shown in diagrams. This is correct when you are building the entire station and platform. If you are not, the excess can be omitted. For example, No. 1 has separate pieces added as a lip to fit platform; omit these if you aren't building the platform. Be sure to make necessary adjustments for all units before you start to build them, working with the diagrams to change dimensions which accommodate the platform edges.*

MATERIALS FOR SPACE STATION Materials required for units and platform are presented separately so you can choose the parts you want to build. However, if you plan to build the entire station, there is greater economy of materials if you buy them all at once. The list does not include tiny amounts which only occur in single units (such as acetate for elevator in Living Quarters), so that it's wise to make comparative lists. Major components are: 2¼ sheets of ½" plywood (each sheet is 4' x 8'); ¾ sheet of ¾" plywood; ¼ sheet of ¼" plywood; ¼" x 18" x 18" of hardboard; 3 (each 4' x 8') sheets of plastic-laminate (Formica brand was used; see General Directions for color); 3' of 1 x 1 pine; 3' of 1 x 2 pine; 1' of 1 x 3 pine; 4' of 1 x 6 pine; 3' of 1 x 8 pine; 2' of 2 x 2 pine; scraps of 2 x 4 and ½ x 1 pine; ¼" x 18" x 30" of mirrored acrylic; dowel in following sizes: 3' of ⅜" diam., 1' of ⅝" diam., ½' of 1¼" diam. and ½" diam., scraps of ⅛" diam. and ⅞" diam.; small amounts of other materials under specific directions.

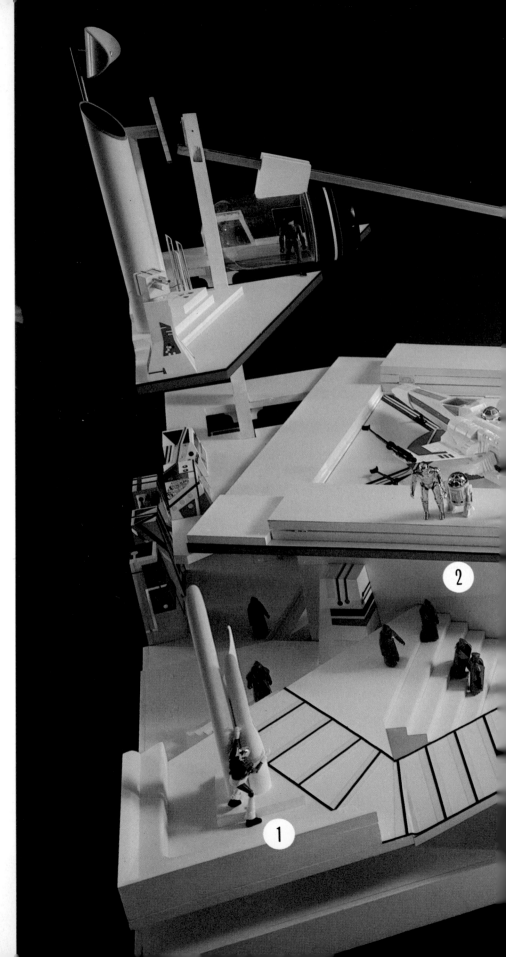

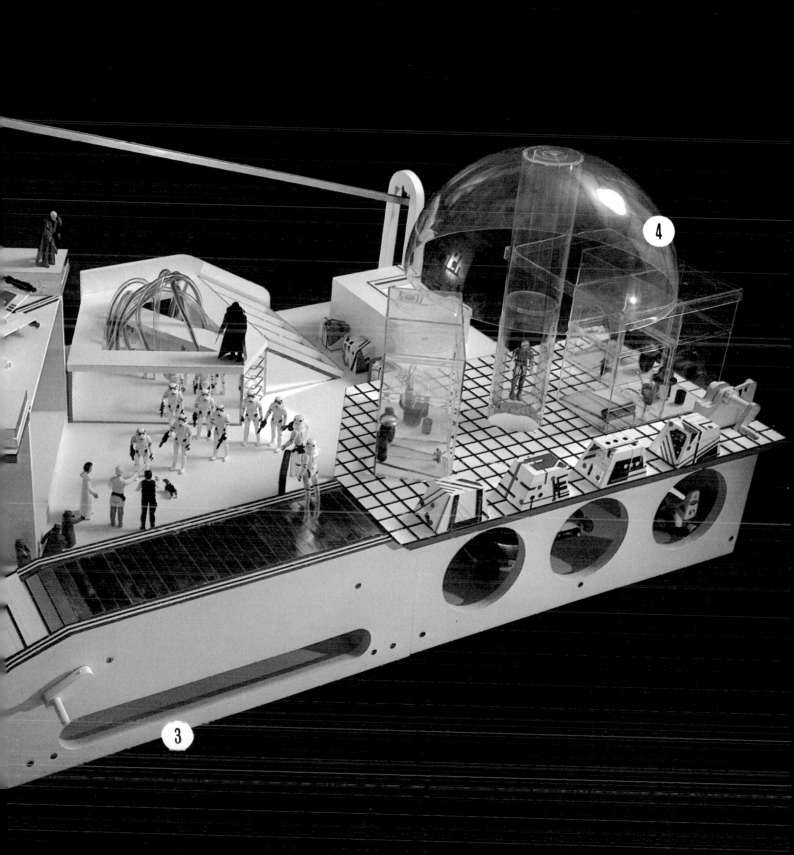

Station Platform

Materials ½" x 36" x 48" plywood; ¾" x 36" x 60" plywood; ⅜" x ⅜" x 16" pine quarter-round molding; 1¼ sheets (each 4' x 8') of plastic laminate (see General Directions at start of project).

Cut ¾" plywood to 36" x 60" (if using large sheet) for platform and ½" plywood to shape shown in diagram for base. Laminate base entirely and only that portion of the platform that is not covered by the base. Carry the laminate under the edges of the base and cement scrap pieces of laminate under the base so that it is level.

Attach base to platform with screws through the underside. If you are building Conveyor-belt Bridge, paint quarter round white and attach after Bridge is finished. If building Monorail, attach Tower Base as indicated in Monorail instructions.

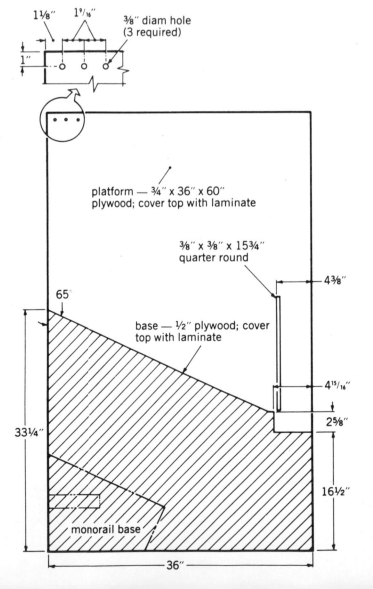

platform — ¾" x 36" x 60" plywood; cover top with laminate

⅜" x ⅜" x 15¾" quarter round

base — ½" plywood; cover top with laminate

1⅛"   1⁹⁄₁₆"   ⅜" diam hole (3 required)

1"

4⅜"

4¹⁵⁄₁₆"

2⅝"

65"

33¼"

16½"

monorail base

36"

1 Park with Drawbridge

2 Rocket Launch Platform

3 Conveyor-belt Bridge

4 Living Quarters

4A Trick Staircase

5 Personnel Launcher

6 Solar Power Unit

7 Monorail

8 Weather Station

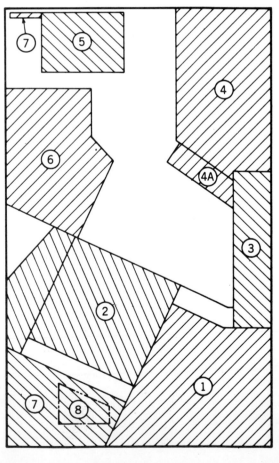

1. Park with Drawbridge

MATERIALS ¼" x 6" x 24" plywood; ½" x 36" x 48" plywood; 2 x 2 x 24" pine; ⅝" x ⅝" x 2' pine quarter round; 24" x 48" of plastic laminate (see General Directions at start of project); PVC pipe, 1" o.d. x 30"; 1" x 4⅝" continuous hinge; scraps of self-adhesive plastic foil.

Follow diagram and cut out all parts. Make both step units together, as one. Use white glue to join the steps together to make unit and clamp until dry. Cover treads with plastic-laminate and then cut apart into two sets of steps as shown in diagram.

Cut out base A and base B. We show base A completely covered with laminate, but you can cover just parts which are not covered by base B and add scraps into covered area to keep base B level. Cover B completely with laminate. Screw A and B together from bottom.

Cut and laminate platform E. Cut out bench parts; assemble and paint. Screw to platform E from underneath. To make sculpture, cut PVC pipe as shown in diagram, using band saw to cut tops at an acute angle. Twist pipe slightly as you push it into saw blade, working slowly to get odd shapes. Cover inside with seld-adhesive plastic foil. Cut sculpture base and paint it. Contact cement sculpture to its base; then cement base to platform. Complete assembly and make drawbridge following diagram. Hinge to unit (if making Conveyor-belt Bridge, make drawbridge to fit onto it).

Drawbridge leads to park area, where a gleaming sculpture of PVC pipe soars into space.

PARK WITH DRAWBRIDGE

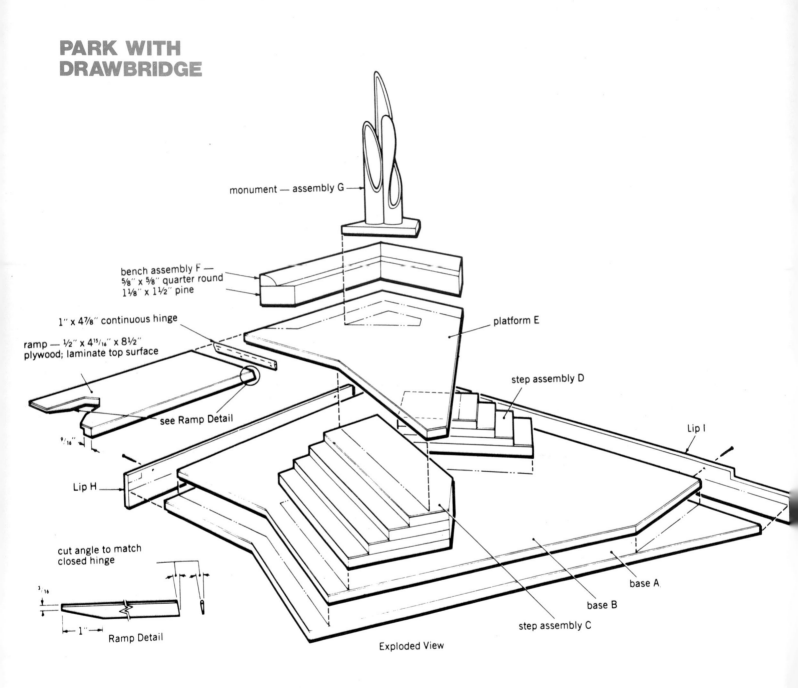

monument — assembly G

bench assembly F —
⅝″ x ⅝″ quarter round
1⅛″ x 1½″ pine

platform E

1″ x 4⅞″ continuous hinge

ramp — ½″ x 4¹⁵/₁₆″ x 8½″
plywood; laminate top surface

step assembly D

see Ramp Detail

Lip I

⁹/₁₆″

Lip H

base A

cut angle to match
closed hinge

base B

³/₁₆

step assembly C

1″   Ramp Detail

Exploded View

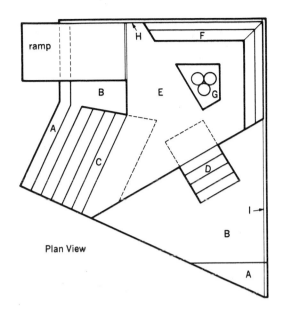

Plan View

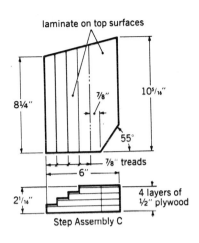

laminate on top surfaces

$8\frac{1}{4}''$

$\frac{7}{8}''$

$10\frac{5}{16}''$

55°

$\frac{7}{8}''$ treads

6″

$2\frac{1}{16}''$

4 layers of
½″ plywood

Step Assembly C

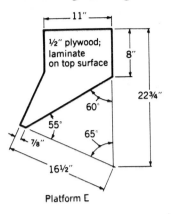

11″

½″ plywood;
laminate
on top surface

8″

$22\frac{3}{4}''$

60°

55°

65°

$\frac{7}{8}''$

$16\frac{1}{2}''$

Platform E

1″ o.d. pvc pipe — cut curves;
line with metallic self adhesive plastic
(3 required)

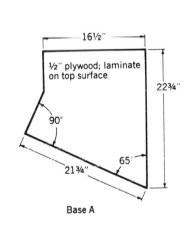

$16\frac{1}{2}''$

½″ plywood; laminate
on top surface

$22\frac{3}{4}''$

90°

65°

$21\frac{3}{4}''$

Base A

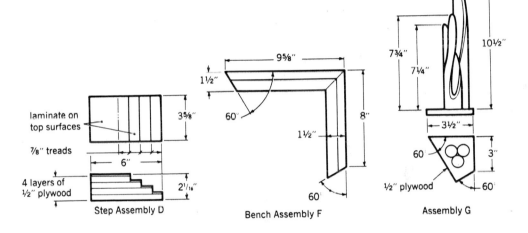

laminate on
top surfaces

$\frac{7}{8}''$ treads

6″

$3\frac{5}{8}''$

4 layers of
½″ plywood

$2\frac{1}{16}''$

Step Assembly D

$9\frac{5}{8}''$

$1\frac{1}{2}''$

60°

8″

$1\frac{1}{2}''$

60°

Bench Assembly F

$7\frac{3}{4}''$

$7\frac{1}{4}''$

$10\frac{1}{2}''$

$3\frac{1}{2}''$

60°

3″

½″ plywood

60°

Assembly G

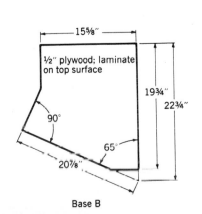

$15\frac{5}{8}''$

½″ plywood;
laminate
on top surface

$19\frac{3}{4}''$

$22\frac{3}{4}''$

90°

65°

$20\frac{7}{8}''$

Base B

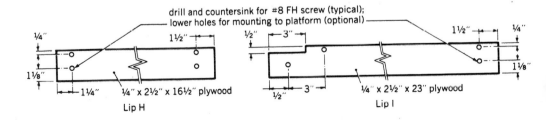

drill and countersink for #8 FH screw (typical);
lower holes for mounting to platform (optional)

¼″

$1\frac{1}{2}''$

$1\frac{1}{8}''$

$1\frac{1}{4}''$

¼″ x 2½″ x 16½″ plywood

Lip H

½″

3″

$1\frac{1}{2}''$

¼″

$1\frac{1}{8}''$

½″

3″

¼″ x 2½″ x 23″ plywood

Lip I

2. Rocket Launch Platform

MATERIALS ½" x 36" x 48" plywood (included optional step); 18"-sq hardboard; ¼" x ¹⁵/₁₆" x 18" pine lattice; ³⁄₈" x ¾" x 24" cut from 1" pine stock; 1 x 2 x 18" pine; 36" x 48" plastic laminate (see General Directions at start of project); four ¾" x 1½" butt hinges with screws.

To build launch platform From ½" plywood, cut out back with slots, 2 sides and bottom. Apply laminate to one side of bottom and inside of two side pieces. Assemble with glue and counter-sunk screws. Apply laminate to the three outside surfaces.

Cut the slides from pine lattice, paint and attach with contact cement in positions indicated. From pine, cut and assemble handle and arms. Drill pilot hole for pivot screws.

From ¼" hardboard, cut moving platform; from pine, cut its slide brackets. Laminate top of platform. Assemble with glue, then cut out channels in sides. Install handle and arms with pivot screw. Place platform and test mechanism. It should stay up without being held and drop with a nudge of the handle. The rounded notch in each bracket may require slight deepening to adjust.

Cut out catwalk. Attach to walls with finish-

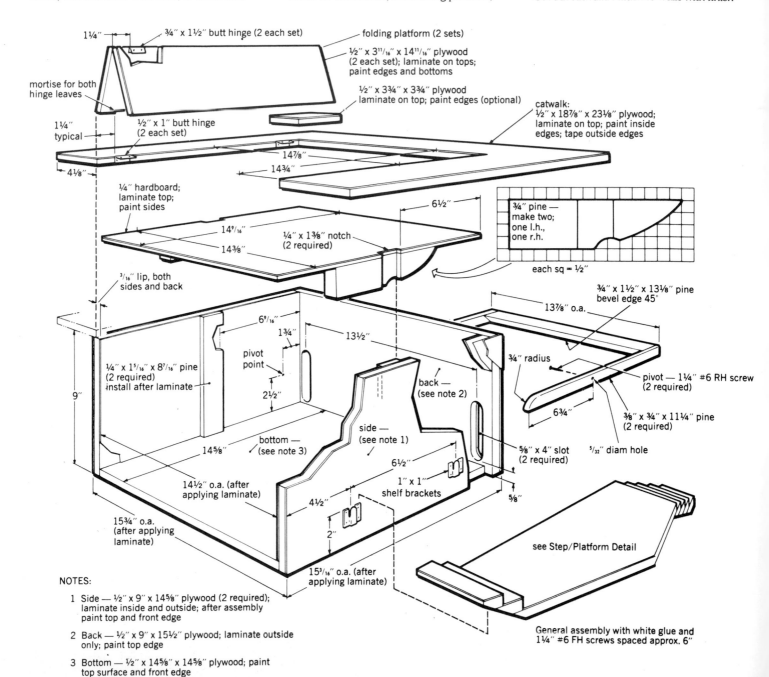

NOTES:

1 Side — ½" x 9" x 14⅝" plywood (2 required); laminate inside and outside; after assembly paint top and front edge

2 Back — ½" x 9" x 15½" plywood; laminate outside only; paint top edge

3 Bottom — ½" x 14⅝" x 14⅝" plywood; paint top surface and front edge

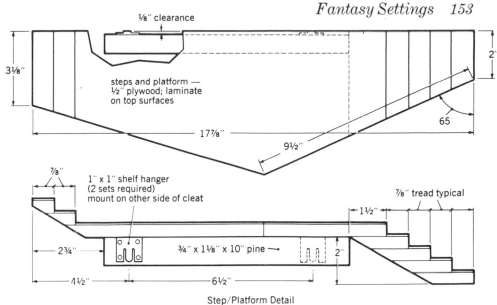

steps and platform —
½″ plywood; laminate
on top surfaces

⅛″ clearance

3⅛″

2″

17⅞″

9½″

65

⅞″

1″ x 1″ shelf hanger
(2 sets required)
mount on other side of cleat

⅞″ tread typical

1½″

2¾″

¾″ x 1⅛″ x 10″ pine →

2″

4½″

6½″

Step/Platform Detail

ing nails and glue so there will be a ³⁄₁₆″ lip along its inside edges. Laminate catwalk and ½″ piece of plywood large enough for four sections of folding doors.

Cut four door sections. Mortise for hinges as shown. Hinge in pairs, each pair to catwalk. Sand, fill and paint edges.

To build steps attached to rocket launch From pine, cut cleat; from ½″ plywood, cut landing and steps (with beveled back edges if band saw is not available). Assemble upper two steps and landing with glue only. Cut angle under steps with band saw. Assemble lower steps; cut angle under them. Attach lower steps to landing and cleats to step assembly. Install 2 sets of shelf hanger plates. Laminate steps and landing.

Rocket is hidden when platform of takeoff site is lowered and the bifold doors are closed.

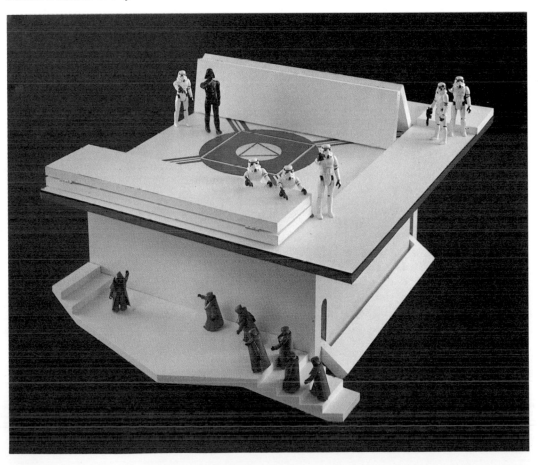

3. Conveyor-Belt Bridge

MATERIALS ½" x 12" x 48" plywood; ¼" x ⅝" x 4" pine lattice; ¾" x 7½" (1 x 8) x 18" pine; ⅜ -diam. x 18" dowel; 18" x 24" plastic-laminate (see General Directions at start of project); 4" x 44¼" piece of canvas; 1 can of spray aluminum paint; eight ¼" -wide rubber bands or 1 sheet of 80-grit sandpaper (to drive wheels if required).

Cut inner parts and assemble with screws as shown. Make canvas belt to fit, then glue treads in place with contact cement which may also be used to hold overlapped ends. Test-fit belt before adding treads.

Cut sides and stretcher blocks. Cover one side of each with laminate. Drill hole for axle in outer side. Attach parts to inner assembly. Spray-paint treads.

Invaders are thwarted by a conveyor-belt bridge between park area and living quarters.

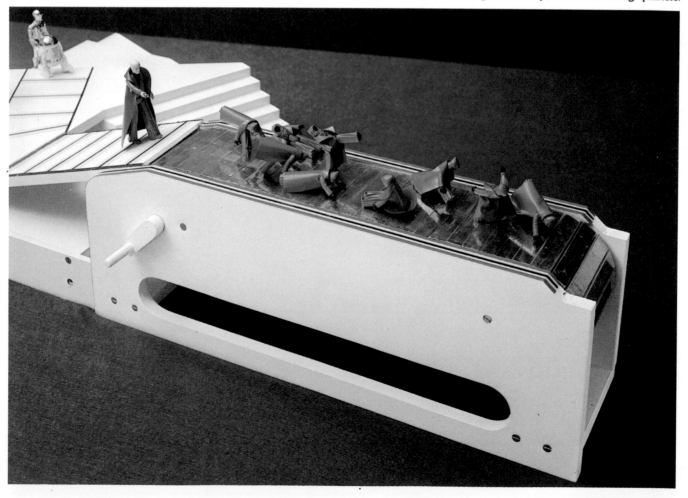

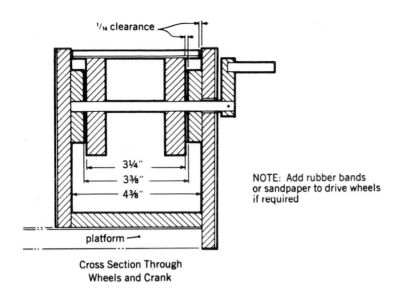

¹⁄₁₆ clearance

3¼"
3⅜"
4⅜"

platform →

Cross Section Through Wheels and Crank

NOTE: Add rubber bands or sandpaper to drive wheels if required

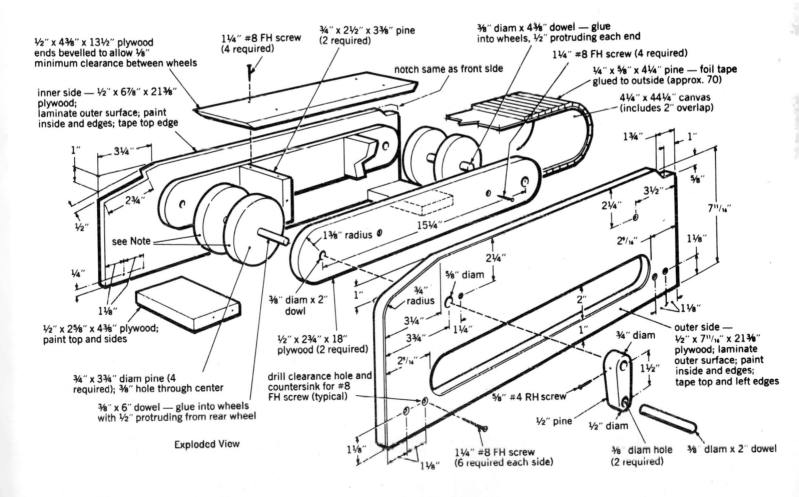

½" x 4⅜" x 13½" plywood ends bevelled to allow ⅛" minimum clearance between wheels

1¼" #8 FH screw (4 required)

¾" x 2½" x 3⅜" pine (2 required)

⅜" diam x 4⅜" dowel — glue into wheels, ½" protruding each end

inner side — ½" x 6⅞" x 21⅜" plywood; laminate outer surface; paint inside and edges; tape top edge

notch same as front side

1¼" #8 FH screw (4 required)

¼" x ⅝" x 4¼" pine — foil tape glued to outside (approx. 70)

4¼" x 44¼" canvas (includes 2" overlap)

1¾"   1"
⅝"
3½"
2¼"
7¹¹⁄₁₆"
2⁹⁄₁₆"
1⅛"

1"
3¼"
2¾"
½"
see Note
¼"
1⅛"

⅜" diam x 2" dowl

1⅜" radius

15¼"

2¼"

1"

⅝" diam

¾" radius

3¼"
3¾"
2⁹⁄₁₆"

1¼"

2"
1"

1⅛"

½" x 2⅝" x 4⅜" plywood; paint top and sides

½" x 2¾" x 18" plywood (2 required)

¾" x 3¾" diam pine (4 required); ⅜" hole through center

⅜" x 6" dowel — glue into wheels with ½" protruding from rear wheel

drill clearance hole and countersink for #8 FH screw (typical)

Exploded View

⅝" #4 RH screw

outer side — ½" x 7¹¹⁄₁₆" x 21⅜" plywood; laminate outer surface; paint inside and edges; tape top and left edges

¾" diam

1½"

½" pine   ½" diam

⅜" diam hole (2 required)

⅜" diam x 2" dowel

1⅛"
1⅛"

1¼" #8 FH screw (6 required each side)

4. Living Quarters

MATERIALS ½" x 24" x 36" plywood; ¾" x 18" x 24" plywood; 24"; x 54" plastic -laminate (see General Directions); 5 clear plastic boxes with lids, each 4" x 4" x 7¼"; 3" -diam. x 36" clear plastic mailing tube; 14" -diam clear plastic hemisphere blue acetate as specified; nylon monofilament. **For elevator crank mechanism** 1¹⁄₁₆ x 2½" x 12" pine lattice; scrap dowel in ⅛", ½", ⅞" and 3" diam.

From ½" plywood, cut top (bevel two edges after lamination), bottom, arched side, front and solid side. Cut 5" -diam. holes in front with jig-saw, then laminate both sides.

Assemble top, arched side and front with glue and screws. Turn upside-down; place bottom on top. Mark position of 3" -diam. hole. Clamp top and bottom together to drill holes with an expansive bit; remove clamp.

Turn unit right-side-up, laminate top and bottom. Attach bottom and solid side to assembled structure.

Cut mailing tube to 22¼" length; cut out bottom and top doorways for elevator. Elevator car consists of ¼" x 2¾" -diam. clear acrylic disc top and same size bottom, hung together by two strips of 2" x 6" blue acetate. Cut out these parts and drill a hole in car top for monofilament. Cement acetate to discs; cement shaft in its holes. Drill 2 holes for monofilament in hemisphere.

Find center of hemisphere and mark 1½"-radius circle with a non-permanent marker and compass. To assemble, place end of monofilament through hole in car top and knot end. Place car in shaft. Thread other end of monofilament through center hole in hemisphere from inside to out, then back in through 2nd hole. Apply cement around top of shaft. Place hemisphere with its marks aligned with shaft edge.

Install elevator crank mechanism (see directions below) and tie end of monofilament to crank shaft.

Attach Trick Staircase (see directions for 4A which follow) to solid side of Living Quarters with contact cement.

Crank mechanism Cut pine parts (since parts are so small, you will find it easier to use larger pieces of pine in right thickness). Assemble, following diagram. If crank axle doesn't turn freely, sand dowel to reduce size slightly. All parts are glued, except those that move (axle and ratchet stop).

Star Wars characters, X-Wing Fighter, Tie Fighter and Land Speeder are all by Kenner; other figures and vehicles shown are by Mego.

LIVING QUARTERS

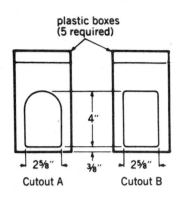

plastic boxes
(5 required)

Cutout A   Cutout B

4"

2⅝"   ⅜"   2⅝"

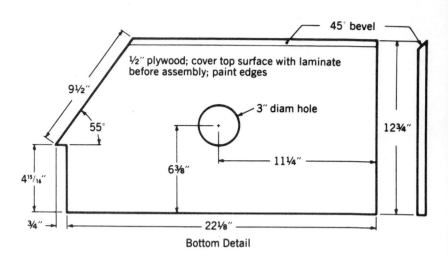

½" plywood; cover top surface with laminate
before assembly; paint edges

45° bevel

9½"

55°

3" diam hole

12¾"

6⅜"

11¼"

4¹⁵⁄₁₆"

¾"

22⅛"

Bottom Detail

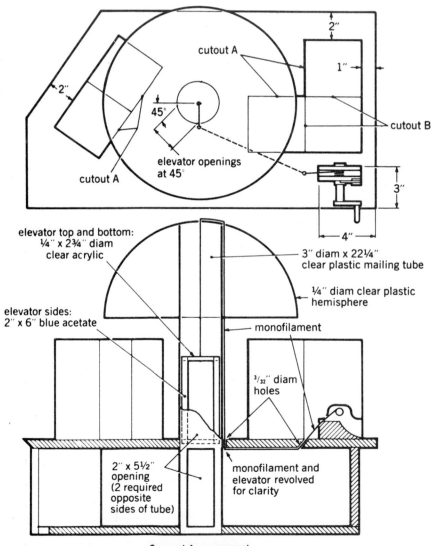

cutout A

2"

1"

2"

45°

cutout B

elevator openings
at 45°

cutout A

3"

4"

elevator top and bottom:
¼" x 2¾" diam
clear acrylic

3" diam x 22¼"
clear plastic mailing tube

¼" diam clear plastic
hemisphere

elevator sides:
2" x 6" blue acetate

monofilament

³⁄₃₂" diam
holes

2" x 5½"
opening
(2 required
opposite
sides of tube)

monofilament and
elevator revolved
for clarity

General Arrangement

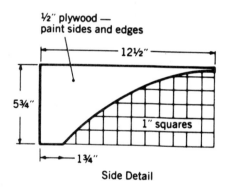

½" plywood —
paint sides and edges

12½"

5¾"

1" squares

1¾"

Side Detail

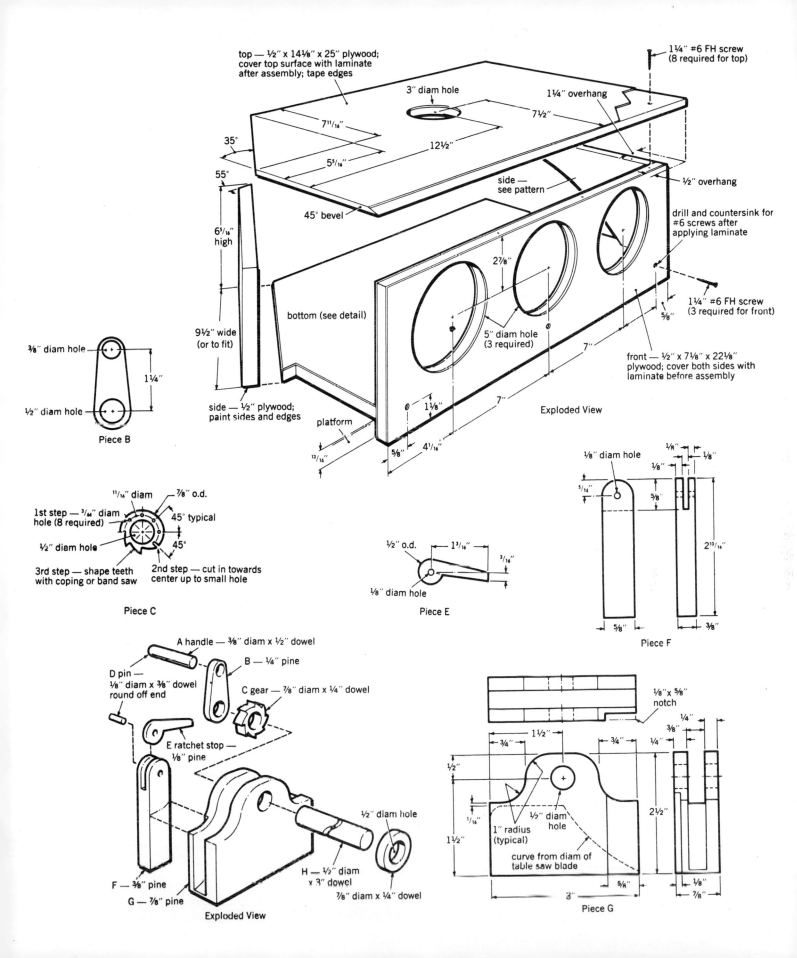

top — ½" x 14⅛" x 25" plywood; cover top surface with laminate after assembly; tape edges

1¼" #6 FH screw (8 required for top)

3" diam hole

1¼" overhang

7½"

½" overhang

35°

7¹¹/₁₆"

12½"

5⁵/₁₆"

side — see pattern

55°

6⁵/₁₆" high

2⅞"

drill and countersink for #6 screws after applying laminate

45° bevel

9½" wide (or to fit)

bottom (see detail)

5" diam hole (3 required)

7"

1¼" #6 FH screw (3 required for front)

5/8"

front — ½" x 7⅛" x 22⅛" plywood; cover both sides with laminate before assembly

side — ½" plywood; paint sides and edges

platform

13/16"

5/8"

1⅛"

4¹/₁₆"

7"

Exploded View

⅜" diam hole

1¼"

½" diam hole

Piece B

¹¹/₁₆" diam

⅞" o.d.

1st step — ³/₆₄" diam hole (8 required)

45° typical

½" diam hole

45°

3rd step — shape teeth with coping or band saw

2nd step — cut in towards center up to small hole

Piece C

½" o.d.

1³/₁₆"

3/16"

⅛" diam hole

Piece E

⅛" diam hole

⅛"

⅛"

⅛"

5/16"

⅜"

2¹³/₁₆"

5/8"

⅜"

Piece F

A handle — ⅜" diam x ½" dowel

B — ¼" pine

D pin — ⅛" diam x ⅜" dowel round off end

C gear — ⅞" diam x ¼" dowel

E ratchet stop — ⅛" pine

H — ½" diam x 3" dowel

½" diam hole

⅞" diam x ¼" dowel

F — ⅜" pine

G — ⅞" pine

Exploded View

⅛" x 5/8" notch

¼"

⅜"

1½"

¾"

¾"

¼"

¼"

½"

1/16"

1½"

1" radius (typical)

½" diam hole

curve from diam of table saw blade

2½"

3"

5/8"

⅛"

⅞"

Piece G

Trick Staircase (to living quarters)

MATERIALS ¼″ x 12″ x 18″ plywood; ½″ x 6″ x 12″ plywood; ¼″ x 1⅛″ x 24″ lattice; ¾″ x ¾″ (1 x 1) x 24″ pine; ¾″ x 1½″ (1 x 2) x 12″ pine; ¼″-diam. x 6″ dowel; ½″-diam. x 1″ dowel; 12″ x 24″ plastic-laminate (see General Directions at start of project); No. 18 wire.

Note *Considerable accuracy is required for the trick staircase to work properly. For best results, use jigs to cut steps with their angled slots, and to drill pivot holes in steps.*

Cut out steps (plus a few extra in case of mishaps) from 1 x 1 pine. Cut ¼″ slot in each, as shown, and then drill for brad and wire pivots. Cut treads and glue in place.

Cut out part E; drill as shown. Connect it to each of the steps with 2¼″ wires.

Cut out sides A and B from ¼″ plywood. With pieces clamped together as shown in Details A and B, drill brad pivot holes and dowel holes.

Cut out part G, ¼″-diam. dowel. Drill ½″-diam. dowels before cutting into ¼″ slices. Also cut the stationary step and rear ½″-plywood block.

With stationary step and rear block in place, insert dowel through its holes and mark positions on it for part G and the collars. Take apart and glue parts on their marks.

Cover the outside of large side A with laminate. Drill dowel holes and countersunk pilot holes for screws through laminate and plywood. Do not drill to expose brad pivot holes, which remain covered with laminate.

Attach block, brace and stationary step to side B as shown. With side A lying on its laminate, place and clamp it near the edge of work surface so that dowel hole is not covered. Place brads in side A's pivot holes and then each step's hole over corresponding brad. Place dowel in its hole in side A. Now attach side B, placing other end of dowel in its hole; glue on stationary step, then glue and screw side A into block.

Insert brads through pivot holes in sides into matching holes in blocks. Cover holes with masking tape.

Cut out part F. Place it on part E in relation to part G; mark. Cut and drill dowel handle; glue in place. Cut and attach step top and landing C.

Attach staircase to Living Quarters as described under Living Quarters (No. 4).

Staircase to living quarters converts to enemy-defying slide with a flick of lever on side.

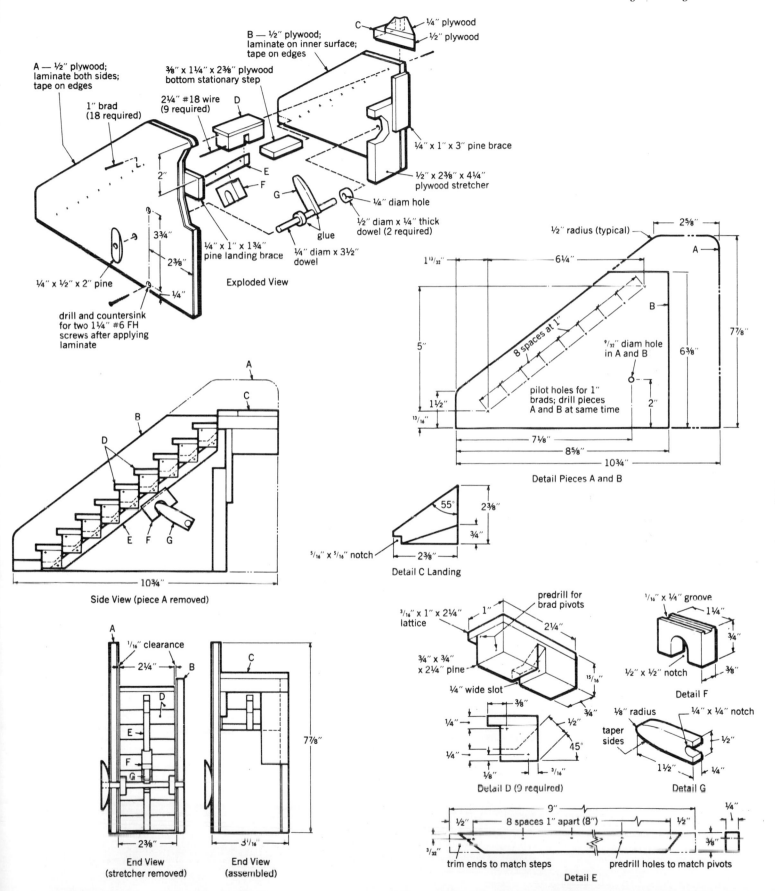

A — ½″ plywood;
laminate both sides;
tape on edges

1″ brad
(18 required)

2″

3¾″

2⅜″

¼″

¼″ x ½″ x 2″ pine

drill and countersink
for two 1¼″ #6 FH
screws after applying
laminate

⅜″ x 1¼″ x 2⅜″ plywood
bottom stationary step

2¼″ #18 wire
(9 required)

D

E

F

G

glue

¼″ x 1″ x 1¾″
pine landing brace

¼″ diam x 3½″
dowel

Exploded View

B — ½″ plywood;
laminate on inner surface;
tape on edges

C

¼″ plywood

½″ plywood

¼″ x 1″ x 3″ pine brace

½″ x 2⅜″ x 4¼″
plywood stretcher

¼″ diam hole

½″ diam x ¼″ thick
dowel (2 required)

A

B

C

D

E   F   G

10¾″

Side View (piece A removed)

½″ radius (typical)

2⅝″

A

B

7⅞″

6⅜″

2″

1¹³⁄₃₂″

6¼″

8 spaces at 1″

5″

1½″

¹³⁄₁₆″

⁹⁄₃₂″ diam hole
in A and B

pilot holes for 1″
brads; drill pieces
A and B at same time

7⅛″

8⅝″

10¾″

Detail Pieces A and B

55°

2⅜″

¾″

⁵⁄₁₆″ x ⁵⁄₁₆″ notch

2⅜″

Detail C Landing

A

¹⁄₁₆″ clearance

2¼″

B

D

E

F

G

2⅜″

End View
(stretcher removed)

C

7⅞″

3¹⁄₁₆″

End View
(assembled)

predrill for
brad pivots

1″

2¼″

³⁄₁₆″ x 1″ x 2¼″
lattice

¾″ x ¾″
x 2¼″ pine

¼″ wide slot

¹⁵⁄₁₆″

¾″

¼″

¼″

⅜″

½″

45°

⅛″

³⁄₁₆″

Detail D (9 required)

¹⁄₁₆″ x ¼″ groove

1¼″

¾″

½″ x ½″ notch

⅜″

Detail F

⅛″ radius

¼″ x ¼″ notch

taper
sides

1½″

½″

¼″

Detail G

9″

½″

8 spaces 1″ apart (8″)

½″

¼″

³⁄₃₂″

⅜″

trim ends to match steps

predrill holes to match pivots

Detail E

5. Personnel Launcher

MATERIALS ½″ x 18″ x 30″ plywood; ½″ x 1″ x 2″ pine; ⅜″-diam. x 6″ dowel; 12″ x 36″ or 18″ x 24″ plastic-laminate (see General Directions at start of project); double-stick foam tape; elbow catch with screws; ⅜″ i.d. flat washers; two springs each ⁷⁄₁₆″-diam. i.d. x 5″; 2′ of No. 18 soft steel wire.

From ½″ plywood, cut out parts for the inner box, catwalk (C) and moving platform (A). Follow Details A, B, C. Cut notch in platform. Glue and nail pine block in place. Install latch catch, fill notch with plug, laminate top surface and then drill for spring dowels.

Use platform as guide to drill ¼″-deep holes in floor of box and underside of catwalk

for same dowels. With dowels in place in floor and the platform on dowels, locate position of elbow section of latch; then mark and install with screw.

Assemble box. Attach catwalk last with platform, dowel, springs and washers in place. Laminate catwalk. Paint inside of box and visible edges. Cut walls of outer box and other remaining parts (all are cut to fit). Assemble as shown; laminate.

Drill and attach 5 stair rungs in location shown in Front Section View, forming rungs out of No. 18 wire as shown in detail in the diagram for No. 5 Solar Power Unit, directions for which follow.

Personnel launcher's platform, spring-operated, catapults figures into space.

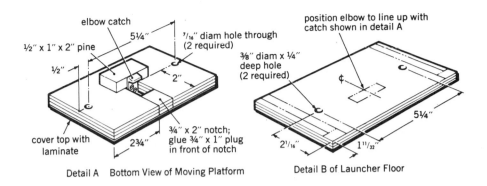

Detail A   Bottom View of Moving Platform

Detail B of Launcher Floor

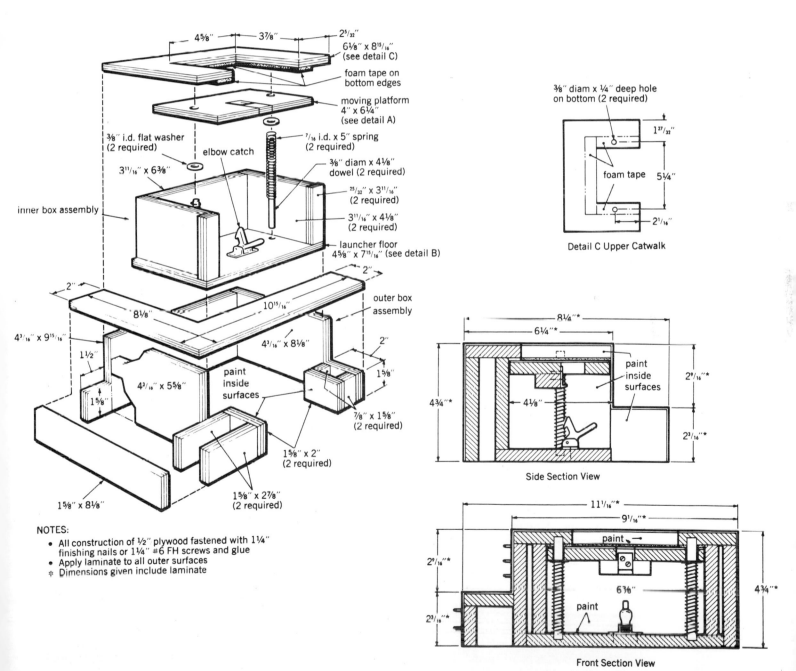

Detail C Upper Catwalk

Side Section View

Front Section View

NOTES:
- All construction of ½" plywood fastened with 1¼" finishing nails or 1¼" #6 FH screws and glue
- Apply laminate to all outer surfaces
- ✻ Dimensions given include laminate

6. Solar Power Unit

MATERIALS ½" x 24" x 30" plywood; ¾" x 12" x 30 " plywood; 1" x 1" x 20" pine; ¼" x 12" x 24" mirrored acrylic; 18" x 36" plastic-laminate; 12' of ⅜"-diam. plastic aquarium tube; 18" of No. 18 soft steel wire; 36" of ¼"-diam. clear acrylic dowel; 18"-wide acetate strips, 1' each of pink, yellow, green and blue.

From ¾" plywood, cut pieces A, B, C and D (all 4" high), with mitered sides following Top View diagram. Also cut 2 triangular sides and cross support for the heat (or sun) collector. From ½" plywood, cut long outer side and base. Drill for acrylic pegs.

Assemble sides around base with heat collector parts. Paint edges and sides that will be visible. Laminate outer surface of outer side. Cut ¼" acrylic mirror: for sides with mitered corners, and for heat collector with top and bottom to fit. Sand cut edges to remove saw cuts, which will reflect in mirrors. Cut top (catwalk) and laminate. Glue mirrors and top in place.

Cut acrylic dowel pegs; insert in base holes. Cut plastic tubing for each pair of pegs. Cut colored acetate in ¼" strips (3" shorter than its tube), slip into tubes and place tubes on pegs.

Trim frame pieces for heat collector from ½" stock. Assemble with glue, pressing pieces together; paint. Glue frame in place with many dots of glue.

Cut and bend wire for ladder rungs. Place tape over acrylic and mark rung holes. Drill holes, remove tape and insert rungs.

Simulated solar panels and distributor pipes provide the space station's "power."

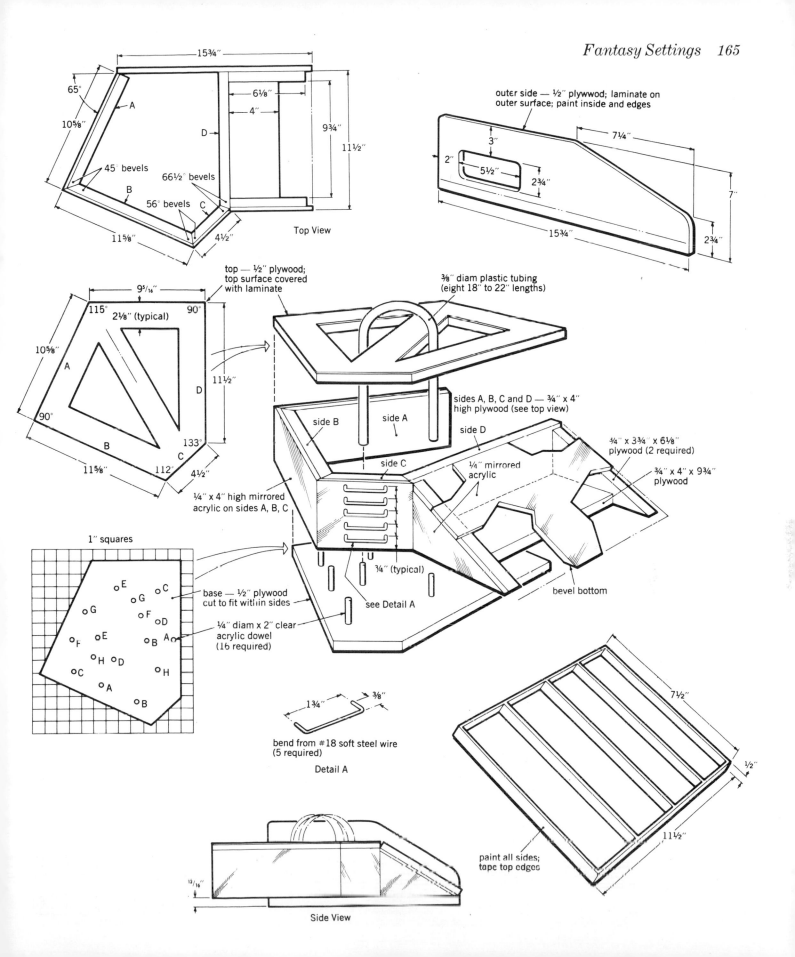

15¾"

65°

10⅝"

A

6⅛"

4"

D

9¾"

11½"

45° bevels

B

66½° bevels

56° bevels

C

11⅝"

4½"

Top View

outer side — ½" plywwod; laminate on outer surface; paint inside and edges

3"

2"

5½"

2¾"

7¼"

7"

15¾"

2¾"

top — ½" plywood; top surface covered with laminate

⅜" diam plastic tubing (eight 18" to 22" lengths)

9⁵⁄₁₆"

115°

2⅛" (typical)

90°

10⅝"

A

D

11½"

90°

133°

B

C

11⅝"

112°

4½"

sides A, B, C and D — ¾" x 4" high plywood (see top view)

side B

side A

side D

side C

¼" mirrored acrylic

¾" x 3¾" x 6⅛" plywood (2 required)

¾" x 4" x 9¾" plywood

¼" x 4" high mirrored acrylic on sides A, B, C

bevel bottom

1" squares

E

C

G

G

F

D

F

E

B

A

H

D

C

H

A

B

base — ½" plywood cut to fit within sides

¼" diam x 2" clear acrylic dowel (16 required)

see Detail A

¾" (typical)

1¾"

⅜"

bend from #18 soft steel wire (5 required)

Detail A

7½"

½"

11½"

paint all sides; tape top edges

¹³⁄₁₆"

Side View

7. Monorail

MATERIALS ½" x 36" x 30" plywood; 30" x 36" plastic laminate (see General Directions at start of project); 1" x 6" x 48" pine; ⅛" x 6" x 18" clear acrylic; ¼" x 6" x 12" clear acrylic; ¾" x ¾" x 4" cove molding; ⅜"-diam. x 6" dowel; ⅛" x 12" dowel; ⅛" x ¾" x 6" aluminum bar; 56½" cut from 6' length of standard shelving bracket; 2½"-sq cardboard; 2 liter plastic Cola bottle; 3 yd. nylon monofilament; acrylic solvent; ⅜"-diam. washers.

Tower with platforms Construct tall tower first, making grooves in the uprights as shown. Cut and assemble uprights and top; add base temporarily. Make certain uprights are parallel. Cut platforms to fit; attach.

From ¼" and ⅛" acrylic, cut car parts. Polish edges. Assemble as shown with acrylic solvent (use as glue). Assemble counterbalance weights, using ⅛"-diam. dowel and washers. Remove base, position car between uprights; replace base. Tie car to counter weights with monofilament. Remove or add washers until car rises with finger touch. Complete base and part E. Attach.

Note *If the monorail is being constructed alone, use piece of ¾" x 11" x 60" plywood as base, with towers screwed or pegged to it.*

Small tower Cut parts from pine and assemble as shown. Drill bottom edge for 3⅜"-diam. dowel, matching holes in platform. Cut two pieces of aluminum bar, each ⅛" x ¾" x 2". Drill as shown in Detail G and cut notches with hack saw. File burrs and round corners. Attach aluminum brackets to appropriate towers. Cut shelf standard to fit between towers.

Monorail car Choose bottle with fewest possible scratches. Pull off base. Cut bottle as shown, then doorway. Cut ring for collar from 1" pine, cutting inner flattened circle first. Cut floor from ¼" acrylic. Polish edges; cement to flattened section of collar.

Cut parts for track slide from pine; assemble. Check fit on track, then attach to car.

Assemble two ends of car on collar; hang car on track and check slide. Use Teflon spray if required to improve it.

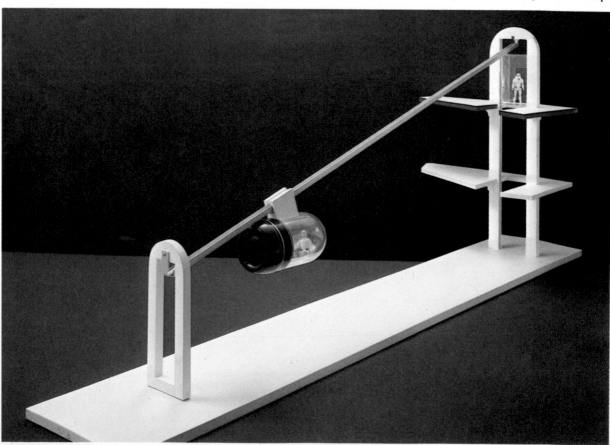

Monorail capsule, made of a plastic cola bottle, is operated manually between stops.

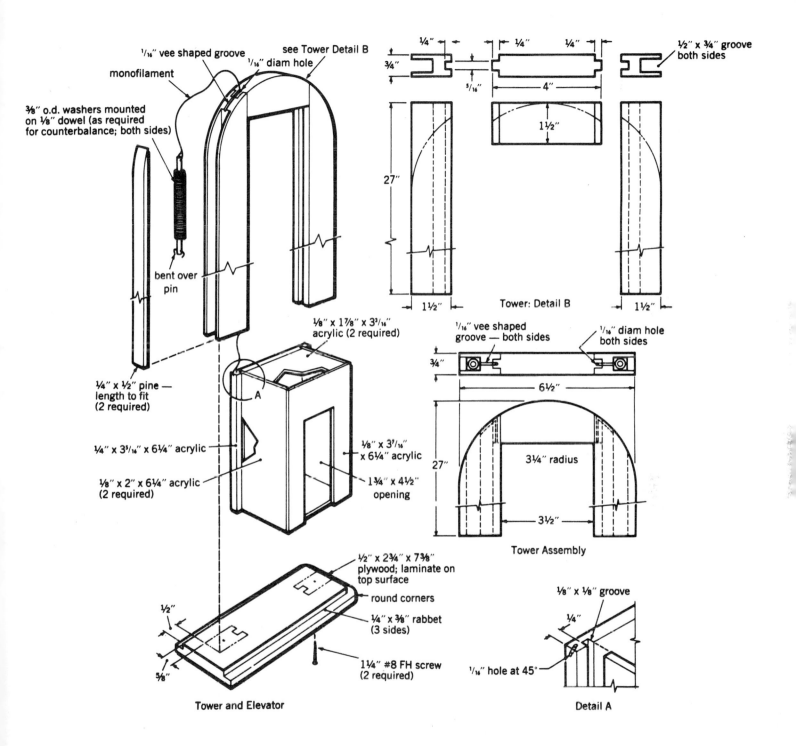

1/16" vee shaped groove

monofilament

see Tower Detail B

1/16" diam hole

3/8" o.d. washers mounted on 1/8" dowel (as required for counterbalance; both sides)

bent over pin

1/4" x 1/2" pine — length to fit (2 required)

1/8" x 1 7/8" x 3 3/16" acrylic (2 required)

1/4" x 3 5/16" x 6 1/4" acrylic

1/8" x 2" x 6 1/4" acrylic (2 required)

A

1/8" x 3 3/16" x 6 1/4" acrylic

1 3/4" x 4 1/2" opening

1/2" x 2 3/4" x 7 3/8" plywood; laminate on top surface

round corners

1/4" x 3/8" rabbet (3 sides)

1/2"

5/8"

1 1/4" #8 FH screw (2 required)

Tower and Elevator

1/4"

1/4"

1/4"

3/4"

5/16"

4"

1 1/2"

27"

1 1/2"

1 1/2"

1/2" x 3/4" groove both sides

Tower: Detail B

1/16" vee shaped groove — both sides

1/16" diam hole both sides

3/4"

6 1/2"

27"

3 1/4" radius

3 1/2"

Tower Assembly

1/8" x 1/8" groove

1/4"

1/16" hole at 45°

Detail A

MONORAIL

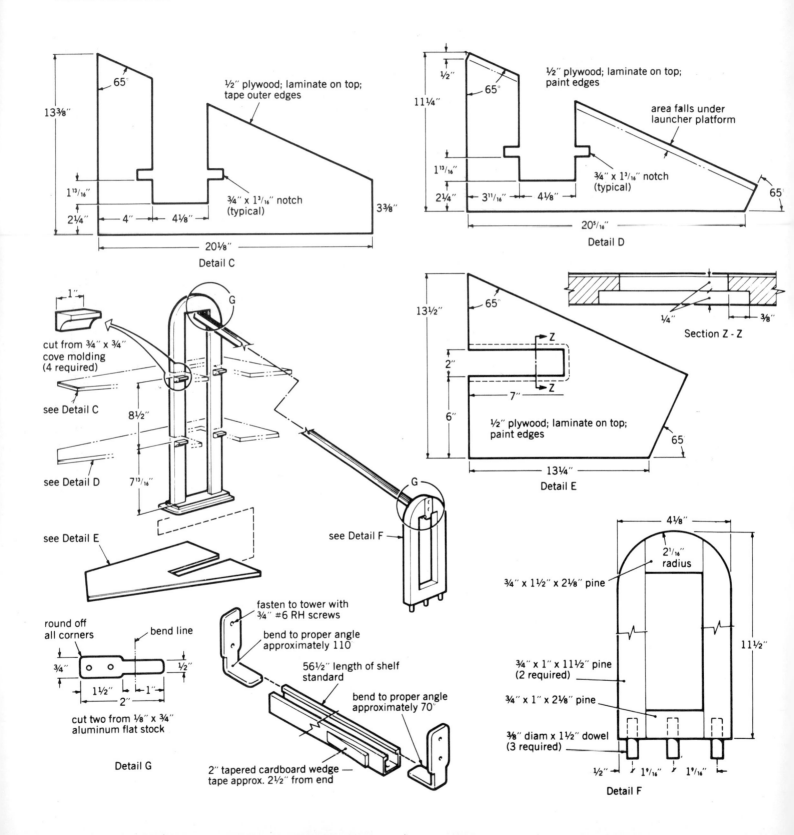

Detail C

65°

13⅜″

1¹³/₁₆″

2¼″

4″

4⅛″

20⅛″

3⅜″

½″ plywood; laminate on top; tape outer edges

¾″ x 1³/₁₆″ notch (typical)

Detail D

½″

11¼″

65°

1¹³/₁₆″

2¼″

3¹¹/₁₆″

4⅛″

20⁵/₁₆″

65°

½″ plywood; laminate on top; paint edges

area falls under launcher platform

¾″ x 1³/₁₆″ notch (typical)

Detail E

13½″

65°

2″

7″

6″

13¼″

65°

½″ plywood; laminate on top; paint edges

Z
Z

Section Z - Z

¼″

⅜″

1″

cut from ¾″ x ¾″ cove molding (4 required)

see Detail C

see Detail D

8½″

7¹³/₁₆″

see Detail E

G

G

see Detail F

round off all corners

bend line

¾″

½″

1½″

1″

2″

cut two from ⅛″ x ¾″ aluminum flat stock

Detail G

fasten to tower with ¾″ #6 RH screws

bend to proper angle approximately 110°

56½″ length of shelf standard

bend to proper angle approximately 70°

2″ tapered cardboard wedge — tape approx. 2½″ from end

Detail F

4⅛″

2¹/₁₆″ radius

¾″ x 1½″ x 2⅛″ pine

¾″ x 1″ x 11½″ pine (2 required)

¾″ x 1″ x 2⅛″ pine

⅜″ diam x 1½″ dowel (3 required)

½″

1⁹/₁₆″

1⁹/₁₆″

11½″

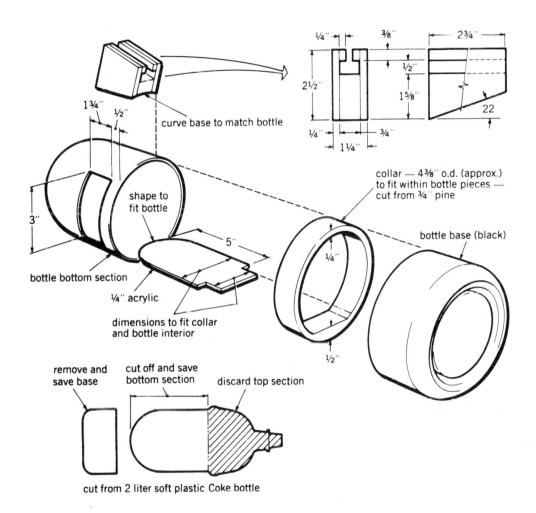

curve base to match bottle

1¾" ½"

3"

shape to fit bottle

bottle bottom section

¼" acrylic

dimensions to fit collar and bottle interior

5"

¼"

½"

¼" ⅜" 2¾"

2½"

½"

1⅝"

22

¼" ¾"

1¼"

collar — 4⅜" o.d. (approx.) to fit within bottle pieces — cut from ¾" pine

bottle base (black)

remove and save base

cut off and save bottom section

discard top section

cut from 2 liter soft plastic Coke bottle

Weather Station
(on upper monorail platform)

MATERIALS 1″ x 8″ x 18″ pine; 3½″ o.d. x 2½″ PVC pipe; 1⅝″ o.d. x 11½″ PVC pipe; ¼″-diam. x 15″ aluminum rod; ¼″ x 6″ x 12″ mirrored acrylic; ⅝″-diam. x 12″ dowel; ¼″-diam. x 12″ dowel.

Follow Plan View to cut pine and to assemble Weather Station base. Drill board as indicated.

Cut 1⅝″-diam. PVC pipe to 11½″ x 45° angle. Use shape of angled end as pattern and cut out ¼″ acrylic mirror.

Cut ⅝″-diam. dowel as shown for solar wind wheel support. Drill pilot hole for screw in facing end. Mark back of mirror (Detail C) to cut wind wheel with jigsaw or band saw. Drill center clearance hole for screw.

From ¼″-diam. aluminum rod, cut Radar Pole and arm. See Detail B to cut mortise and tenon hinge with hacksaw. Drill both parts and connect with brad cut to ⅜″. Lightly peen cut end after brad is inserted.

Cut curved sound reflector from 3½″ PVC pipe (Detail A) with jig, coping or band saw. Sand and drill center hole for ¼″-diam. arm. Slip onto arm as shown.

Cut ¼″-diam. acrylic dowel as shown and polish cuts.

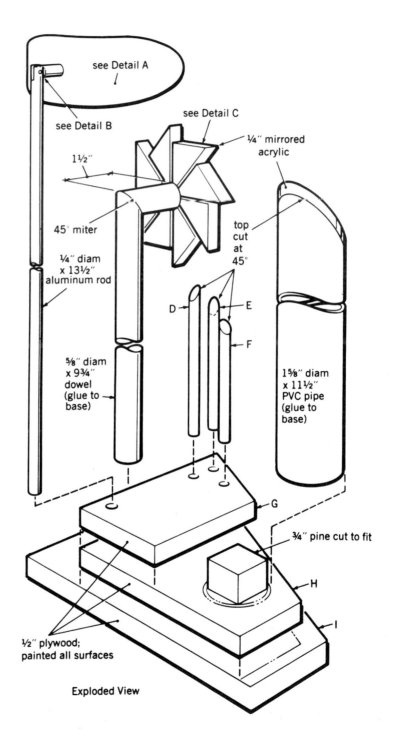

see Detail A

see Detail C

see Detail B

1½″

¼″ mirrored acrylic

45° miter

top cut at 45°

¼″ diam x 13½″ aluminum rod

D

E

F

⅝″ diam x 9¾″ dowel (glue to base)

1⅝″ diam x 11½″ PVC pipe (glue to base)

G

¾″ pine cut to fit

H

I

½″ plywood; painted all surfaces

Exploded View

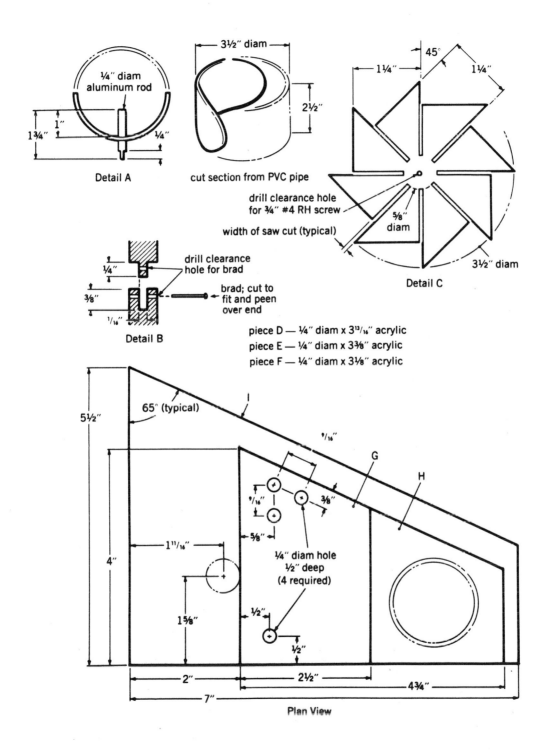

¼″ diam
aluminum rod

1″

1¾″

¼″

Detail A

3½″ diam

2½″

cut section from PVC pipe

drill clearance hole
for ¾″ #4 RH screw

width of saw cut (typical)

45°

1¼″

1¼″

⅝″
diam

3½″ diam

Detail C

¼″

⅜″

1/16″

drill clearance
hole for brad

brad; cut to
fit and peen
over end

Detail B

piece D — ¼″ diam x 3¹³/₁₆″ acrylic
piece E — ¼″ diam x 3⅜″ acrylic
piece F — ¼″ diam x 3⅛″ acrylic

5½″

65° (typical)

I

9/16″

G

H

9/16″

⅜″

1¹¹/₁₆″

⅝″

¼″ diam hole
½″ deep
(4 required)

4″

1⅝″

½″

½″

2″

2½″

4¾″

7″

Plan View

Computer Banks

Computer banks are shown throughout station. They are built from scrap lumber, following diagram. Paint each white and decorate with self-adhesive plastic as described under General Directions at start of project. To make the same number as shown, you'll need to build 8 small computer banks, 5 large computer banks and 6 computer consoles.

Beds and Other Furniture

Beds and other furniture are built from odds and ends, to suit the space station motif. The bed construction is shown in diagram. For three beds (as shown in Living Quarters photograph) you'll need ½" x 6" x 12" of green acrylic and ½"-diam. x 12" of black acrylic dowel. Follow diagram to build beds.

For other funiture, you'll need a small tube of artist's Mars Black paint and epoxy, white glue **or** glue for acrylics to glue acrylic to wood. Ideas for furniture as shown are: **for lamps,** use round head 1"-diam. shank button, shaded with oval wooden bead with blunt ends for base (paint base beads black); **for one table,** use 1" diam. x 1" dowel base, paint black and place 1½"-diam. shank button with dish face covered with self-adhesive plastic foil and rim painted black on dowel base; **or for other table,** use same dowel base painted black and flat-face shank button also painted black; **for vases,** use colored glass 1" beads or oval bead with flat ends or aluminum marker caps or ¾"-round enameled beads, all with leaves cut from green, pink, and yellow acetate.

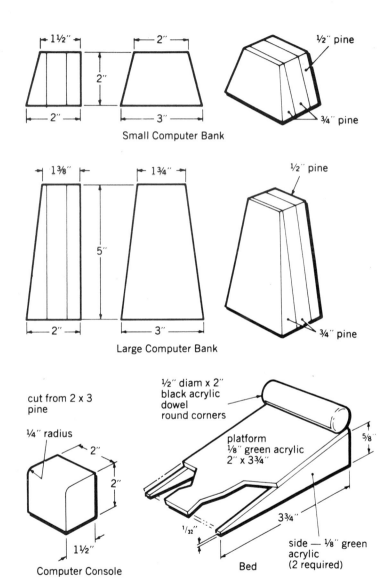

Small Computer Bank

½" pine
¾" pine

Large Computer Bank

½" pine
¾" pine

cut from 2 x 3 pine
¼" radius

Computer Console

½" diam x 2" black acrylic dowel round corners

platform ⅛" green acrylic 2" x 3¾"

side — ⅛" green acrylic (2 required)

Bed

Portable dollhouse

*No more wondering what you'll do
with your little doll when you take her visiting!
Bring along this cunning dollhouse.
Basically, it's a self-contained cardboard (or wooden)
box, with an ingenious drop-down
front and an eye-hook catch that latches it in place for
carrying (even has a handle). No costly
furnishings to buy — you make them all
yourself, easily and inexpensively,
from fabric scraps, spools, clothespins and
the like. Nothing is fragile or
hard to replace, so the furniture can go along too.*

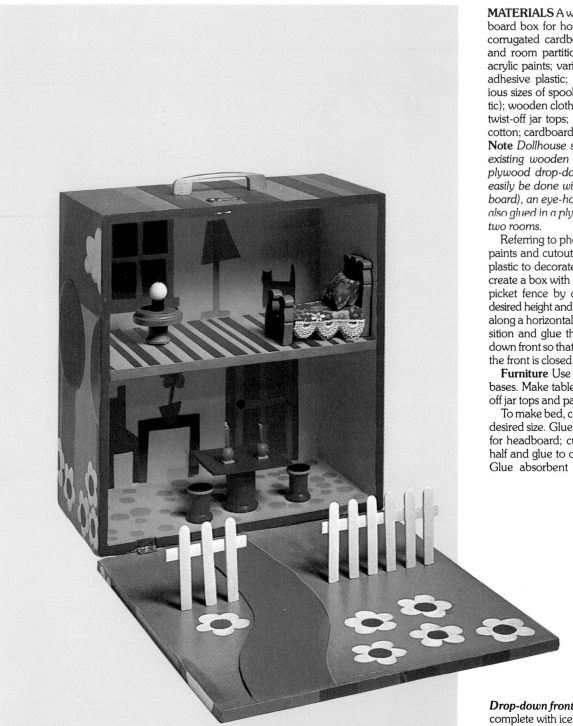

MATERIALS A wooden or corrugated-cardboard box for house; scrap ⅜″ plywood or corrugated cardboard for drop-down front and room partitions (optional); white glue; acrylic paints; various colored scraps of self-adhesive plastic; ice-cream-pop sticks; various sizes of spools (can be wooden or plastic); wooden clothespins; fabric scraps; metal twist-off jar tops; wooden beads; absorbent cotton; cardboard scraps.

Note *Dollhouse shown was made from an existing wooden box. We added a hinged plywood drop-down front (which can also easily be done with one of corrugated cardboard), an eye-hook catch and a handle. We also glued in a plywood floor-ceiling to make two rooms.*

Referring to photograph, use bright acrylic paints and cutout shapes from self-adhesive plastic to decorate dollhouse. If you have or create a box with a drop-down front, make a picket fence by cutting ice cream sticks to desired height and gluing them, evenly spaced, along a horizontal stick as in photograph. Position and glue the fence in place on drop-down front so that it clears any furniture when the front is closed.

Furniture Use spools for stools and table bases. Make tabletops of cardboard or twist-off jar tops and paint bright colors.

To make bed, cut cardboard in rectangle of desired size. Glue two clothespins to one end for headboard; cut two more clothespins in half and glue to opposite end for footboard. Glue absorbent cotton to cardboard and

Drop-down front becomes a tiny yard, complete with ice-cream-stick picket fence and painted-on grass, walk and flowers.

cover with a scrap of fabric for bedspread. Make a separate pillow and stuff with cotton.

For candlestick, use a small wooden bead with a tiny square of cardboard for base. Cut a birthday-cake candle to size and insert in hole in bead.

Referring to sketch for more dollhouse furniture suggestions, use plastic pin boxes or any other small boxes for bureau and coffee table. Cut plastic spray-can tops along front edge for chairs and add a fabric-covered cushion. Join two halved spray-can tops with a fabric-covered cardboard rectangle for couch, adding covered button forms for throw pillows. Pushpins are legs for table, chairs and couch.

Drapes are strips of fabric with a scalloped valance tacked in place; curtain rods are drinking straws.

Make large mirrors from plastic tops covered with silver self-adhesive paper.

The floor lamp's base is a spray-can top cut to shape, the pole is a dowel and the lamps are toothpaste-tube tops hung from a strip of plastic (cut from can top) and string. Toothpaste-tube tops also make attractive vases.

The rug is just a square of fabric.

To make some very modern-looking furniture, try using plastic packing materials. Cut the shapes with a coping saw or knife or both, lightly sandpapering the cut edges. Add beads, nailheads or whatever for feet, knobs and trim and mark drawers, doors and other components with felt-tipped pens.

All latched up and ready to go, it's a compact little package she'll be proud to carry along.

CHAPTER 6

General Instructions

Throughout the book an effort has been made to connect instructions of any kind directly to the projects where they are used. With knitting and crochet, which appear in so many places, this was not possible, so we have brought the basics together in the chapter that follows. In addition to refresher courses on these subjects, you will find a complete chart of embroidery stitches used in the book, and directions for making fringe, plus the fundamentals of woodworking.

Contents

Refresher courses
in knitting & crochet

General Information   **179**

Knitting basics   **180**

Crochet basics   **182**

Embroidery Stitches   **184**

Basic Pointers
on Woodworking   **185**

Refresher Courses
in knitting & crochet

NEEDLES AND HOOKS

Knitting needles come in a variety of styles, each designed for a specific use. Straight needles are for knitting back and forth. Double-pointed (dp) needles have points at both ends, are sold in sets of four, and are for knitting in rounds; one alone may be used in making cables. A circular needle, pointed at both ends and flexible in the center, is for knitting either in rounds or back and forth on more stitches than could be conveniently worked on dp or straight needles.

NEEDLES		HOOKS	
U.S.	**English**	**U.S.**	**English**
0	13	1	0
1	12	2	1
2	11	3	1½
3	10	4	2
4	9	5	2½
5	8	6	3
6	7	7	3½
7	6	8	4
8	5	9	4½
9	4	10	5
10	3	11	5½
11	2	12	6
13	0	13	6½
15	000	14	7

ABBREVIATIONS AND TERMS

beg	begin or beginning
ch	chain
dc	double crochet
dec	decrease
dp	double-pointed
hdc	half double crochet
inc	increase
k	knit
lp	loop
p	purl
pat	pattern
psso	pass slipped stitch over
rep	repeat
rnd	round
sc	single crochet
sk	skip
sl	slip
sp	space
st	stitch
tog	together
tr	triple
yo	yarn over

ASTERISKS (*) are used to indicate that a group of stitches or steps are to be repeated the specified number of times. *K 2, p 1, repeat from * twice means you should knit 2, purl 1, knit 2, purl 1, knit 2, purl 1.

GAUGE refers to the number of stitches (and sometimes rows) that make up 1″ of the knitted fabric. Each set of directions lists the gauge obtained by the designer when she worked the pattern with the yarn and needles specified, and is the gauge upon which the directions are based.

MULTIPLE means the number of stitches that are worked across to form one pattern.

The number of foundation stitches must be divisible by the multiple.

PARENTHESES ( ) are used to enclose directions for larger sizes, as listed at the start of each set of directions. They also may indicate that the group of stitches which they enclose are to be repeated the number of times stated immediately after. (K 2, p 1) 3 times means you should knit 2, purl 1, knit 2, purl 1, knit 2, purl 1.

WORK EVEN means to continue the same stitch, without increasing or decreasing.

KNITTING

CASTING ON

Make a slip knot on needle about two yards from end of yarn — allow plenty!

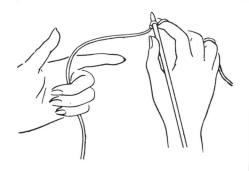

Hold yarn end in palm of left hand.

Loop end of yarn around your left thumb from front to back; wind yarn leading to ball loosely around fingers of right hand.

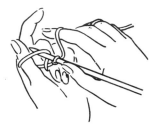

Holding needle in right hand as you would hold a pencil, insert the needle into loop on thumb from front to back.

Pass the yarn in your right hand around the needle from back to front.

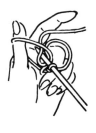

Draw yarn through, slip loop off thumb, pull to tighten. One stitch is cast on.

KNIT STITCH

Holding needle with cast-on stitches in left hand, second needle in right, yarn in back, insert needle into first stitch from left to right, front to back.

Pass yarn under and over the right-hand needle. (You may find it more comfortable to support both needles with your left hand in this step.)

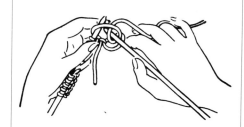

Draw loop on right-hand needle through the stitch on left-hand needle.

Slip the stitch just worked in off the left-hand needle. One knit stitch made.

PURL STITCH

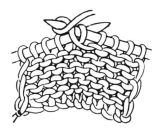 

Holding needle with stitches in left hand and second needle in right, yarn at front, insert the right-hand needle into first stitch from right to left, back to front. Pass yarn over and under right-hand needle, draw loop through, slip the stitch just worked in off the left-hand needle.

Stockinette stitch is produced by alternating knit and purl rows. It has two different surfaces; the smoother of the two is considered the front, or "right" side. In "reverse stockinette," the back of stockinette knitting is used as the "right" side.

INCREASING

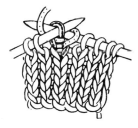 

To increase in *knitting,* knit the stitch as usual, but do not slip the stitch just worked in off the left-hand needle. Instead knit again in the same stitch, inserting the needle into back of stitch. Now slip the stitch worked in off the left-hand needle.

To increase in *purling,* purl the stitch as usual, but do not slip the stitch just worked in off the left-hand needle. Instead purl again in the same stitch, inserting the needle into back of stitch. Now slip the stitch worked in off the left-hand needle.

DECREASING

To decrease in *knitting,* knit two stitches together from left to right.

To decrease in *purling,* purl two stitches together from right to left.

BINDING OFF

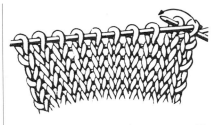

Work the first two stitches as you would in a regular pattern row. Insert tip of left-hand needle from left to right into the first stitch worked, which is now on the right-hand needle.

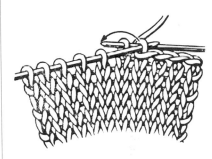

Pass the first stitch over the second stitch and off tip of right-hand needle — one stitch bound off. Repeat until as many stitches are bound off as the directions call for.

AS YOU WORK

MULTICOLOR DESIGNS are handsome and fun to knit. When working with more than one color, always carry the unused strands on the wrong side. In changing colors, pick up the new strand from under the dropped strand to prevent a hole in your work. If strand is carried for more than three stitches before it is to be worked, twist it with a strand being used every fourth stitch to avoid long, loose threads on the wrong side.

SUIT THE EDGE STITCH to the pattern and the edge shape. When working plain stockinette or garter stitch, the first stitch of each row may be slipped without working it to obtain the less bulky, smooth "chain edge." When working a more intricate pattern stitch or shaping an armhole, neckline, etc., every stitch should be worked to produce the "closed edge."

JOIN A NEW BALL of yarn with a knot at the seam edge wherever possible. When crocheting, join a new thread as follows: Leaving a 4" end, draw up a loop, draw end through, and pull to fasten. Draw up another loop in same stitch and proceed as directed.

CROCHET

FOUNDATION CHAIN

Make a slip knot on hook, held in the right hand. Thread yarn over left ring finger, under middle, and over index fingers, holding short end between the thumb and middle finger.

Pass hook under and over yarn and draw it through loop on hook. Repeat for as many stitches as the directions specify.

SINGLE CROCHET

Insert hook into second chain from hook (or, within a row, into stitch under the two upper strands).

Pass hook under and over yarn and draw it through the chain or stitch. Two loops on hook.

Pass hook under and over yarn again and draw it through the two loops. Single crochet completed.

HALF DOUBLE CROCHET

Pass hook under and over yarn, insert hook into third chain from hook (or into stitch, going under the two upper strands).

Pass hook under and over yarn and draw it through the stitch. Pass hook under and over yarn again and draw it through the three loops on hook. Half double crochet completed.

DOUBLE CROCHET

Pass hook under and over yarn, insert hook into the fourth chain from hook (or into stitch, going under the two upper strands).

Pass hook under and over yarn and draw it through the chain or stitch, then pass hook under and over yarn again. Draw yarn through the first two loops on hook. Pass hook under and over yarn again and draw it through remaining two loops on hook. Double crochet completed.

TRIPLE CROCHET

Pass hook under and over yarn twice, insert hook into the fifth chain from hook (or into stitch, going under the two upper strands).

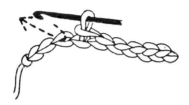

Catch yarn and draw it through the chain or stitch.* Pass hook under and over yarn and draw through two loops, repeat from * twice more. Triple crochet completed.

SLIP STITCH

Insert hook into second chain from hook, or into stitch to work within or across a row. (Insert hook into corresponding stitches of two edges to be seamed.) Pass hook under and over yarn.

Draw a loop through both the chain (or stitch) and the loop on the hook.

HOW TO MAKE FRINGE

For each fringe tassel, hold tassel strands together and fold in half. With crochet hook, catch the loop end of the gathered strands and draw it through stitch or space, at edge of project, as instructions specify. Draw strand ends through loop and pull to tighten.

EMBROIDERY
STITCHES

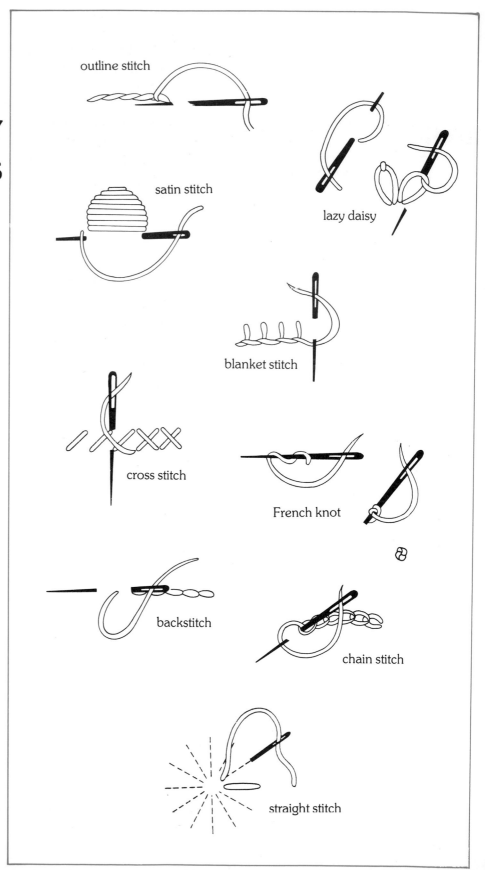

outline stitch

satin stitch

lazy daisy

blanket stitch

cross stitch

French knot

backstitch

chain stitch

straight stitch

BASIC POINTERS ON WOODWORKING

MATERIALS AND TOOLS Table saw; saber saw; jigsaw or coping saw; drill with assorted bits; screwdrivers; C-clamps; wood putty; awl; nail set; try square; vise; utility knife; white wood glue; medium through very fine grades of sandpaper; for natural finish, white shellac or clear satin polyurethane; for painted finish, pigmented shellac primer and paint as listed in specific directions; screws, nails or hinges as specified for individual projects.

NOTE *Wood required and special tools are listed under specific projects.*

MAKING PATTERNS Enlarge pattern (see instructions in conjunction with individual projects). To make 1 item, draw pattern directly on grid marked on wood. If you are making several of a given item, make a paper pattern as described. Mark from paper pattern by placing sheet of carbon paper face down on wood with pattern on top; go over outlines with pencil to mark on wood. For dark woods, buy special white carbon paper in art-supply stores.

CUTTING WOOD Cut curves with jigsaw or coping saw. For matching parts, clamp together and cut as one if using jigsaw (coping saw won't cut multiple thicknesses). For broad curves and straight cuts, use saber or table saw.

DRILLING Use an awl to mark and start holes for drilling. Clamp wood to scrap to prevent splintering as bit comes through bottom. Clamp and drill matching parts at one time. Drill holes in scrap to test-fit dowels. Drill lead or pilot holes and countersink holes for flathead screws.

NAILING Use finishing nails for thick wood, wire brads for thin; length should be at least ⅛″ shorter than parts to be joined. Drive nails slightly below surface with nail set after nailing. For added strength, glue joints to be nailed.

ASSEMBLING Test-assemble; check parts that should be square with carpenter's try square. When parts fit, assemble by gluing, then screwing or nailing. Clamp with scrap between clamp and wood; wipe away excess glue immediately with damp cloth.

SANDING AND FILLING Sand smooth before finishing. Fill nail holes or countersunk screws with putty and sand smooth. Fill plywood voids or wood defects in same manner.

FOR NATURAL FINISH Apply 2 coats polyurethane or shellac, sanding and dusting between coats. Add more coats for high gloss.

PAINTING Apply 1 coat primer, then 2 coats paint, sanding and dusting between coats.

INDEX

Airmobile 61

Balloon mobile 60
Bath splashers 58
Bean-bag toss toys 68
A bevy of bears 14
Big Girl & Big Boy 54

Canny pig 79
Clown marionette 63
Clown mobile 60
Country-cousin doll 52
Cradle twins 62
Creature kites 74

Dachshund pals 24
Dotty Dinosaur 85

Fake-fur hand puppets 34
Family of elves 36
Floppy Pup, Hopalong Bunny
& Brown Bear 20
Foam-ball finger puppets 71
Football & basketball pillows 76

Gas station—at your service! 84
Giraffe toy chest 88

Heartthrobs 55
Honey bunnies 26

It's Supercity! 114

The knitted family 48

Lonely Leo 28

Music-box crib pillow 59

Noah's Ark cradle & animals 90

Outer-space Station 144
Owlish pencil caddy 77

Panda pendant 66
Pine Unicorn 87
Pinky the Pig 17
Portable dollhouse 173
Pup & piggy pull toys 65

Rocking pony 86
Rudolph 25

Satin-smooth teddy 29
Seesaw table 89
Shaggy Sheep 31
Shoe bank 64
Socko the Hobbyhorse 78
Squeezable foam blocks 72
Squiggly dragon 82
Sweet Sue 50
Switch-a-roo Uggie Wuggies 22

Teaching board 70
Tumbly Tiger 18

Velour teddy friends 30

Whirligig on wheels 67

Zippy Zebra 19

TECHNIQUE INDEX

This supplementary index divides projects by the techniques used to make them, so that you can more quickly find those that suit your skills and interests. When two techniques are almost equally involved in making a toy, it is listed under both: e.g., Shaggy Sheep is basically sewn, but its coat is made by hooking rug yarn into a burlap covering.

SEWING/EMBROIDERY

Bean-bag toss toys 68
A bevy of bears 14
Big Girl & Big Boy 54
Country-cousin doll 52
Dachshund pals 24
Fake-fur hand puppets 34
Family of elves 36
Floppy Pup, Hopalong Bunny & Brown Bear 20
Football & basketball pillows 76
Heartthrobs 55
Honey bunnies 26
Music-box crib pillow 59
Rudolph 25
Satin-smooth teddy 29
Shaggy Sheep 31
Socko the Hobbyhorse 78
Sweet Sue 50
Switch-a-roo Uggie Wuggies 22
Velour teddy friends 30

CROCHET/KNITTING

The knitted family 48
Pinky the Pig 17
Squeezable foam blocks 72
Tumbly Tiger 18
Zippy Zebra 19

STITCHING ON CANVAS (or the equivalent)

Lonely Leo (bargello) 28
Shaggy Sheep (hooking rug yarn into burlap) 31

SIMPLE CONSTRUCTION (craft-hobby level)

Airmobile 61
Balloon mobile 60
Bath splashers 58
Bean-bag toss toys 68
Canny pig 79
Clown marionette 63
Clown mobile 60
Cradle twins 62
Creature kites 74
Foam-ball finger puppets 71
Owlish pencil caddy 77
Panda pendant 66
Portable dollhouse 173
Pup & piggy pull toys 65
Shoe bank 64
Socko the Hobbyhorse 78
Teaching board 70
Whirligig on wheels 67

WOODWORKING

Dotty Dinosaur 85
Gas station—at your service! 84
Giraffe toy chest 88
Noah's Ark cradle & animals 90
Pine Unicorn 87
Rocking pony 86
Seesaw table 89
Squiggly dragon 82
Teaching board 70
Whirligig on wheels 67

MAJOR CONSTRUCTION (play settings to build)

It's Supercity! 114
Outer-space Station 144

DESIGNS

M. Albert 70, 88

B. Brown 22-23

T. Compos 86

S. DeGaltoni 17, 28, 76

A. Deminez 21

E. Dobbins 73

C. Ein 24

W. Einsel 79

L. Hobbs 25

B. Isenberg 87

R. Jager 60 (right)

B. McDermott 59

C. McLoughlin 60 (left), 67

D. Olson 77

K. Orr 27

B. Oslow 61, 69

K. Ozarow 174-175

S. Penrod 18, 19

J. Perrin, Jr. 71

A. Priestley 35

S. Renick 30

J. Russell 37

E. Sayles 58, 62, 63, 65, 75

W. Schields 51

P. Scholtz 53

M. Scranetta 66

E. Swinickse 31

R. Tarnoff 15

S. Von Steckleberg 49

J. Walker 89

M. Wein 29, 64, 78, 84

Woman's Day Staff 54, 55, 83, 85, 91, 100, 116-135, 146-166

PHOTOGRAPHY

J. Arnold 174-175

B. Ollman 35, 53, 54, 62, 63, 64, 65, 66

S. Owen 91, 100, 146-166

C. Schiavone 24, 31, 51, 58, 61, 67, 70, 71, 78, 89

Woman's Day Studio 15, 17, 18, 19, 21, 22-23, 25, 27, 28, 29, 30, 37, 49, 55, 59, 60 (2), 69, 73, 75, 76, 77, 79, 83, 84, 85, 86, 87, 88, 116-135